THE Low-Maintenance House

by Gene Logsdon

Rodale Press, Emmaus, Pennsylvania

Book design by Sandy Freeman

Illustrations by Sally Onopa

Library of Congress Cataloging-in-Publication Data

Logsdon, Gene.
    The low-maintenance house.

    Bibliography: p.
    Includes index.
    1. Dwellings—Maintenance and repair.
I. Title.
TH4817.L64   1987   643′.7   87–9489
ISBN 0–87857–718–1   hardcover

2   4   6   8   10   9   7   5   3   hardcover

CONTENTS

ACKNOWLEDGMENTS

The world has always regretted that I did not play college football seriously, win the Heisman trophy, lead the Cleveland Browns to the Super Bowl, and then become the winningest coach in pro-football history, but I did not entirely miss out on that kind of action. Producing this book has been equally as much a team effort. All I had to do was play Walter Payton, running up the middle every so often. Carol Hupping did the quarterbacking, often throwing for a first down on third and eight when I failed to get enough yardage. When I did make considerable gains it was due entirely to excellent blocking up front from assistant editors, secretaries, researchers, designers, and copy editors who never get the glory they deserve: Cheryl Tetreau, Barbara Emert, Roger Moyer, Sandy Freeman, and Tina Whyte. Special teams coach Tom Gettings and his photographers supplied pictures with a little outside help from Dennis Barnes. I thought I could see head coach Tom Woll over on the sidelines shake his head doubtfully once or twice, but he kept sending in plays until we finally crossed the goal line with the finished book.

G.L.
January, 1987

CHAPTER 1

IN SEARCH OF THE LOW-MAINTENANCE HOUSE

Though I have done more construction work than the average home-owner, I hasten to state right now before I cover this book with hand-split infinitives or paint its pages with purple prose or pour one footer full of concrete conclusions, that I am no expert in the art and science of low maintenance. I am a typical homeowner, which means that my roof may sometimes leak, my faucets drip, my plaster crack, my chimney choke with creosote, my gutters fill with leaves, and my walls streak with vile discolorations that emanate mysteriously from the fingertips of little children. My expertise in these matters is to appear helpless until my wife takes care of them. If that were not the case, I could not have motivated myself to do the research this book demanded. I, as much as you, want off the treadmill of playing Mr. Fix-it every weekend. The only thing I like to fix is a good lunch.

What I have learned first of all is that there probably isn't any such thing as a truly low-maintenance house. Some are just more low maintenance than others. In low maintenance, we deal in comparisons. As I take you on a journey from the bottom of your footer to the peak of your roof to show you how to avoid maintenance problems, or cope with them in an easier way, I would love to tell you that a basement wall has been invented that won't ever leak; wood siding that won't ever need paint or stain; trees for your lawn that grow fast to precisely the height you want, then never grow larger, but continue to sport beautiful leaves that vanish before they hit the ground in fall. Alas, miracles are rare indeed. Some basement walls resist leaking longer than others. Some woods weather better than others. No tree is perfect for landscaping. Even when some new material or construction method appears to promise 30, 40, or 50 years of low maintenance, we have to remember that these products and methods haven't been around long enough to prove such a test of time.

Secondly, I learned that low maintenance can mean solving one problem while creating another—or choosing between the lesser of two disadvantages. What you gain one way you may lose another. Gutters fill with leaves, plug up, and the water cascades down to the lawn or to ornamentals below like a little Niagara Falls. Put screens on the gutter and the gutter can't plug up. But the water racing off the roof cascades none-theless *over* the screen and makes little Niagara Falls anyway. One company (Raingo, 7034 East Court Street, Davison MI 48423), using a more imaginative approach, puts a novel outlet in the downspout that is sup-posed to funnel leaves out of the spout, but not the water. Unfortunately, the leaves do not always cooperate.

Vinyl siding presents us with another set of low-maintenance trade-offs. Vinyl is a relatively new siding material with wonderful advantages inside and outside the house. Vinyl siding is a quick way to cover an old wood house and rid yourself of the job of painting every five years or so. It is a good low-maintenance alternative in this respect. But what the vinyl salespeople are slow to tell you, and the house paint salespeople very quick to let you know, is that vinyl is a pretty good vapor barrier. Vapor barriers are handy to have on the inside of the house, but not necessarily on the outside. Warm air from inside the house meeting cold air from the outside somewhere in the wall can create condensation, which gets easily trapped inside the vinyl siding and won't dry out. Therefore, the paint people insist, the vinyl siding remains in good shape, but the old wood frame inside may be rotting away not so slowly. Since most vinyl siding is fairly new, the full effects of its vapor-barrier capabilities on the house have not been experienced. People who paint, especially with a latex paint (latex allows the wall to "breathe" a little), opt for high maintenance on the siding, but low maintenance on the framing underneath. People who choose vinyl siding opt for low maintenance on the outside and take their chances on what happens to the house's framing.

A third lesson important to homeowners seeking lower maintenance is that there are more products available than hardly any one person knows about. I am sure this is true, because it was not long after I started my search that I found building contractors with much more experience than I have who would prick up their ears at the mention of some of the more esoteric products. When I mentioned glazed clay roofing tiles in many colors to a roofer I was interviewing, he started asking me more questions than I could ask him! Hardly any of the contractors I talked to were aware of marble wall tiles with a new adhesive that makes them easy for do-it-yourselfers to apply. With these new tiles, do-it-yourselfers can overcome the higher price of marble instead of using some other higher-maintenance wallcoverings. If the people in the business can't keep up with new products, obviously the rest of us are even more desperately ignorant of them. I have therefore made it the main goal of this book to include as many promising low-maintenance materials that I could get wind of. (They're throughout the text and repeated in Appendix A for quick reference.) I slacked off a bit on vinyl wallcoverings, however, when I found that even in our little village there were nearly 400 catalogs of samples to choose from! You'll just have to do that kind of choosing on your own.

But as much as I have tried to emphasize products and materials, I have resisted the temptation to make this book just another repair and fix-it manual. As I researched, I was amazed at how many newspaper columnists, magazine editors, and book authors of the handyman variety appeared to be unaware of the amount of existing simple how-to information. Whenever you have to buy something to repair or renovate or add on, the product's label generally gives you much better how-to instructions than can be given in a book, since those instructions will be specific to the particular material or method being employed. In fact, so aware are manufacturers of the influence of the written word, that you can literally be inundated with how-to directions and brochures from the dealer you buy from. Given all this, I have passed along such how-to information only where a particular method is critical to low maintenance, such as in installing ceramic tiles in a bathroom. There are several ways to install them, but if the tiles are expected to last a long time without loosening, you will have to avoid the easier ways and stick with the proven methods.

Also I have included how-to information where the method is not only critical to long life and low maintenance, but when in my experience the method is not well known, such as installing standing-seam metal roofing. You will probably never install this kind of roof yourself, but you should at least know that the method is fairly simple if you have a strong back. By the same token, I do not descend into the details of sheet vinyl installation on floors because rapid innovations are making the tried-and-true methods obsolete. Most of the leading vinyl floor manufacturers now have installation methods for certain kinds of vinyl flooring that are so simple you need only a pencil, measuring tape, and scissors to do the job. And the company will guarantee you can do it or they will replace anything you ruin by mistake!

How Not to Be Penny-Wise and Pound Foolish

Recently I stopped at an apartment complex under construction at the edge of a fairly large and rapidly expanding city, mostly because I could hardly believe my eyes. The size of the complex could only be described as colossal. Some 800 buildings (I was told) were going up, almost as fast as mushrooms, each containing six apartments, renting for about $350 a month. Young professionals were renting the units as fast as they became available—in fact clamoring to move in even before they were finished. The apartments were considered "nice for the price," the new occupants said, and far enough out of the city to provide at least the illusion of "countryness" while still close enough to their jobs to make commuting fairly practical. Most of the renters were moving from similar apartments that were about 20 years old and already showing deterioration, just as these new ones would 20 years hence. Slapdash flimsiness and bare minimum standards were evident everywhere to the traditional builder's eyes. I kept asking myself if it would not have been to the builder's advantage, as far as his reputation was concerned, to invest in a little quality, to make the buildings last a little longer.

I was not thinking big enough. A little calculation showed why cutting corners in a large apartment complex really paid. If the builder could save just $500 on each of the 4,800 apartments, that meant $2.4 million saved! Obviously, the renters didn't mind, nor even know how cheaply their apartments were built. These were temporary homes for temporary people on the move, affordable, comfortable, and attractive enough, and besides, most of the time the occupants wouldn't be there. Why not cut corners? Even the tax system favors it. These apartments can be depreciated faster than they deteriorate.

Minimizing Building Standards— Save Now, Pay Later

It is only when these minimal standards for housing are carried over to the single family home that a clear loser can be pinpointed. The builders of large numbers of tract houses still benefit from lowering per unit cost even slightly, but for the homebuyer, minimal standards spell trouble: endless high-maintenance costs and poor resale value. With the costs of material and skilled labor ever rising, the pressure to lower standards even further exerts itself. The National Association of Home Builders (NAHB) has begun to speak well of wooden foundations for houses and wants to increase minimal spacings between wall studs from 16 to 24 inches, reduce the thickness of plywood for floor and roof sheathing, and get rid of floor joist bracing and plate sills. Although NAHB likes to say that reducing the costs of homebuilding allows more people to own their own homes, the reduction to the homeowner is slight and could mean costly maintenance work in the future. If a builder erects 100 houses a year and can save $2,000 on each one by easing building codes, that's $200,000 saved. For the individual homeowner, the $2,000 is penny-wise but pound foolish.

A good treated wood foundation costs "a few hundred dollars" less than a masonry foundation, builders tell me. Although treated wood has been in use successfully for 40 years, it has not been used in underground foundations that long. Wood foundations are touted as being dryer than masonry, but this is a debatable issue. The key to a dry basement is good drainage (see chapter 2), not the wall material. And to depend upon a thin skin of plastic on the exterior wood foundation to keep water out is something of a risk—fill dirt and stones settling around the foundation might tear or crack that skin. But even if the wood foundation has some advantages, why would a homeowner take such a risk to save just a few hundred dollars on what is by far the hardest part of the house to repair?

Before you decide to save money by using ⅜-inch plywood for roof decking instead of ½ inch, as some builders are tempted to do, check with a lumberyard to see how much you are actually saving. According to my calculations, on a moderate-size house it's about $200. Is it worth it? The thinner plywood will not hold the nails nearly as well, and roofing will loosen and blow off more easily. If you put that ⅜-inch decking over rafters spaced 24 inches apart instead of the approved 16 inches, then you are also asking for roofs sagging under snow load.

Crossbraces between floor joists do not really add to the strength of the floor, or so some carpenters maintain, but the braces make the joists— and therefore the floor—more rigid, and in case of not-so-dry joists, prevent them from warping and making the floor uneven. By not using them, you save maybe $75. Then as a reward for your penny wisdom, you may have to endure squeaky spots in the floor or cracks in the tile floorcovering forever. Even if that doesn't bother you, contemplate this scenario: Some day in the future, you need desperately to get your house sold and you finally have a buyer just about ready to offer you a price you can live with. She steps on the squeaky board, and it sends a signal to her that the house might not be as solid as she thought it was. She decides to keep house hunting.

Another corner-cutter advocated by the penny-wise is literally a corner-cutter. The corners of a conventional stud wall are composed of three studs, the main purpose of the third being to provide a place to nail interior drywall or wallboard. Cost cutters want to eliminate the third stud and attach the drywall at the corner with metal drywall clips. Common sense says such a wall corner will be weaker and subject to cracking. What is saved? A few studs—peanuts for the homeowner, though in a year's work, the saving adds up for the builder.

Another questionable practice is nailing roofing directly over rigid insulation in a cathedral ceiling situation. In this case, roof decking is nailed to the rafters, rigid insulation is laid down on the decking, and then the shingles are nailed through the insulation into the decking. It is much better to add another layer of plywood *over* the insulation before nailing on the shingles. The nails will hold much better. And without it, reroofing—trying to remove shingles from the insulation without harming the latter—can be a real pain. Since the amount of cathedral ceiling is usually small in relation to the whole roof (except on high-priced mansions designed with lots of cathedral ceilings, in which case money is no object anyway), the low-maintenance investment in the second layer of plywood will pay better dividends, not the least of which is more insulative value where you need it the most.

I also wouldn't recommend using No. 14 electrical wiring, even if codes allow it, because the difference in price between that and the superior No. 12 is hardly $50 on a small- to moderate-size house. Using the lighter No. 14 only means reduced voltage at the end of a long circuit. Also, if you are given a choice between, say, 150-amp service to your circuit box and 200 amp, take the higher even if your electrician says you can "get by" with the lower. You don't know what increased electrical current you may need in the future, and the difference in cost is negligible—only about $50.

I, myself, think plastic plumbing pipe is great stuff. But it saves only a couple hundred bucks per house. Is that worth the risk in northern climates where extremely cold temperatures freeze pipes? You can unthaw a copper pipe much easier than plastic. Copper will withstand several freezes, usually, before it ruptures from freezing water. And a minor fire that could destroy plastic pipe might not hurt copper at all. If you do use plastic, use plenty of fasteners so it doesn't sag and retain water when you have to drain it to avoid freeze-up.

In remodeling you are apt to run into a special problem when connecting new pipe to old. Most older homes were plumbed with galvanized steel. But copper is much better and easier to install, so you really should use it in remodeling. The problem is that copper and galvanized steel will corrode each other if connected directly. Use brass connectors to keep the other two metals separate, since brass will not corrode in contact with either of them. You could instead use new plastic piping—chlorinated polyvinyl chloride (CPVC) or polybutylene—that will handle hot water, but it is not approved by many housing codes. Check codes closely when doing plumbing, as they vary from place to place. For example, one way plumbers connect copper to galvanized steel is with a dielectric union. It involves soldering a brass flange to the copper pipe with a neoprene gasket between the brass flange and the connecting galvanized coupling. If this pipe needs to be grounded, the gasket breaks the ground, and some local codes require a continuous ground.

Because of the corroding relationship between copper and steel, use only copper, brass, or plastic hangers for copper pipe, and steel or plastic for galvanized pipe.

Some builders would like to reduce 2-by-8-inch sill plates that are bolted to the foundation to 2-by-4-inch size, or eliminate them altogether in favor of metal strapping to anchor studs to the foundation. That would save you something less than $100. I not only wouldn't do it, but advocate going in the opposite direction. If possible, build the stud wall on the ground with a 2-by-4-inch sill nailed across the bottom of all the studs. Then set the whole wall frame up on the 2-by-8-inch sill and nail it down. No toenailing of studs into the sill. The double sill ought to forever prevent rot due to moisture moving up from the foundation to the wall. And that strip of insulation you should put between the foundation and the sill keeps out cold that would be hard to deal with in a sill less wall. Also, it is very nice to have that continuous sill to nail exterior siding to all around the bottom, not just at the studs. And it is extremely handy to nail bracing to the sill temporarily when putting up the stud wall.

Which Framing for Economy? Which for Durability?

Low maintenance in housing always brings up this question: Which framing technique gives the better house for the money, stud construction or post and beam? Because of all the variables the argument is never settled to everyone's satisfaction. According to government statistics, the average life of a conventionally built stud house is about 75 years. The life of a timber frame is at least 300 years and some over 1,000 years old survive. But a house can be poorly built or well built by either method.

Stud framing looks flimsy and in fact is flimsy until you get all the diagonal braces and plywood sheathing nailed on. By comparison, try mortising a 4-by-4-inch brace into two 8-by-12-inch post beams. Then drill a hole through the mortise-and-tenon joint and drive a dry white oak pin slightly larger than the hole through it. Now you know what solid is. And as the dry pin swells and the greener beams shrink, the joint tightens so solidly that a hundred years from now, your descendants will not be able to take the frame apart.

In the pragmatic society in which we live, a well-built stud house is certainly strong enough for any home and provides an easier way to insulate walls, install plumbing, and run electrical wiring. But we feel

Insulated wall panels are erected over the exterior of the timber framing of this house, sealing the frame from the weather and at the same time leaving the lovely timbers exposed inside.

squeamish about those frail studs held together by all those nails. We hide them behind layers of sheathing. On the other hand, mortised-and-tenoned posts and beams have structural integrity. We know it even if we don't know carpentry. We proudly leave the beams exposed whenever possible, for all to see. Their beauty, if nothing else, is justification for their cost.

Actually, post-and-beam construction need not cost more than stud construction. Jeff Arvin, of Riverbend Timber Framing, Inc. (9012 U.S. 223, Blissfield, MI 49228), a small business that makes posts and beams and last year built 60 timber frame houses, says: "We're competitive with stud houses any time, and most of the time we can beat the pants off them." As a rule-of-thumb estimate, Riverbend puts the cost of its post-and-beam house shells (with siding, windows, doors, and roofing in place and weather-tight) at about $20 to $22 a square foot. The post-and-beam framing skeleton alone comes to about $7 to $9 a square foot. Riverbend uses oak, but other manufacturers use maple or pine. Many other woods will work if not exposed to the weather or excessive moisture.

Although post and beam appears to use more wood, there is about the same amount used in stud construction. But studs and other dimensional lumber require a great deal more sawing and therefore waste in sawdust and scraps. Logs that are too knotty for boards might yet make good beams. Post and beam allows for more flexibility in design especially for solar heating, which requires large areas of windows or solar panels. Post and beam also lends itself well to the newly popular concept of the "great room"—combining living, dining, and kitchen areas into one large, open area with vaulted ceiling, dominated by a superefficient, low-maintenance large masonry heater of the Finnish or Russian design (see chapter 14).

A Nail Is Not a Nail Is Not a Nail

Benjamin Franklin gets credit for a saying actually first written down 100 years earlier by George Herbert, and just as applicable today: "A little neglect may breed mischief: for want of a nail the shoe was lost; for want of a shoe the horse was lost; for want of a horse the rider was lost." The same applies to a house with the addition of one word: For want of a *proper* nail, etc. Using the wrong nail in the wrong situation can indeed breed mischief.

The size of a nail is designated by the word penny or the letter d preceded by a number. A 6-penny or 6d nail is 2 inches long, and a 60-penny or 60d spike is 6 inches long. The rule of thumb in choosing the proper nail size is that a nail's length should be about three times the thickness of the board being nailed, but this is not a hard-and-fast rule. A better way of saying it is to be sure the nail goes into the base wood or other material to which a board is being nailed a little farther than the thickness of the board. In making gates, for example, where 1-inch boards are being nailed into 1-inch boards, the nail needs to penetrate through both boards by ½ inch and be bent over.

Common nails are made of common steel, rather soft and bendable. They are far less likely to break or chip with a bad hammer blow, sending a piece of metal flying into your eye. But they are very prone to rust and therefore are never used where the heads are exposed. If they are so used mistakenly, as on siding, rust will soon streak down the wall from every nail. So for roofing, siding, and many other specific uses, choose nails that do not rust—galvanized steel, aluminum, and in some cases, copper.

Common nails have smooth shafts, but where extra holding strength is required, as in flooring or roofing, nails will have threaded, ringed, or spiral shafts to grip the wood better. Even some very small nails, such as panel nails or trim nails, have these spirals to give added gripping strength to their comparatively small diameters. Some of these nails are very brittle, too (like panel nails), and a misplaced blow can send a chip of metal at you. Wear protective goggles. Old common roofing nails had smooth shafts, but the new ones used for metal roofs have rings or threads and should be used.

Scaffold nails have a double head so that they can be pulled out easily. Masonry nails have spiral shafts and are extra hard for nailing into concrete or masonry units or in some cases even stone. Here again watch your eyes. Instead of threaded flooring nails, cut nails are often used, and are also called flooring nails. They look like old-fashioned nails with their square wedge-shape shaft instead of a round shaft.

Finishing nails and casing nails have very small or virtually no heads at all so they can be driven neatly below the wood surface and covered with wood filler.

A very long ring shank spike is used to fasten joists and headers to poles in pole construction. These spikes are also very brittle and will not bend. And once driven into a pole, they are virtually impossible to pull out.

When you go to the hardware store, don't be afraid to ask if there is a special kind of nail you should be using for the job at hand. At a good old-fashioned, family-operated store, the proprietor will know.

Board, Linear, or Square?

Be sure that when a price is quoted to you, you know whether it is in board feet, linear feet, or squares. A board foot is a piece of wood 1 by 12 by 12 inches (it is a little less actually, since all commercial lumber measures less than its stated size). A price per linear foot is the price per running foot no matter how wide or thick the board. Thus, a 1-by-6-inch board priced at 35¢ per linear foot is equal to 70¢ per board foot. Most siding and roofing is sold by the square, and a square is equal to 100 square feet. A square will take more siding or roofing than the actual width times height of the boards or panels used, because you have to overlap them. For example, a 1-by-6-inch length of cedar siding actually covers only a little more than 4 inches, because the other 2 inches of width lap the board below.

Good Lumber Makes Good Framing

The quality of the lumber affects the soundness of the house's frame and also affects your pocketbook considerably. Make sure you are buying what you want to buy. Economy studs are 77¢ each right now (1986) in my town; good quality studs are $1.22. This is not to say that economy studs, cautiously used, cannot make nearly as solid a frame as the more expensive ones. But make sure "you get what you pay for." Boards for trim, door and window frames, etc., should be nearly free of knots. A No. 2 ponderosa pine 1 × 12 costs 85¢ per foot, versus 46¢ for a No. 3. In wood siding, knots can be critical. For low maintenance, buy top grade and then demand that top grade be delivered. In cedar siding, some knots are unavoidable, but if the knots are tight, they will generally be okay.

Some builders and homeowners make a big production out of scrutinizing the lumber delivered for the prospective new home. They demand quality, and they are not afraid to reject a load of lumber if they find a knotty board or two not up to the grade standards they have specified. Since even the best lumber today leaves a lot to be desired, this may be a good practice, especially if you are dealing with a lumberyard you are not familiar with. But by the same token, there's probably no such thing as a load of lumber these days that doesn't have some defects.

"Well, it gets to be a kind of little game we play," one lumber dealer confided to me when I asked about the problem. "On some guys, we'll send out something less than the best the first time because they are going to send it back no matter *how* good it is just to try to show they are no pushover. Then we deliver what we planned to send in the first place. Another time, we'll send out the best we've got and when the builder sends it back, we'll rearrange it and send it out again. He's made his point and that's really all that matters."

I don't know which side to be on in that situation, but the lesson is not to be afraid to reject crooked, knotty sapwood-edged boards if you're paying for better.

A Good Builder Can Make All the Difference

A stable lifestyle is a great advantage for building low maintenance into a home. It is also invaluable in dealing with lumberyards, building contractors, etc. If you are a stranger in a new community, it is difficult to know which builders build good houses and which just get by. The community knows, but it may take a while before you find out because people won't talk frankly to strangers. If you are in a hurry to get a house built, as is generally the case, proceed with extreme caution. All the good builders will probably not be able to get to your house for at least a couple of months or more. A builder who can start tomorrow requires more checking into. In almost every case, it is better to rent a while and learn the local scene. When in doubt, hire a *bonded* contractor who can legally be held responsible should something go wrong.

In buying an existing house, knowing the reputation of the builder is invaluable. Houses built by so-and-so will be good buys, and that kind of quality is often not reflected in the price. But other houses, built by another so-and-so with a reputation for poor work, may be selling at approximately the same price. Only the people who have lived in the area a rather long time know who built what.

Building Codes for Minimum, Not Quality, Standards

Building codes became necessary when communities were no longer stable. In new suburbs where all the inhabitants come from hundreds of miles away and will be moving out in a few years to someplace another hundreds of miles away, there is no communal knowledge to guide people, to distinguish the honest from the dishonest. In place of communal knowledge, rules and codes must be promulgated and enforced, bloating the regulating bureaucracy even further.

Interestingly, when building codes came to our unusually stable community, it was the more honest builders who fought them. They argued quite rightly that codes established minimal standards and minimal standards sanctify mediocrity. Mediocre builders can undersell good builders. The upshot is that newcomers hire mediocre builders thinking themselves protected by codes, and they get mediocre houses. Natives continue to hire good builders and save money in the long run.

New Designs Haven't Withstood the Test of Time

Finally, do not be overly influenced by new house designs that appear to promise lower costs in heating but are short on long-term proof of low maintenance and durability. I have observed people who decide that, for example, a brick or stone home would be "too expensive," but who then turn around and pour more money into a weirdly shaped wood house that promises to reduce fuel costs by making use of the sun. What they save in fuel turns out to be less than the interest on the increased building costs they pay out. And because the house violates certain traditional notions about load-bearing walls, the only way the house can be built conveniently and at moderate cost is with wood, which generally means some kind of regular maintenance. I don't care how durable a natural wood wall may be, you are tempting the fates by building great expanses of it two and three stories tall into the wind and the weather. There are even visionary architects who make a point of denigrating masonry—stone and brick—because they think masons make too much money and amateurs cannot learn how to work with these materials. The first is arguable; the second is downright wrong.

The visionary architect is very important to society, without him or her new ideas would never be tried. But the right partner for a visionary architect is a rich client. The rest of us should watch and learn our lessons. A simple rectangular form with a moderately steep roof is a proven shape for a house. Any deviation from that is going to cost more money no matter how much the phrase "low cost" is ballyhooed. Beware of glowing descriptions of new house designs in which the word "cantilevered" is used profusely. Octagonal houses, round houses, tower houses, rambling floor designs that sprawl over half an acre, floors that jut out over the landscape all may be wonderful houses to look at, but they will cost more per square foot unless very cheap materials are used. Even if that should not be the case, unless you can find a builder experienced in that type of house design—which isn't easy in many localities—it will cost you more because the builder and his workers are going to be learning as they go along.

We still have a lot to learn about underground houses and about some of the odd-shaped aboveground houses designed to catch the maximum winter sun and the minimum summer sun. The latest findings seem to show that underground homes are not cost efficient, even if they don't lead to terminal cabin fever. Much better is a home that just snuggles into a hillside away from the prevailing winds—a design idea that has been used effectively in northern dairy barns for centuries. And it will be very interesting to observe how well these new glass and wood, asymmetrical, sheer-sided trapezoidal and rhombic-shaped houses will hold up in 50 years, if windstorms don't blow them over sooner than that. Just from the standpoint of fashion, if not obsolescence, they may be impossible to sell. I keep thinking of a quote from David Pye, the famous English woodworker: "If you want to enable someone to sit, it will be idiotic to proceed in the way that students of design are sometimes advised to do—to think out the whole problem from first principles as though all the people who for the last 4,000 years have been making and using chairs were half-wits. Where the problem is old, the old solutions will nearly always be best . . . because it is inconceivable that all the designers of 10 or 20 generations will have been fools."

So, too, of houses. Pye admits that new technology can sometimes change that general rule, but experience shows that "new" technology has a strange way of coming back around to prove traditional experience. Cheer for new developments in housing, but let the people who can afford it do the experimenting.

An example: David Wright is a well-known architect and builder whose name is almost synonymous with passive solar houses. Wright made his name designing and building low-cost, energy-efficient homes using nearby low-maintenance materials as much as possible. He is especially famous for the adobe houses he built in the Southwest and low-energy redwood homes in California.

It is interesting to look at the house he built and lives in *now*. (I'm reading from an article in the February 1986 issue of *Harrowsmith*.) The exterior of the unusually shaped house is cedar shakes and metal roof with

David Wright's latest house, featuring four different heating systems.

enameled steel window frames. This gets a B+ to an A- for low mainte-nance, and it is the best compromise with cost—chosen, perhaps, because installing stone or masonry on such an odd-shaped house would have been difficult.

But inside Wright has no less than four different heating systems. His "backup" is radiant ceiling electric heat, the same as I have, which is, in my opinion, far and away the lowest-maintenance heating system of all, though it is also a high energy consumer. To cut down on that high energy use, Wright burns wood in a big monolithic fireplace. Water is heated via a coil around the fireplace and also by way of preheating tanks in the solar attic, in addition to an electric water tank. Hidden in the ceiling and floor joists are flexible plastic pouches that contain eutectic "solar salts" as they are now called, a combination of materials (mostly sodium sulfate) with a freezing-melting point of 73°F. I'm not in a position to judge the merits of such a system, but I will add that in the article even Wright does not recommend it to others.

To mesh the workings of the somewhat complicated heating system, there is a remote sensor to monitor the temperatures of the solar salts, outside air, solar attic, preheat tank water, and fireplace water coil. There are adjustable dampers and fans to move air—five modes, including one for summer that draws cool air from the first floor and flushes it out through the skylights. Both the water storage tanks and the electric water heater located in an alcove off the master suite's immense walk-in closet are "cloaked in thick batts of insulation." Thermal venetian blinds cover the double-glazed windows. After describing all this, the writer concludes: "In the end, a pittance is spent on hot water."

Well, that depends on how you count dollars. Wright's electric bill for 2,500 square feet of living space was quoted at between $40 and $75 a month during the winter. The house cost $140,000 to build. What part of that went into the complicated heating-cooling system is not given, but I'm sure it is considerably more than the cost of conventional methods. And it demands regular maintenance.

By comparison, my winter electric bill for 3,000 square feet in a much colder climate is about $110 a month, heating with a simple wood stove and using electric heat only very sparingly. I would venture to suggest that the interest on the money differential between my wood stove/electric system and Wright's complex solar/wood/eutectic salts/electric system would more than pay for the electricity he presumably is saving. And my larger house, a simple rectilinear brick house with the bottom floor nestled into a hillside, cost only half that much to build. Of course, mine was a built in 1975 and his in 1980, but I know that the price of wood and bricks didn't go up appreciably during that five-year time period.

Such naivete should not be blamed on Wright, of course, nor should his true costs be compared unfavorably with conventional housing, since he is admittedly experimenting with new ideas. But a comparison with conventional methods proves sobering to those who would jump too enthusiastically into new energy-saving methods.

To Sum Up: Some Low-Maintenance Planning Advice

1. If you have to make a choice, choose quality over quantity.

A good rule to follow in building for low maintenance is to price your house in the planning stages using quality construction methods. If that price is beyond your credit rating, *cut the size of your house, not the quality*. It is almost a law of human nature that people will build their houses just a little larger than they can afford, no matter how rich they are. Why space equates with wealth, power, grandeur, or status in the human mind is beyond me, but so it does. What is the use of having a nice, easy-living home if one must then spend hours of extra time cleaning the damn thing or worrying about getting a maid who will clean it? Not to mention the extra money spent to heat and cool all that status-loving space. Mansions end up as funeral homes. Castles become museums.

2. Consider remodeling instead of building or buying new, for affordability *and* quality.

I don't think higher initial cost should be a deterrent to building low maintenance into a home—even a banker understands that since brick can last several hundred years without maintenance, its initial higher price over wood may end up costing less in the long run. Rather, I think that it's the time involved, or perhaps the timing of the work, that forces home-owners to choose the high-maintenance alternative.

A perfect example of what I mean is the woodworking shop that my son and I built. I had my heart set on laying up stone walls since we could get the stone for free. But it was the usual story. We experienced delay after delay, and it was late fall before we got a good start. I'm sure we could have laid the walls (between my son and his friend, who helped, I think we could figure out how to do anything), but we were rank amateurs at it and we'd still be laying up stone in January. Even with an experienced mason, which we couldn't afford, it would have meant going into winter without a roof overhead. So we put up a stud wall. Stud walls are fast. At least they *seem* fast, although by the time you hang the exterior and interior layers over it, I wonder. And so it is with houses.

There's usually the wait for the loan to clear. Then, if you are moving into a new house, there always seems to be the necessity of moving NOW. Husband is already at his new job. Wife and kids are in the old house, waiting. Or husband can't find a house that fits his low-maintenance ideals in the right location. The old house won't sell. Or the new house one has picked out can't be vacated until its current owner finds another place to live. With pressures of time and timing on us, we shrug, say to hell with it, and buy or build the best we can, in the time allotted.

For this reason, remodeling a house may be a more economically practical way to achieve low maintenance than building new, as contradictory as that at first seems. You are more in control. You remodel at your own pace, taking on no more than your schedule and bank account can handle at one time. Current economic conditions favor remodeling anyhow. Homes bought at super high prices in the '70s and early '80s are difficult to sell at that price, if at all, in most areas. "Trading up" to a better home is not as financially feasible as it used to be, so homeowners "remodel up" instead.

Staying put, whether forced by finances or deliberately chosen (many people are opting to put down roots rather than continuously move around the country as they climb the corporate ladder), can be a tremendous money-saver whether one is building new or remodeling. Having decided to settle down for good, you can *plan* low maintenance and move slowly to achieve it economically.

Can't afford brick? Plenty of free brick is available for the cleaning, if you know where to look. All it requires is your spare time. Learn masonry and lay brick yourself. Learning is not hard—learning to do it *fast* is. But you don't need to be in a hurry. Brick, stone, and decorative block are not really so expensive; union masons are. A builder told me the other day in a moment of discouragement that he was going to quit. "A union block layer costs me $1,150 a week including all his benefits, and if he lays brick, he costs more," he bemoaned. "That's more money than I make!" I don't really begrudge a mason those wages—most of them wear back braces after 15 years at it, and they don't make that kind of money every week anyway. But you can easily see how valuable your own labor becomes, however much slower you are, if you have a stable lifestyle that allows you to work several years, if necessary, on your new home or on remodeling your present one.

Landscaping is a good example. If you buy a new home already landscaped, you are paying plenty for that shrubbery whether you know it or not. Once settled in (or while leisurely building a new home), you can start your own trees, ornamentals, and lawn of the best low-maintenance varieties that you might not otherwise be able to afford (see chapters 7, 8, and 9).

The same kind of economics applies to interior remodeling. Ceramic tile is gorgeous stuff. But it is expensive, comparatively, and gets a good deal more expensive when you hire a skilled tile setter to install it. I think ceramic tile is worth that cost anyway, but if you don't and are not pressed to finish that bathroom NOW, you can easily learn to install the tiles yourself and bring the cost way down (see chapters 11 and 12). You'll be slow, but no matter. Ceramic tiles, especially the small ones, have a quality about them in a finished wall, floor, or countertop that even when laid amateurishly (that is, not quite perfectly straight and square) still look great. And will still last forever.

3. Paying more initially for durability and low maintenance is a good investment in the long run.

Low maintenance and durability are not the same thing. A clapboard house can last a couple of centuries and some in New England have, but they must be painted every five to ten years. Nevertheless, durability is the main characteristic of low-maintenance materials. For this reason, if no other, low maintenance means higher initial cost usually, but a good long-term investment.

Many times I have tried to devise a formula for expressing the true cost of using long-lasting low-maintenance materials compared to cheaper stuff. Simply put, it would be: initial cost plus maintenance cost equals true cost. The problem with that formula is that when interest rates are high, the interest on money saved from using cheaper materials or methods might nearly equal the money saved by avoiding maintenance with higher initial cost. That would mean that by using cheap materials or methods initially, you might lose the weekends made for Michelob, which you will spend instead painting, patching, plugging, etc. What *really* tips the scales in favor of higher cost initially comes as the house grows older and/or must be sold. You may be able to keep a minimum-standards house in shape by constant painting, patching, plugging, etc., but it will always look painted, patched, and plugged, too; it will not hold its value; and it will not sell well. Conversely, the low-maintenance house will increase in value and sell faster at a profit.

An example: Owner A built a minimal-standards house ten years ago, for let us say, $40,000. B went ahead and spent $10,000 more for more quality and low maintenance. In ten years that $10,000 meant B paid out perhaps $12,000 in interest. In the meantime, A had to spend $4,000 in maintenance that B saved, but is still $8,000 ahead in the financial game. Then comes sale time. A's property won't move at all for a year, while A is frantically driving 60 miles one way to a new job. He finally sells for $35,000. On the other hand, B sells his house in three months for $65,000. And no maintenance problems to hassle him in the meantime. Doesn't take much of a calculator to figure out who won that game.

Part 1
The Low-Maintenance Exterior

CHAPTER 2

FOUNDATIONS

FIRST

I asked a lumberyard proprietor the other day if he would build a wooden foundation for a home *he* was going to own. Wooden foundations are very much in the talk stage now, and many are actually being built. Since this man was in the lumber business, I figured he'd have nicer things to say on the subject than the concrete man down the street. He did. But not much.

"Depends," he replied, smiling at me cagily. "If I were building a split level into a well-drained hillside—where one wall is exposed on the bottom floor—I would think a wood foundation appropriate. The key is good drainage. If you have it, a wood foundation is feasible. And if you decide on one, the codes are quite strict on good drainage. Then if you use a good pressure-treated lumber like the Wolmanized brand we carry, you should be okay. As any farmer can tell you, a wood post, even untreated, rots hardly at all down in the ground. It's the part of the post at the soil surface where oxygen is plentiful that rots fast. And treated wood takes care of that."

Maybe so. But none of the reputable builders in this area will recommend wood foundations, partly because the excellent drainage necessary is hard to achieve in our heavy clay soil and humid climate. I picked up a copy of the 30-day limited warranty on Wolmanized residential lumber, which the lumber dealer had recommended for foundations. After the warranty statement, there is the following disclaimer: "Warrantor shall not be liable hereunder for damage to Wolmanized residential lumber used in foundation systems, in water immersion applications . . . .Warrantor shall not be liable for . . . the natural characteristic of some wood to check, warp, or twist, or for any incidental or consequential damages."

19

Wood Foundations

Good pressure-treated lumber is great stuff, don't get me wrong. It will resist decay and termites and it can be used in contact with the ground. I have used Wolmanized lumber that way on a pole barn and it shows no decay in eight years. We used the lumber to build the deck on our house ten years ago, and it has survived well in all kinds of weather. (The greenish cast from the copper in the preservative can be painted over with a dark stain to give it a more natural wood finish look.) But in foundations, treated wood has not yet stood the test of time.

One of the chief reasons for hesitancy over wood foundation walls has to do with lateral strength, not decay, and is the main reason the searcher for low maintenance ought to be dubious about not only wood, but concrete block as well. A friend of mine tells a sad tale about the house he built. On the back and side walls of his split level, he used 12-inch concrete blocks for extra strength, rather than the usual 8-inch ones. The house was already well along in construction when a heavy cloudburst filled the ground cavity around the walls with water. The builder had neglected as yet to provide for fast drainage away from the wall. Hydrostatic pressure in the column of water against the wall was so great (and always is) that to my friend's unbelieving eyes, it bowed those 12-inch concrete blocks 4 inches at the center of the back wall, racking the half-finished house so all the door frames were out of square. What would hydrostatic pressure have done to 8-inch walls in that situation, or a flimsy wood-paneled foundation wall?

The Importance of Good Drainage

Experienced builders install the tile drain down along the base of the footer as soon as they put in the footer. "And get that tile down at the *base* of the footer all the way around," emphasizes Kenny McClain who built our house. "If it's even half a foot up the side of the wall, water can lie under it and cause problems." As soon as the roof is up, make sure there is spouting to carry roof water away from the house in case of heavy rain before backfilling and grading are completed. Even after fill dirt is in place against the wall, a problem can present itself. After three years or so, the backfilled dirt will settle lower than the lawn out from the foundation. When this happens, in a downpour the rain that runs down the house walls lies against the foundation rather than running away from the house, and it may cause trouble.

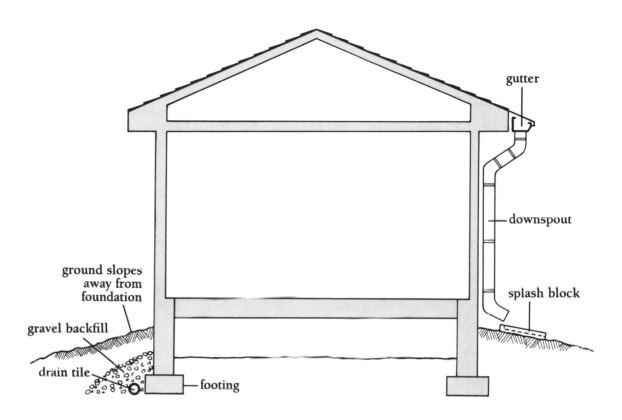

gutter

downspout

splash block

ground slopes
away from
foundation

gravel backfill

drain tile

footing

Hydrostatic pressure coupled with the tendency of some heavy clays to expand when wet can be quite strong even after backfilling, if the weather is unusually wet and the freshly backfilled dirt is saturated with water. The November of 1985 was the wettest on record in our locality. "There was so much water in the ground that drain tile couldn't carry it away fast enough, and I'm awfully glad I didn't have any block foundation walls in progress," says McClain. "I'm sure they would have fallen in. It does happen."

A good drainage system is the key to a dry basement.

Block versus Poured Concrete

When you are building or renovating, you can always find block layers who will quote a price for a block foundation a little cheaper than a poured concrete one. But it will take them longer to finish during that crucial time when your excavation is exposed to the weather. If they do the job right, that is, fill about every fourth row of blocks with concrete and bond the wall tight with reinforcing rod through the blocks, the cost will come close to the cost of poured concrete. Moreover, block walls require more waterproofing than poured concrete. The blocks need to be plastered on the outside up to grade line and then coated with tar, at least. Better than tar, which eventually dries out and forms tiny cracks, are various concrete sealers on the market. Thoro System Products (7800 Northwest 38th Street, Miami, FL 33166) is a well-known manufacturer of such products. Another sealer that is much better than tar for damp-proofing is Owens Corning's Tuff-N-Dri (Fiberglass Tower, Toledo, OH 43659). It is a polymeric coating that is sprayed onto the outside foundation walls. The coating is somewhat elastic and does not crack if there is shrinkage in the wall, as tar does. And it remains elastic at below freezing temperatures, too.

Although you also ought to coat the outside of poured cement walls with tar at least, such walls are not as porous as concrete block and do not require plastering. Another advantage of poured concrete is that once the forms are pulled, the dirt can be filled in over the footer tile (which should have about a foot of gravel directly over it first for good drainage) immediately, and the ground around the house can be graded right away.

Waterproofing the Foundation

A new way to drain away water and keep foundation walls drier is with waterproofing panels or mats, which are installed on the outside of the walls after they have been conventionally waterproofed. The interior of the panels or mats is expanded polystyrene or high-density fiberglass that quickly drains or wicks water entering through the exterior filter fabric, down to the tile drain. Thus, hydrostatic pressure is relieved. The panels are also insulative and protect the waterproofing on the foundation wall from harm during backfilling. (But the panels are not meant to take the place of regular waterproofing.) If drainage problems are severe, manufacturers suggest using both the panels and gravel. Cost ranges from 50¢ to $1 per square foot but manufacturers claim that the products are cheaper than hauling and installing gravel over the tile. These panels seem like they're a good investment, but only time will tell. Manufacturers include: American Wick Drain Corporation (301 Warehouse Drive, Matthews, NC 28105); Eljen Corporation (15 Westwood Road, Storrs, CT 06268); Geotech Systems Corporation (100 Powers Court, Sterling, VA 22170); JDR Enterprises (725 Branch Drive, Alpharetta, GA 30201); Mirafi Inc (P.O. Box 240967, Charlotte, NC 28224); and Owens Corning (Fiberglass Tower, Toledo, OH 43659).

Where drainage away from the house is less than perfect, and waterproofing the outside foundation is not enough to stop leakage through the wall, waterproofing the inside wall can help. Thoro System Products, mentioned above, sells some of the most advanced products for the job.

Insulating the Foundation

A low-maintenance foundation wall needs to be insulated well on the outside. Rigid 1-inch foam panels are placed over the entire 8-foot wall, and good builders like to put a second 4-foot layer around the top half of the foundation wall. The blue panels with a higher R-value than the white are almost always worth the extra cost for a house.

Pouring Concrete Foundations

In pouring the concrete walls, you can save some of the cost by using the wood in the forms for house construction later on. But the trend now is toward aluminum forms (which originated in Japan) because they are light, easy to use, and virtually indestructible, lowering the cost of poured concrete walls considerably. These forms also allow for easy installation of reinforcing rod and wire.

Another clever aspect of the metal forms is that some are designed to leave an imprint of bricks on the inside wall, complete with recessed mortar joints. After the forms are removed, one can go over the wall with a paint roller—any color you desire—and paint the "bricks" without touching the "mortar lines." The effect is barely discernible from the real thing unless you look closely, and it results in an attractive wall of 100 percent low maintenance and durability.

This is a perfect example of how low maintenance can also mean low cost. Leave it to the Japanese. You will hear it often in this book: We ignore the primal beauty of masonry, metal, and sometimes wood in favor of decoration with fake masonry, metal, and wood. Even concrete blocks need not be ugly, as I try to make apparent in the next chapter. Nor is it always prettier to cover concrete walls and floors with some kind of paneling or tile. For example, at Ohio Dominican College in Columbus, the walls of underground halls and rooms are the poured concrete itself, unadorned or sometimes tinted, the form seams boldly evident. The effect is most attractive. This idea could fit tastefully in home decor, too. Low maintenance and low cost.

Making Concrete Better

Improvements in concrete are being made all the time. There are chemicals that can be added to make it set up faster or slower than normal. The latest trick is an additive that makes the concrete workable without water or with only a very small amount of water. When you consider that

The Proper Concrete Mix

The standard concrete mix is 5½ bags of cement (94 pounds each or 1 cubic foot) per cubic yard of concrete, which works out to approximately one part cement to five parts aggregate, the aggregate usually being two parts sand and three to four parts gravel.

How do you tell if the concrete is wet enough? The traditional test is to dump a cupful upside down on a level surface. If the concrete holds its shape fairly well, it has the right consistency. If it slumps out flattish, it is too wet. If it doesn't slump at all, it is too dry. I like it a trifle on the wet side because it works easier. But if concrete is too wet, it will make a weak wall.

conventionally you need about 5 gallons of water for every sack of cement, you can understand the savings in transportation costs alone.

Incidentally, you won't save much money trying to mix concrete yourself, except on very small jobs. I paid $40 a cubic yard for ready-mix (1986). I found that if I had had the gravel and sand hauled in, bought the bags of concrete myself, and rented a mixer, I would have had to actually pay that $40 for the privilege of doing all that work of mixing myself. And I wouldn't have gotten the consistent quality of ready-mix either. Rarely I hear stories of ready-mixers who cheat on the proper amount of cement, or (more often) whose sand is dirty and therefore won't bind into a solid concrete, but I doubt this happens very often. The cheater would be too soon out of business.

Tinting

Integral color in concrete (pigment added directly to the concrete during mixing) gives much better results if white portland cement is used, unless you want dark colors. White portland cement and white sand make a pure white masonry mortar that can be used with almost exotic effect. I once laid a slate floor in an entryway with white mortar, and it was a real showstopper. White portland cement and pigments to color concrete add considerably to the cost, but no more expense or maintenance will be necessary on that wall.

CHAPTER 3

EXTERIOR WALLS

The shell of your house, the exterior, is by far the most important part of it in terms of low maintenance. That's why this chapter bulges formidably fatter than the others. If we could design books for low maintenance, the pages of this chapter would be made of tougher paper than the rest, because they are the ones you will thumb through most often.

At a party, four building contractors were asked which kind of house exterior they thought gave the best low maintenance, per dollar spent.

"There is no such thing as a low-maintenance home," the first one said, jokingly. That was the last thing they agreed on all evening.

"I suppose, *per dollar spent*, an igloo in the Arctic would win first prize," a second volunteered. "Three trained people can build a nice one in a couple of hours if there is plenty of wind-packed snow around. And the walls are unbeatable insulation, both for sound and temperature."

"Give me a cave anytime," said a third. "Now *that's* low maintenance."

Then they got down to serious arguing.

"All things considered, a natural wood siding that requires no painting is the best for the money."

"Yeah, until the woodpeckers drill holes in it like they are doing in some wooded areas."

"Stone or brick lasts forever and never needs paint."

"Well, brick just might need a sealer coating. Besides brick costs too much."

"The only reason brick costs more is that most builders gain their experience as carpenters, not masons. Because they have to hire masons and because wet crews are so dependent on the weather, they just automatically jack up the price more than the materials justify."

"Hoo, boy. You sound like you've been talking to the Brick Institute.

"The best siding for the money would be native lumber [like oak, pine, locust, or any wood that holds up fairly well in the weather]: rough-cut vertical board and batten, nailed on green from the sawmill, and stained after it dried out a little. But vertical board and batten isn't popular right now.''

"A lot of this board and batten is oak, and carpenters don't like to work with oak even though it nails fine when green and is much more durable than pine."

"Watch the Amish if you want to see the best homes for the money. One I know just built a new home. Redwood siding and a roof of standing seam galvanized metal. Can't beat that for low maintenance. But it doesn't look stylish."

"What have you guys got against aluminum siding? The new baked-on colors don't fade like they used to."

"Just pray it doesn't hail and dent it all to hell."

The argument was still in progress at 2:00 A.M. But there was one more question that was most illuminating. What kind of houses did *they* live in? Coincidentally perhaps, all four lived in brick houses.

Brick

Although the four building contractors at the party all had brick houses, that does not mean that brick is the very best low-maintenance exterior (with all the variables, there is no best), but the arguments in its favor are quite compelling. From an ecological point of view, much energy is used in making brick. But once made properly, brick can last indefinitely. A 2 × 4 rots eventually and not all the breakdown can be economically recovered as available energy. A brick, properly made, remains available as a brick possibly for centuries. Nor is there a shortage of suitable clays to make brick. And because bricks are so durable, millions of them are available from outmoded buildings for reuse.

Of course, brick is not forever, or not nearly as forever as some natural stone (see later in this chapter). If the outer surface of bricks (especially old bricks not baked as completely as modern ones) wears away, the inner brick is generally soft and may deteriorate rather rapidly in the weather. Even when bricks endure for centuries, the mortar between them will not, and repair becomes necessary. But building consultants, architects, and carpenters vastly exaggerate the difficulties of most repair work on old brick buildings.

As for the assumed high price of brick compared to other exterior wall sidings, it depends on how you count your pennies. "Where else can you buy something for 4¢ a pound that will last forever," quips Harold Snyder of the Claycraft Company, which produces brick in Ohio. Actually brick *itself* is not necessarily more expensive than any other good exterior wall material. Depending on the type of brick, expect to pay from $140 to $225 a thousand. There are about six bricks per square foot, so that means,

---

Cut Those Vines Back

Do not let vines grow on brick walls, picturesque as that might seem. The tendrils grip into the mortar and suck out moisture necessary to the longevity of the wall. Accelerated deterioration may be the unhappy result.

---

using 18¢ brick as an example, a square foot of brick costs about $1.08 plus the cost of mortar. Rough cedar siding *starts* at about 95¢ per square foot, not counting a penetrating stain treatment. Redwood is considerably more. Vinyl siding was last quoted to me at $180 a square or $1.80 per square foot.

The expensiveness of brick is in the labor. Country bricklayers may charge as low as $14 an hour, but union bricklayers work for between $20 and $30. A bricklayer at $20 an hour, laying 10 square feet an hour, costs you $2 a square foot for labor. Thus, the total cost of the brick would come to over $3 per square foot. Labor for wood, aluminum, or vinyl siding would be considerably less—not counting painting, staining, or upkeep. The old rule of thumb among contractors in my local area is that a house with a brick exterior costs $1 more per square foot than a wooden exterior, and since good wood and good brick have both been rising in price, that rule probably still holds. Even if the difference is now $1.50, as some contractors figure, then on a 1,600-square-foot house you are talking about $2,400 more for brick. Can you think of a better building investment, really? No more worries about your home's exterior walls for the rest of your life, barring an earthquake or bomb. And if you have to sell, you stand a good chance of getting that investment back, with interest.

Speaking of earthquakes, brick does have less tolerance to a foundation settling than does wood. Wood will give a little. Brick and other masonry walls crack when they give.

Color and Texture Choices

You have a greater—much greater—selection in color and texture with brick than with stone, block, or wood. Belden, one of several brick companies in Ohio, alone sells at least 200 different kinds of brick, Jim Platt of the Mideast Regional Brick Institute in Canton, Ohio, tells me. New colors and textures are constantly being developed, and the different brickyards guard their formulas as closely as famous restaurants guard their recipes. Bricks are in fact fascinating enough to justify a book on them alone, not only geologically, but historically and culturally as well.

(I had better state some place that I have absolutely no connection, financial or otherwise, with any brick manufacturer. If I sound like I'm selling brick it is only because I like brick—I live in a Belden brick house—and because I've found the subject interesting. You will too, if you start researching.)

Bricks have been made and used since ancient times. Brick walls in England still stand, made by the Romans before the birth of Christ. If you begin to keep a sharp eye out for brick, you will notice breathtaking artistry in older buildings: stunning arches, pillars, door and window frames, inlaid designs, graphics, numbers, names—all done with variously colored bricks. The different methods of laying up a wall are named by country of origin: Dutch bond, English bond, Flemish bond, etc. The English love red brick and brought the architecture with them to this country. So did certain German immigrants later, building their red brick houses, churches, and schools in the Midwest in stubborn defiance of the almost unlimited forest around them, which they doggedly burnt to get rid of. In American cities with Polish neighborhoods, you find many old yellow brick houses. Homesick Polish immigrants wanted yellow brick because back in Poland that is the color their clays produced. In the Art Deco rage of the '30s, glazed brick became popular, and you will still find houses made of it in sections of New York City—dirty, but indestructible.

One reason some older brick homes do not last "forever" or even for 100 years without maintenance is that not all the bricks in the exterior wall were baked uniformly hard as they should have been. Softer ones deteriorate and have to be replaced. They are softer because the position they occupied in the old kilns did not always provide for even heating.

Almost all brick is machine-made today, one way or another. Wire-cut brick is very straight and square on the edges; sand-molded brick is more rounded and softer to the eye, though not structurally any softer. Most brick today is baked very hard, at least a very hard $\frac{1}{16}$-inch skin. If it's softer inside, as much older brick was, sandblasting is a mistake, because when exposed, the soft inner brick will deteriorate in the weather. Sandblasting is seldom a good idea anyway because it wears the brick away. There are cleaning compounds used now that contain muriatic acid. Professional crews apply them, usually in a spray, to clean off brick.

Soft bricks absorb more water than hard, but can be treated with silicone compounds to waterproof them. Not many new bricks today need waterproofing. People who say their bricks leak will find that the water is coming through the mortar joints, not the brick itself. Silicone coatings will help that problem. Formerly, in the days when brick walls were truly brick walls and not brick veneer as is mostly the case today, the inner bricks were very soft and cheap. Exposed to the weather, they deteriorate rather rapidly. If you are getting brick for reuse from an old house, be aware of this.

Bricks today may be solid or cored, the latter having holes in them to make them lighter and to grip the mortar better.

Mortar

The quality of the mortar is just as important to the durability of the wall as is the brick or other masonry unit used. Quality covers a wide range of definitions, from proper mixtures to proper application. Mortar is composed of masonry cement or a mixture of masonry cement and portland cement or a mixture of portland cement and hydrated lime. Seven different combinations are identified by type: M, S, N, O, K, and for reinforced masonry, PM and PL. These are very important to architects and builders, but for practical purposes, the homeowner is best off to buy pure masonry cement rather than fuss with mixtures.

Mix masonry cement with clean masonry sand at the rate of 1 part cement to 2½ parts sand. The sand proportion can vary from 2¼ to 3½ parts, but the greater the amount of cement the stronger the bond will be, especially below grade. Add to that enough water to make a good plastic workable mixture. Achieving the optimum plasticity is the key to strong, long-lasting mortar and is the difference between a good mason and a poor one—for which you pay the same money. The mortar must be neither too

Brick for Fireproof Walls and Flues

One of brick's main advantages is only partially realized in home residences. Brick won't burn. This is why there is such a renaissance in brick in architectural, institutional, and public buildings. Brick backed by concrete block passes the strictest fire codes. Masonry salespeople love to point out, quite rightly, that owners of commercial buildings quickly recoup the extra cost of brick and go on to save thousands of dollars—in insurance costs alone.

Homeowners do take partial advantage of brick's fire safety feature by using it in fireplace walls and chimneys. There has been a recent backing away from stainless steel flues by many wood stove users. Stainless steel flues are more expensive than masonry but much cheaper to install so the overall cost is less. But though approved by all codes, stainless steel is guaranteed for only ten years. Most often it will last longer than that, but the danger is that once the flue is in place, who will replace it in ten years just to be on the safe side?

Stainless steel flues have not had a very good record. Of 23,000 chimney fires in stainless steel flues, a fourth of them spread to the surrounding structure according to a survey done by the U.S. Consumer Product Safety Commission. A good masonry chimney won't let that happen. According to some experts, intense heat can cause the inner lining of a stainless steel flue to buckle and lose its insulative power and then a chimney fire might set the house ablaze. The danger is especially critical where wood or fake masonry chimneys are built around the steel flue. A brick chimney is not only safer, but especially when built inside the house rather than on an exterior wall, it acts as a giant heat sink, absorbing heat rising with the smoke and adding considerably to the efficiency of the stove or fireplace.

wet nor too dry (see the box "The Proper Concrete Mix" in chapter 2). Once a brick has been set in its bed of mortar so that the mortar bulges out to fill the joint properly but not drip down the side, it is then tapped gently to level, if necessary. Then it should not be readjusted later on—even a minute or two later—as this can break the bond between mortar and masonry.

Water that is highly alkaline or acid (lime water, for example, in the first instance, and sulfur water in the second) should not be used, as it can cause mortar to discolor later on and stain the wall—very noticeable if colored mortars are used. But this is a rare problem.

Joints can be finished off several ways. Indented joints, or raked joints as they are called, give pleasing visual textures to a wall, but the indentation should not be more than ½ inch, or water is encouraged to lie on the joint, possibly seeping into the wall rather than draining off. Raked joints are seldom advised for high snow and rainfall areas, but my house has raked joints, and we experience calamitous rains on occasion, with no ill effects.

Building *Real* Brick Walls

Homeowners and carpenters resist masonry walls because of real or assumed inconveniences in running electrical wiring or plumbing in them, and because masonry has poor insulation value. So they build a wooden frame house and veneer it with brick—building two walls, in effect.

Today, only a few gallant souls argue against doing this and build a *real* brick house, one with two or three runs or "wythes," as they are called, of brick or brick backed by concrete block—doing away with the wood stud walls altogether. A neighbor, Fred Frey, whose family has been in the construction business for years, bought an old farmhouse recently and remodeled it into a stunning modern home, where the accent is definitely on low maintenance. The roof is old-fashioned standing-seam metal (more on that in chapter 4), and the exterior is brick. On the new addition to the house, the brick is backed by the customary stud wall, but the old part of the house was already brick—inside and out. Frey added a third wythe of brick so that all the brick was of the same kind.

With a rigid foam insulation in a cavity between the new brick and the old, Frey doesn't believe the old part of the house is any harder to heat than the new. On the interior, some of his old brick walls have simply been plastered right over the interior brick. Frey says a real brick wall of two wythes should cost only about a third more than a stud wall with an exterior wythe of brick—less if the interior brick is left as is (that is, neither plastered nor paneled), to become the interior wall.

John Thorndike, who built his own real brick house a few years ago near Athens, Ohio, agrees. He built his walls of two wythes of standard brick with a 2-inch space between for polyurethane insulation with a high R-value. "If you use a moderately priced brick and 2 inches of polyurethane, the cost of materials will be 25 to 30 percent higher than the *least* expensive 2-by-4 stud wall with 4 inches of fiberglass insulation, exterior sheathing and siding, and interior gypsum wallboard," says Thorndike. "But the masonry wall will be superior on almost every count, *including insulation*."

That being so, if you used high-quality wood wall materials, the material cost of real brick versus a brick veneer or a high-quality wood siding would not be much different. The labor cost would still keep the brick wall more expensive, but not much.

Brick for Do-It-Yourselfers

And that brings up brick's other major advantage. It is *very* amenable to do-it-yourself builders. Americans don't realize this because we basically spring from a wood culture. Wood is probably the most useful material on earth, and our nation has grown up surrounded by acres and acres of it. Many of us grow up learning the basics of wood construction—the operation of ax, saw, hammer and nails are as familiar as tying our shoes. Consequently, when we turn to building, we naturally turn to wood. Carpentry is our inheritance. On the other hand, we tend to view masonry as an esoteric art, and masons have been only too glad to encourage that mystique. While it is true that the more decorative kinds of brickwork demand both engineering skill and artistic talent, that is also true of carpentry.

As Thorndike says, and I quote from his delightful article on brick in *Country Journal* (April 1980): "At its simplest, bricklaying is something a 10-year-old child is capable of learning, and there is no reason for home builders to shy away from it. Anyone who has ever wished to build his own small castle should now feel free."

The advantage of brick for the spare time do-it-yourselfer is that, first of all, anyone can lift a brick. A brick is, as the computer generation likes to put it, "user-friendly." That is certainly not true of concrete block. Secondly, in the process of building with brick, you can quit anytime and not have to worry about rain, as you might with a wooden wall. You can work at any pace that suits you. (But you can't lay brick in below-freezing weather unless you add a quick-drying agent to the mortar, and even then I'd be leery.)

The basic mechanics of laying a brick wall are the same as laying concrete blocks, requiring only that you know how to measure accurately and plumb with a level and string. Hundreds of books tell how. For an all-brick wall, the kind most favored by masons today, is the two-wythe kind like Thorndike's. (This is despite the Brick Institute's attempt to interest builders in a one-wythe wall in place of studs, which it says can be practical. And, of course, you can always go to a three-brick thickness if you like to lay brick.) Weep holes through the bottom of the outside wythe carry off any moisture that might gather in the cavity between the two wythes of brick. Insulation is installed in the cavity as the wall mounts, and about every 2 feet vertically and 4 feet horizontally metal wall ties or crossties are laid in the mortar joints connecting the two wythes to improve strength. These ties will conduct some cold through the cavity to the inner wall, but at $3/16$ inch in diameter, not much.

Brick Paneling

If you like brick but think it is too expensive and not insulative enough, there's a new product in brick paneling for exterior siding, called Pan-Brick (Pan-Brick, Inc., 3030 Saskatchewan Drive, Regina, SK S4T 6P1, Canada). These panels are real bricks only ½ inch thick bonded to isocyanurate foam board on plywood. The panels have an R-value of 8.7 and cost about $6 per square foot installed. The bricks will last, and the foam board is supposed to, but only time will tell. The paneling is applied with drywall screws and the holes are sealed.

Another curious real brick panel is Perma-Panel (U.S. Brick, Michigan Division, 3820 Serr Road, Corunna, MI 48817). A panel, 48 by 16 inches, is composed of polystyrene insulation glued to an aluminum frame upon which ½-inch-thick bricks are set on little ledges so that there is a ⅜-inch space all around each brick. The panels, minus the bricks, are nailed and/ or glued to the wall, adhesive is applied to the aluminum, then the thin bricks are set into place and grouted. The whole system is a way to lay brick without learning how to be a bricklayer. The polystyrene backing adds insulation. No footing is necessary to support this lightweight kind of brick wall. "Moisture must not get between the panel and the substratum," say the instructions, which means you've got to have expert caulking and flashing of all potential openings. Personally, I think it would be more practical to learn to lay brick.

Concrete Masonry Units

If, in the pursuit of low maintenance, you should think twice before using concrete block for belowground foundation walls, you might want to think again before using it in aboveground walls. Except in the Southwest where houses traditionally are less often built of wood, and in certain other areas where a combination of warm, mildewy weather and termites make wood risky, people tend to avoid concrete block for their homes but use it voluminously in their public and commercial buildings. Masonry's fire safety and therefore reduced insurance rates overcome our notion that they are ugly and provide poor insulation when we are considering non-residential buildings. We can also readily see the tremendous advantage of masonry for low maintenance in, say, a supermarket wall. But in our houses, the verdict remains: too ugly, too hard to insulate.

We may be shortchanging our homes.

Today walls of concrete masonry units need be neither ugly nor poorly insulated. A visit to a large concrete block manufacturer will dispel that notion in a hurry. There are over 100 different precast masonry units made besides the standard 8-by-8-by-16-inch block, not counting all the decorative blocks used for screening walls, garden walls, and the like, nor counting the many beautiful and colorful pavers for sidewalks and driveways. You can even buy concrete blocks that come with insulation in their cores (see the box "Insulated Concrete Block" on page 35).

The standard block, along with a few other routinely made sizes, can be laid in at least 42 recognized patterns, from what is called ashlar to basketweave, to give even a plain old ho-hum block wall more dramatic visual impact. You can buy concrete brick the same size as clay brick at a much lower price. This unit, and larger ones, are available with rough-textured slump or split faces that very nearly resemble cut stone in a wall. Many other textures are possible. To avoid the plainness of the standard block, manufacturers now make fluted, ribbed, scored, recessed, beveled, serpentine, and taper-faced block. Some of these blocks are so cannily designed that when laid in a wall the mortar joints are not evident, and many people do not realize they are looking at a block wall.

There is even an acoustical block for extra sound absorbance. Slots on the face of this block, which also make a decorative pattern, conduct sound into the block's hollow core, muffling the noise. Acoustical block is used around bowling alleys, noisy factory rooms and gymnasiums, but might be a possibility in a children's playroom.

Any block can now be ordered in various colors. The aggregate used can produce various earth tones itself, but the latest advances are in mixing mineral oxide pigments with the concrete. Tan, buff, red, brown, pink, and yellow are now practical. Green and blue are expensive, and so far no method has been found to keep blue permanent. If you don't want colored block, you might choose colored mortar instead. It's more practical than colored block because it is much cheaper to color than the block, and for a lot less cost the effects achieved can be nearly as dramatic. Iron oxide makes red, yellow, brown, or black mortar; chromium oxide makes green; cobalt oxide, blue; and carbon black, black or gray.

Glazed Concrete Block

Glazed concrete blocks are another choice rarely given consideration in homes—many people are not aware that they exist. Although expensive, companies with an eye to the ultimate in low maintenance and dramatic color use them on commercial buildings. Walls around institutional indoor swimming pools are often done in glazed masonry where sanitary but beautiful permanent finishes are desired. Both smooth and textured glazed faces are made in several sizes and shapes. Why they are not used more in kitchen, laundry, and bathroom walls can only be explained to me by our preference for wood houses. My only experience with glazed masonry was years ago when we used them for part of the walls in a Grade A dairy milkroom. Their use was thought to be most extravagant for a milkhouse, but we were able to secure them as seconds because of some slight defect, so they cost little more than plain concrete block. The smooth glazed faces were extremely easy to clean compared to the concrete block around them. They were a beautiful pale green color— a little pleasure to look at each day at the beginning and end of work.

Sources of Block—and Information on It

Not all the various kinds of concrete block are available from every manufacturer. Most of the outlets you will buy from do not make their own block, as in years gone by, but order from a large manufacturer. If you want something the larger manufacturer in your area does not make, the company will invariably refer you to one that does. Since shipping concrete long distances is cost prohibitive, you might not be able to get precisely what you want, except at considerable extra expense. But as with clay brick, if your order is large enough, your local manufacturer may be only too glad to custom-make it for you.

He will also have in his office brochures and pictorials displaying some of the latest ideas in masonry, published by the National Concrete Masonry Association. (Their address is 2302 Horse Pen Road, Herndon, VA 22070. No one with an address like Horse Pen Road could possibly steer you wrong, right?)

Also, if you are thinking seriously of building or remodeling with low-maintenance masonry construction, by all means get a copy of the *Concrete Masonry Handbook for Architects, Engineers, Builders,* by Frank A. Randall, Jr., and William C. Panarese (Portland Cement Association, 5420 Old Orchard Road, Skokie, IL 60077). Even though written for professionals, this book is easy to understand, with many precise drawings of how various masonry walls should be built. And even if you are not doing the work yourself, a copy is handy to have around. Your builder's background will no doubt be in carpentry, and I have a notion there are timely instructions in this book even he may not be aware of.

Insulating a Masonry Wall

Insulating a masonry wall can be as simple as backing it with a stud wall and proceeding conventionally, but new developments are making

Insulated Concrete Block

There is a new concrete block available that will considerably increase a load-bearing concrete block wall's R-value—from less than 1 to 5 or more depending on block density. Called Insul Block, it is a concrete block whose hollow core is filled with an expanded polystyrene liner. The block is almost entirely divided by this insulative barrier, which not only increases thermal resistance but virtually eliminates condensation within a wall, sometimes a problem in concrete block walls (see the section entitled "Leaking," later in this chapter). Though the block looks weak because the two sides are connected only by a narrow bridge at the bottom, it is code-approved for any load-bearing wall situation that an ordinary block can be used for.

Split and scored face block are available, and integral colors can be added as in any concrete block. Used with ½ inch foil-backed gypsum board on furring strips, a standard 8-by-8-by-16-inch Insul Block wall has an average R-value of about 9, depending on block density. With 1 inch of expanded polystyrene and ½ inch of gypsum board, R-values range between 10 and 13.4, again depending on block density. A 2-inch cavity wall with 2-inch polystyrene board insulation in the cavity and an outside brick veneer or stone exterior would give higher R-values yet. Ten- and 12-inch-wide Insul Blocks with these additions have appropriately higher R-values, the highest being 12 to 15 depending on the density of the block.

Insul Block is entirely maintenance-free unless you paint it and should at some point want to change the color or need to add a fresh coat of paint. It is manufactured by Insul Block Corporation (55 Circuit Avenue, West Springfield, MA 01089).

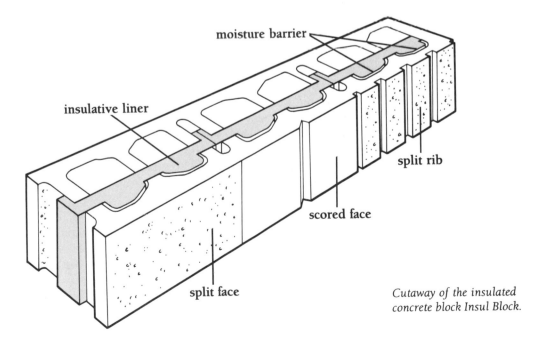

Cutaway of the insulated concrete block Insul Block.

all-masonry load-bearing walls just as easy to insulate as frame walls. To appreciate these developments, one must first realize that insulating a house for energy savings is not yet as cut-and-dried as the R-value maniacs, as I call them, have led us to believe.

The R-value maniacs leapt into instant prominence back when oil prices skyrocketed by saying that if an R-value of 12 in a wall conserved energy and saved money, then an R-value of 24 would make one rich and teach "them damned A-rabs a thing or two." So we all dutifully buttoned up our homes until we found that they were so tight you could barely close a door without popping an eardrum, and inside environments were becoming polluted because there was so little ventilation. Having spent more money than we would have spent trying to insulate the damned A-rabs out of our lives, we then had to spend even more money getting the house (and us) to breathe healthfully again while still trying to preserve the supposed savings of all that extra insulation.

What we have learned now is two things: First, heat loss through walls is only a minor part of total heat loss—only 10 to 26 percent of the whole in single family residences. Roofs, floors, windows, and doors (the latter often left open for 5 minutes at a time by children trying to make up their minds whether to go back outside or come in) are more critical areas. (See *The Concrete Approach to Energy Conservation* from the Portland Cement Association, 5420 Old Orchard Road, Skokie, IL 60077.)

And second, once R-values of about 12 are reached in walls "adding insulation beyond that level would be cost-effective only in very cold climates," say the editors of *Rodale's Practical Homeowner* magazine.

Furthermore, with new electronic gadgetry, architects are learning that the conventional way of figuring heat and cold transfer in a building does not necessarily apply for heavy masonry construction. Because masonry has a much greater heat storage capacity than lighter (wood) construction, it does not respond to temperature fluctuations as fast as wood. Heat transfer is calculated upon the assumption that there is a constant difference between extreme outdoor and indoor air temperatures—"steady state response" in architectural terms. But because heavy masonry walls act as heat or cold sinks or reservoirs, they temper the actual difference between indoor and outdoor temperatures, which in fact are fluctuating all the time. This is called, and can now be measured as, "dynamic thermal response."

In controlled tests, a heavy masonry wall subjected to an outside cyclic temperature variation of 60°F had heat flow rates calculated by the steady state method to be 32 to 69 percent higher than when calculated by the dynamic thermal response method. In other words, steady state gives an unfair comparison with wood of the same U-value. That's why a masonry building with the same heat transfer values (U-value) as a lighter wood building will be cooler than the latter on a hot summer day. Heat gain in a wood house peaks at about 4 P.M. but not until 8 P.M. in a masonry house of the same U-value, when it is cool enough to open a window or step outside. What's more, the peak is considerably higher in the wood house than in the masonry.

It is not difficult to get close to R-12 insulation value in an all-masonry wall anymore. One way is to use furring strips inside with 2-inch batt insulation between them and also to fill the hollow cores of the block with bulk insulation. Add on interior paneling and you are then in the R-13 range. Cavity walls filled with 2 inches of insulation between two wythes of masonry result in an R-value of about 10.

Cost of Concrete Block

The cost of a concrete block can vary from place to place, and the cost of the labor to lay them can vary even more. Right now, in 1986 in Ohio, the cost of a standard 8-by-16-inch block is 73¢ or less, depending on how many you order. Total cost of construction, including labor and mortar is right around $1.70 per standard block.

Fluted, scored, and other fancy load-supporting block are, of course, higher priced. For example, a gray fluted 8 × 8 × 16 costs $1.47 not counting labor; a brown fluted of the same size, $1.68; and a white fluted $1.85. In local outlets in my part of the country, plain Insul Block is $1.40 each, a little higher for the same block with decorated faces. Decorative block for screening or garden walls is $1.26 each and up.

Pricing masonry units is not much help until you know who's going to lay them. City union masons charge a good bit more than country non-union. Of course, a highly paid professional mason will usually lay block fast and well, justifying his high wage.

Mortaring

Much of the quality of a masonry wall depends on the mortar work. A block is laid in place on its bed of mortar and against the preceding block's head so that the concrete oozes just so-so to fill *all* the mortar space and bulge out a little. Otherwise, holes in the mortar may result in water penetration or a weak joint. The amount of mortar laid down for a bed or buttered on the block's head before laying is important. In some instances, even the *way* the mortar is laid down is dictated by building codes (see the *Concrete Masonry Handbook*, noted in Appendix B). Globs of mortar dropped on the scaffold and allowed to dry partially should not be thrown back on the mortarboard. Mortar splattered against the wall will have to be cleaned off. Wait until it is partially dry, scrape off with a trowel, then when the spot is dry, rub it out with a broken piece of block.

In laying up a cavity wall, you need to be careful not to drip wet concrete down into the cavity where it would block water from going out weep holes and interfere with the installation of insulation boards in the cavity. (To prevent this from happening, you can lower a board that's the width of the cavity down into the cavity. Suspend it by a wire at each end of the board and hook these wires over the top block line you are working on. Then the concrete will fall on the board, which you can later lift out.)

MASONRY EQUIPMENT

It is a good idea to have a catalog of masonry equipment even if you don't intend to do the work yourself. Such catalogs are very educational. They display tools the neophyte never realized there was a job for. They are also excellent for mail ordering hard-to-find tools seldom available locally. The one I have, free for the asking, is from the Masonry Specialty Company (4430 Gibsonia Road, Gibsonia, PA 15044). Another good one I have heard about is Goldblatt Tool Company (P.O. Box 2334, 511 Osage Street, Kansas City, KS 66110). Catalogs provide a choice of *quality* tools usually. To the beginner, a trowel is a trowel is a trowel, but a professional will tell you it is foolish to buy a cheap one.

Controlling Cracking

With masonry walls, the biggest low-maintenance worry should not be insulation but quality construction to avoid cracking. Although concrete appears to the neophyte to be a very inert material, it actually shrinks as it dries, just like wood does, only much less, of course. If the blocks have nowhere to move, then they crack along the mortar joints. In fact, large expanses of block walls are almost bound to crack, but that alone is of no significance if the cracking is controlled. You can control cracking by doing a number of things.

First of all, to discourage cracking and to make the wall stronger, fill the entire top row of block with concrete. Some masons also "grout" or "bond" a row in the middle this way, too. Then install reinforcing rod or mesh of various kinds in the solid concrete vertically or horizontally or both. But the main way to control cracking is to leave control joints here and there in the wall. Control joints are not mortared in the usual manner, and when the wall moves, it cracks along this unmortared or partially mortared joint where it is unnoticeable and relatively harmless. Your builder should know all about these matters, of course, but it doesn't hurt for you to have your masonry handbook in hand. Control joints are not nearly as crucial in smaller single-family residences as in large stretches of masonry blocks, like apartments, but it is good to be aware of them.

A top bond beam should be built into every house wall—that is filling the top row of block completely with concrete (called grouting), and usually, adding reinforcing rod to interlock the bond beam with the wall beneath it. Sometimes a bond beam is added to the middle of the wall. In basement walls, about every fourth row of block ought to be bonded and reinforced. In hurricane and earthquake country, building codes require steel rod reinforcing vertically and horizontally throughout block walls.

Leaking

Moisture transmission through masonry must also be dealt with properly. The objection that concrete blocks "leak" is almost always an exaggeration, but occasionally a driving rain will penetrate some concrete blocks, usually through a flaw in the mortar joint. Stucco (see below) is one way to waterproof block. A cavity wall is also very effective—if water gets through the outer wythe, it runs down the cavity and out the weep holes. Various concrete sealers and paints on the market (see chapter 2) also take care of the problem.

Condensation of water within block walls in very cold weather can cause frost buildup. Proper insulation almost always avoids this problem, but in very cold climates in high humidity situations (like in a laundry room), frost buildup might occur in the wall. An inside vapor barrier is the antidote.

Surface Bond Masonry

A new way of building with concrete block reduces the cracking problem in concrete block walls and all but eliminates the possibility of leaking. If the method becomes popular, the *Concrete Masonry Handbook* will have to be partially rewritten.

"Surface bond masonry," as it is called, allows the erection of block walls without mortar in the joints. The first row of blocks are laid in mortar on the footer *very* level, and then the rest of the blocks are dry-stacked. Anybody who has a strong back can do it. Once the walls are dry-stacked plumb and square, reinforcing rods are inserted at intervals in the concrete block, and the hollow cores around these rods are filled with cement. Then the surfaces of the block are plastered with a special concrete mixture strong enough to make a wall the building codes approve of.

Years ago when an obscure scientist in the U.S. Department of Agriculture first announced success with this process, everyone thought they were hearing another eager researcher trying to publish before he perished, but 25 years later the method is in practice. Many builders are still wary, and block layers are uneasy about using this method.

The secret to this method is in the fiberglass shavings and acrylic bonding additives that are mixed into the portland cement. The glass fibers are about an inch long and add great tensile strength to the concrete.

Other additives increase strength, moisture resistance, and insulating effect. Despite all this strength, the surface bonding actually still has a bit of give to it, which is one reason why it is not apt to crack. A second or third coating may need to be applied, depending on which specific product is used. The brand I'm familiar with is Surewall (W. R. Bonsal Company, P.O. Box 241148, Charlotte, NC 28224). Ask your concrete block manufacturer what is available in your area.

"The method works, really works," says Fred Smith, president of Fostoria Concrete Products, Inc., in Fostoria, Ohio. "But we've had a hard time getting the idea accepted by builders in this area." One minor drawback is that without the ⅜-inch mortar joints, customary measurements that have become so habitual in block construction don't apply. An 8-foot wall, for example, "won't lay up right," as one builder complains. It takes 12 standard blocks to lay up an 8-foot wall. Each measures 8 inches tall only if you count the mortar joints, since a block actually measures 7⅝ inches tall. With dry stacking, some additional odd-size block is necessary if the usual 8-foot wall is to be maintained.

Stucco

If and when surface bond masonry becomes a popular way to put up masonry walls, it will be especially suitable for stucco exteriors, since the surface bonding material can be mixed with the stucco (which is precisely what contractors are doing). But whether blocks are mortared or dry-stacked, stucco over them (or over metal lath on wood for that matter) is one of the cheapest, and in my opinion, prettiest of low-maintenance exteriors. We used to live in a stuccoed house. When it was about 25 years old, I brightened up the white stucco exterior with a new coat of cement paint, but the walls didn't need it for any maintenance reason. Applying stucco by hand is hard work, but the rough textures require little plastering skill to achieve. In fact, professionals use machines to blow on stucco through a hose.

A new or clean concrete block wall will take stucco very well without need of metal mesh or lath. Wet the wall first for good bonding. The base coat should be about ⅜ inch thick and left plenty rough. A second coat should be about ¼ inch thick and textured to suit your preference. The concrete plaster can be tinted with various colors to save painting.

With the new surface bonding cements, stucco offers increased advantages in addition to not having to mortar the walls. Surewall, for example, offers seven colors in its surface bonding cement and its finish coat to avoid the need for painting: Antique White, Natural White, Pale Yellow, Pearl Gray, Sandstone, Suntan, and White Jade. It also offers six textured finishes, from Light Lace to Travertine. Who ever thought humble stucco would hobnob in such snooty company?

Stucco over Exterior Insulation

Of greater significance than pretty colors and a nice finish is the new insulative qualities of these materials. The products being pioneered by the surface bonding companies allow for better insulation of masonry walls, and this insulation is on the exterior of these walls, where it is most effective.

A coat of surface bonding cement is first applied to the raw masonry wall. Then, using special adhesives and mechanical fasteners, polystyrene insulation panels are attached to the wall, and one or more coats of stucco are applied over the insulation. Lathing with metal or glass mesh is not necessary. Because of the resiliency of the insulation board and the adhesives used, the wall can move without cracking the surface coating. (Control joints are required in most cases.)

Manufacturers claim that this type of insulation increases heating and air-conditioning efficiency because the heavy masonry building mass inside the insulation envelope remains at a more stable temperature relative to outdoor fluctuating temperatures. This increased ability of masonry to act as a heat sink makes the insulation method especially interesting for

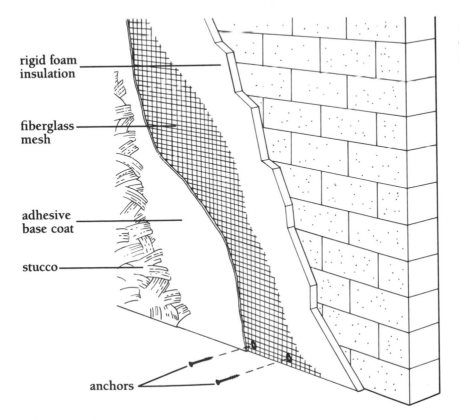

rigid foam insulation

fiberglass mesh

adhesive base coat

stucco

anchors

Cutaway of stucco over exterior insulation over masonry wall.

passive solar systems, where heat from the sun needs to be stored effectively for nighttime winter use, and cold nighttime temperatures stored for daytime summer use. In fact, builders of passive solar homes pioneered the use of surface bond masonry on the masonry walls they built into their homes.

Two inches of polystyrene board stuccoed to the outside of a standard concrete block wall gives a total R-value of 10.56 (counting the R-value of the stucco and the block along with the polystyrene).

Other recent refinements in exterior insulation and stronger plasters make stucco look even more attractive for the future. Manufacturers like Penbar, Inc. (2808 North 2 Street, Minneapolis, MN 55411), apply their acrylic-improved concrete to *extruded* polystyrene rather than the expanded kind. Extruded foam has a tighter cell structure, less moisture permeability, and more compressive strength. Moisture could become a crucial problem in exterior insulation board and stucco finishes because, to use the words of the experts, "water may get behind the insulation, and when it freezes and expands, the system can delaminate from the substrate." ("Delaminate from the substrate" means, in plain English, that it can come loose from the wall.) Extruded polystyrene has an R-value of 5 per inch, exceeding expanded polystyrene.

Penbar calls its exterior insulation/stucco system "the energy envelope," touting the superior advantages of applying insulation on the exterior wall over insulation on the interior wall. Its exterior insulation can be applied to masonry, wood, even metal. Special adhesives glue the insulation board to the wall. Fiberglass mesh is then fastened to the insulation board with galvanized nails. Then, special mechanical anchor assemblies go through the mesh, the insulation, and into the wall to anchor all solidly. A bonding agent is paint-rolled onto the mesh, the fiber-reinforced base coat of concrete is then applied, and finally, the finish coat is put on. The last operation is to spray on a clear or colored sealant. Penbar's stuccos are available in varying shades of red, yellow, buff, orange, green, brown, and black, mixed integrally into the cement. The resulting stucco finish is advertised as being maintenance-free.

Dryvit (Dryvit System, Inc., P.O. Box 1014, One Energy Way, West Warwick, RI 02983) was used over brick on two Rodale Press buildings to add insulative value and to spruce up the exterior. The finish has held up well for the three years that it's been there. In the process, at least 6 inches of insulating foam was applied to the outside of the brick, and the large, warehouselike buildings are now energy efficient. Fuel bills have gone down appreciably. And Roger Moyer, a former Rodale employee who worked in one of the buildings, says that the appearance of the buildings was completely changed: they went from run-down brick to neat and modern. And as a bonus, he adds, the Dryvit has made the buildings quieter because the foam and stucco exterior provides more of a sound barrier to outside noises than did the plain brick.

Being what economists call a contrarian, I can't help bringing my mental attitude toward the economy into the realm of philosophy and architecture. I am pessimistic about the long-term endurance of exterior insulation boards glued to house walls, even though there appears to be no problems. The improved stuccos will certainly last because even the unimproved ones do. But in 20 years will "delamination from the substrate" become a problem? It is a fair question to ask, I think. When I ask it, I'm assured my worries are unjustified.

Stuccolike Materials for Patching, Anchoring, Waterproofing

There are other improved, super-strong concretes on the market that can be used for stucco or, if too expensive for that, are perfect for patching, anchoring, and thin-coat waterproofing. Kan Kote, Inc. (P.O. Box H, Parker, PA 16049), has been around for a decade in the professional builder's market, but only recently for the general consumer. Thin mixtures will waterproof and seal masonry and stone, even wood. With the addition of sand, it makes a cement with strength enough to endure considerable flexing and movement. Another stucco product, Advocote (Coatings International, 5123 Woodlane Circle, Tallahassee, FL 32303) will, like Kan Kote, stick to just about anything and has remarkable tensile strength. I bent a piece of sheet metal to which it was stuccoed over 45 degrees from straight before the stucco cracked. Another stronger-than-concrete product is Rockite (Hartline Products Company, Inc., 2186 Noble Road, Cleveland, OH 44112).

Natural Stone

A classic example of the low-maintenance house is the magnificent stone mansion that the famous architect Charles Greene built in the 1920s for D. L. James near Carmel, on the California coast. The roof is tile (more on that in chapter 4), and the rest of the exterior is stone entirely, hauled (by horse and wagon) from a nearby quarry. Even the roof guttering is tile and stone. The foundation is a natural outcropping of bedrock that underlies the site. The stone itself, practically free for the hauling, is of a rather nondescript gray-brown, but when laid by an artist, walls become breathtakingly beautiful. (Greene directed the laying of every stone, and when the masons laid a part of a wall while he was absent, he had it torn down because it didn't quite match the texture he was striving for.) Greene also demonstrated that irregularly shaped stones could be adapted to any form an architect could dream up. He used them to frame round windows, to

The D. L. James house near Carmel, California, built by Charles Greene in the 1920s.

make large and small arches, for the sills under windows, for grottoed door frames, for chimneys and parapets. You have to see it to believe it; the photo here doesn't do it justice. (You can read the article "The James House: Charles Greene's Masterpiece in Stone" in *Fine Homebuilding* magazine, December 1984/January 1985.)

The James house—castle, really—was of course extremely expensive to build, but one can use the lessons it teaches to build a very fine but a more humble-size home quite cheaply. Greene, who came out of the arts and crafts movement of the early twentieth century, was following in that tradition: make use of as much of the natural materials around you as possible. On such a rocky site as he built on, a person in spare time could start laying up stone on the natural bedrock—the stone free for the breaking and lifting—and raise a house to the roofline without spending much more than the cost of mortar.

Slipforming

Even stone walls built with slip forms, where you can't really see the pattern you are creating too well until you take the form away, are very attractive, as anyone understands who has seen Scott and Helen Nearing's home or read their books on the subject of stone walls. "A slipformed house can be built for less than two-thirds the cost of a similar house made of wood and will compare favorably with mason-built stone houses in terms of durability and attractiveness," says the book *Back to Basics: How to Learn and Enjoy Traditional American Skills* (Reader's Digest Association, 1981). Still more money can be saved by building a two-wythe "sandwich" wall with insulation in the cavity (as I talked about earlier in this chapter when I discussed brick and masonry walls) and letting the inner wythe serve as the inner wall. This practice is best suited for the walls that surround a large fireplace. The heat of the fire will be absorbed into the heavy stone walls and radiate back out over a long period of time. If, on the

Scott and Helen Nearing hand-built all the stone buildings on their homestead by using the slipforming method. Wooden forms hold the stone vertically in place as mortar shoveled in between the stones cement them together. Once set, the forms are removed.

other hand, an inside wall is to be paneled or otherwise needs furring strips, these are embedded in the concrete as the form is filled, against the interior side of the form. In this case, the stones are laid mostly to the exterior side of the form, and the interior side is filled with concrete only. There are many good books on slipforming stone walls, including the Nearings' account in their book *Living the Good Life* (Stackpole Books, 1970) and *Build It Better Yourself* (Rodale Press, 1976).

Commercial Stone

If you purchase any of the commercially marketed natural stone, you can figure spending roughly up to twice the cost of brick by the time the stone is laid up into a wall. Here in Ohio, this is partially due to the easier availability of brick. A significant part of the cost of brick or stone is transportation. If you live near a marble quarry but far from a brickyard, the prices of both might be more equal. But generalities don't always hold. Italian marble used to be cheaper than domestic marble because Italians earned less for their work than Americans. Now it's because the Italians have perfected new machinery to quarry, cut, and polish marble more efficiently. These new technologies, says Robert Hund of the Marble Institute of America (33505 State Street, Farmington, MI 48024), are now being adopted in the United States and should mean lower prices for domestic marble in the future.

This is especially good news for low-maintenance housing, because hardly any material is at once more long lasting and beautiful. Because of its cost, we generally think of marble for interior use (more on that in chapter 11), but it is also used extensively for exteriors of commercial businesses, which have the money to spend. Owners of these buildings feel it's worth the extra money up front; because there's less maintenance over time, in the long run the cost is lower.

There are over 1,000 different types and varieties of marble, some denser than others, of many, many colors: Belgian Black, Cipollino Dorato, Craig Pink Tennessee, Golden Antique Travertine, Norwegian Rose, Nuvolato Apuano, Pakistani Onyx, Rose Alhambra, Rouge Royal Rose, Vermont Imperial Danby, White Italian.

Commercial stone can usually be bought either as cut stone or as rubble. Cut stone has square, flat sides and edges for easier laying, and the pieces come in varying sizes of squares and rectangles to make any number of wall patterns. Thickness is generally about 3 inches for veneer walls but can be ordered as much as 6 inches thick. Rubble refers to broken pieces of the stone, 3 to 6 inches wide, to be laid up with random mortar joints. Rubble gives a more natural stone appearance and is far prettier to me, but to each his own. Rubble, of course, takes more masonry skill to lay but is cheaper per square foot to buy.

Your best bet, however, especially when money is a chief concern, is to use whatever stone is available nearby, be it quarry stone, creek stone, or fieldstone. If you worry that the local stone is not durable enough, you can easily check with local builders or examine old buildings that used the stone or ask a geologist. Granite, marble, slate, schist, gneiss, sandstone, limestone, and even basalt, which is very hard to break, are the kinds of stone most often used.

Durability

No general statement is possible concerning the durability of different kinds of stone. It is easy enough to say that limestone lacks durability in moist climates, and some books say just that, but it ain't necessarily so. Indiana limestone is very durable, as all the old buildings at Indiana University demonstrate. The limestone from quarries in my neighborhood may or may not deteriorate. Some pieces in my retaining wall have broken up after exposure to the weather, especially those in contact with the soil, but other chunks do not. After awhile, you can tell the durable stuff from the not-so-durable. But in mortared walls and chimneys, both kinds seem to last quite well. I know of a building constructed of this limestone at least 50 years old that has not one crack or fractured stone in it.

Sandstone sometimes is not as durable as, say, granite or basalt. "It'll only last a hundred years," one builder says sarcastically. A silicone sealer may be advisable. It's a good idea in this regard to talk to more than one source of information or more than one owner of such houses. The brick and masonry people argue a lot about whether or not their products need sealing.

Cutting Stone

Masonry saws with abrasive wheels or diamond blades will cut some kinds of stone, especially sandstone, another reason the latter is popular. Saws cost $300 and up. Mechanical stone splitters, from $200 to $600, work well on some stone, particularly paving stones, but a sledgehammer is a lot cheaper. Cutting and shaping stone takes skill. Every kind of stone is different. But there is a grain and also fracture planes in stone that enable one to learn to shape a stone for a particular place in the wall. More often than not, you can make a groove in the rock with a stone chisel, and then when you break the rock with a hammer, the fracture will follow the line of least resistance, which is the groove you made.

Facsimile Stone Made of Concrete

In an effort to utilize the beauty of stone while avoiding its weight, imaginative manufacturers are making stones out of concrete. They tint the concrete to resemble the color of the original stone and cast it in molds. Some from the L. B. Stone Company (Box 276, Apple Creek, OH 44606) were used in the new library in our town and to me are very attractive. Years ago I went through the L. B. Stone Company's fascinating little factory, which is owned and operated by Bob Bixler, quite a fascinating fellow himself. (When not making concrete rocks, he likes to run steam locomotives.)

Molding the concrete rocks is mostly a hand operation, which is why the fake stone costs more than the real stuff. But the method allows Bixler to duplicate any rock from anywhere. When he travels, he keeps his eyes open and has brought back specimens from all over the country. The *exact* texture of the rocks is imprinted on the molds, and then when the concrete is poured into them and dries, the hardened surface looks remarkably real, even though it is but the shell of the real rock, flat on the back for easy installation on the wall. Installed, the facsimiles weigh 8 to 12 pounds per square foot; in comparison, brick weighs 28 to 30 pounds. A favorite place to use them is in interior walls around a fireplace, where there is not sufficient foundation under the floor to support real brick or stone. Outside, they can be attached to a masonry or wood wall (same as for brick), where there is not enough solid footer to support stone or brick. There is also a stucco unit applied about the same way.

The salespeople at Northwestern Masonry, a leading distributor of all kinds of stone and masonry supplies in our area, advise caution in the

Builders of traditional adobe houses found a clever way to prevent rainwater from wetting the walls and thereby weakening the adobe walls. They hollowed out a few of the horizontal roof timbers so they could act as gutters, collecting roof water and dumping it out beyond the walls.

exterior use of these concrete stone products. The fake stones are thinner than brick and moisture might penetrate them, say the salespeople. They like to see the concrete stones used under an extra large overhang and/or given a silicone sealing treatment.

Adobe

Like the igloo, the adobe house is low maintenance only in a specific climate—very dry, in adobe's case. Adobe, which is sun-dried mud—a mixture of sand, silt, clay, and chopped straw—is really a very soft brick, and it resembles brick in many of its properties. But unlike brick, it will deteriorate in a humid climate. In the dry areas of the Southwest, where it is traditional, adobe is practical, durable, and easy to maintain. There are adobe walls still standing that are over 500 years old, some perhaps even 1,000 years old.

Traditionally, adobe is plastered over with the same clay used to make the adobe bricks. Traditionalists are trying to revive this kind of plastering, but it is not as maintenance-free as using ordinary stucco, especially for an exterior finish. Stucco goes on over adobe as easily as over concrete block, although for exterior walls, metal lath (chicken wire will work) is nailed to the adobe wall first. The scratch coat is then applied, and a second brown coat put over it. Usually a third finishing coat is then applied as in regular stuccoing. On the inside, metal lath is generally not used. A coat of fibered gypsum plaster is troweled on, followed by a second and final coat of unfibered gypsum plaster.

Insulating Value

Contrary to popular opinion, adobe is not a good insulating material, at least in R-value measurements. But like brick and concrete its bulk provides great thermal stability—slow to heat up and cool down. On a hot day, it is cool in an adobe house. If the night grows chilly, as happens in the Southwest, the adobe house radiates the heat absorbed during the day and maintains a comfortable temperature. In cold weather, the walls will absorb the heat of a hot stove and radiate it back after the stove fire goes out. In technical terms, adobe has a very good "dynamic thermal response," a term I used earlier. To increase its insulative value, you can add polystyrene or polyurethane panels over the adobe and then stucco the panels as previously described. Some builders spray 2 inches of polyurethane foam over the exterior adobe walls and stucco over it after it hardens.

Look closely at the top center of this modern adobe house and you'll see an interior gutter system built into it to direct rainwater away from the walls.

Adobe Bricks

Making adobe bricks is easy but making enough for a house is strenuous labor. The best way is to make forms out of 2-by-4 lumber (4-by-10-by-14 inches or 4-by-12-by-14 inches are the usual dimensions for the usual 10- or 12-inch-thick walls). Two-, four-, or six-unit gang molds are the handiest.

There are easy methods to determine if your clay soil will make good adobe, but if you are a beginner, you would be wise to seek advice. Suffice it to say, this is one instance when you do *not* want organic matter in the soil that keeps it loose and friable. If you live where adobe is practical, advice should not be hard to find, and if you don't, you probably shouldn't be making adobe anyway. At any rate, making your own adobe bricks is more practical (but not much) than making your own concrete blocks, because all the ingredients you need are available, cheap, and easy. Stand the hardened bricks on edge to dry in the sun. Curing time is ten days minimum. Store bricks so that rain cannot hit them directly, but with the edges open to good air circulation, and stack in such a way that pressure from the weight will not ease them out of shape.

Mortar for adobe bricks is made of the same clay used for making the bricks but the straw is left out.

Keeping It Dry

Water is the great enemy of adobe, which is why an adobe house is built the way it is. We Easterners never understand why those timbers protrude from the side of an adobe house near the roofline. In a real adobe house, those protruding timbers are hollowed out at the ends to draw off water that gathers on the nearly flat roof. Today not all the timbers are hollowed for drains, or *canales*, as they are called; usually only the end ones are. The roof is nearly flat so as to expose the least amount of expanse to falling rain, and therefore reduce runoff to the minimum. The walls rise above the roofline to ensure that all the water is funneled through the canales to drip harmlessly out away from the wall, not run down the wall or splash against it.

Metal Exteriors

One of the most low-maintenance homes ever built was the Lustron in the late 1940s, the brainchild of Carl Strandlund. Strandlund had the idea of manufacturing houses in factories, shipping them to the building

One of Carl Strandlund's Lustron houses, built in the late 1940s. Studs, joists, trusses, walls inside and out, and even the roofing tiles were made of steel.

site and erecting them, ready to move into, in less than three weeks. (Another of those "new" ideas that isn't really new at all.) The Lustron was noteworthy because it had hardly a speck of wood in it. Studs, joists, roof trusses—everything—was steel. Exterior and interior wall panels were *porcelainized* steel, which gave the Lustron its distinctive look in sprightly pastel colors. Even the roof shingles were porcelainized steel. The house, which came in several models, was impervious to the weather. Maintenance, inside and out, amounted to wiping with a wet rag. Some people simonized their Lustrons! Porcelain will chip, of course, but it can be touched up with enamel. More major repairs can be handled admirably with auto-body putty, and if the houses would have caught on, auto repairmen would have discovered another way to make a living.

But, alas, they didn't. The government pumped millions of dollars into the project and hence it became a political football, not without the usual suspicions and allegations of scandal. But mostly, Strandlund was way ahead of his time. People of a Wood Culture were not accustomed to thinking of life in a steel house, and though lovers of Art Deco found Lustrons most interesting, if not downright attractive, the ordinary homebuyer thought they looked like colorful diners, or White Castle hamburger joints in technicolor. Only something less than 5,000 Lustrons were built, but many of them still stand, virtually indestructible. Retrofitted with more insulation in these days of higher fuel costs, the Lustron makes a wonderful starter home, say people who still live in them. The only item in the original houses that didn't perform well was the combination clothes washer/dishwasher!

I hope though, that Strandlund's main contribution to homebuilding—a cheaper process of porcelainizing steel—will not be ignored. Enameling, as this process is called when artists do it on copper, is an ancient craft, with a potential for limitless colors and patterns, some of breathtaking beauty. Finding a way to reduce costs enough so the process could be used in commercial manufacturing led to the avocado-colored refrigerator, whose passing no one laments. But with a little imagination, the process could be used for interior walls, and yes, exterior ones too, impervious to wear and moisture and extremely attractive.

Steel Houses of the '80s

Steel homes are very much back in the news now, and this time the public is more favorably disposed. Not too surprisingly, the attraction to all steel homes is in the South, where mildew, rot, and termites exact such a price from wood, and where wood's superior insulative properties are not as necessary.

Madray Building Systems (P.O. Box 712, Okechobee, FL 33473) has been in production only two months at this writing, and, says Trudy Kogut, who not only works for Madray but is also building one of the

The Madray house, a modern version of the steel frame house, displaying here its steel skeleton.

The finished Madray house looks very much like a conventional prefabricated house.

houses, "we've just been overwhelmed with inquiries and orders from all over the world."

Madray makes and sells structural steel components for the frame of the house. Choice of exterior and interior finish is left to the homeowner, but if you want metal siding (and roofing), the firm sells Galvalume (from Bethlehem Steel) in several colors. Galvalume is steel that is plated with an aluminum/zinc alloy. The finish is guaranteed for 20 years. "The finish 'bleeds' if chipped by a rock," says Kogut, "which means that it runs back together to cover the blemish." Galvalume also has good durability in the salty air of oceanside locations, where ordinary galvanized metal will deteriorate rather rapidly.

The framework of a steel home will remind you of the toy erector sets children used to play with, only full size. Because of the way the pieces go together, at least with Madray and I presume the others (see below and in Appendix A), proper squareness and straightness is automatic. You don't have to fiddle around with a level all the time.

A Madray house frame can be erected in less than an hour, using unskilled labor, as the company demonstrates before TV cameras. Cost is very competitive with wood homes. "Frankly, as a single mother with three children, it is the only new home I've found that I can afford," says Kogut. The company is not yet publishing final cost figures, but it appears the house will cost less than $25 a square foot, not counting heating and air-conditioning units. "Another advantage is that you can stockpile the components until you have enough money to start building and they won't wrap, swell, rot, or split," says Kogut. "Or you can build the frame and let it stand until you can afford the rest without worrying about the weather."

The steel frame allows for 6 inches of insulating space inside the walls. "Walls and roof have an R-19 rating," says Kogut, "and you can add more insulation if you want." The exteriors can be wood-paneled, stuccoed, or whatever. "Stucco is very popular here in the South," says Kogut, "and works well with our homes to make an extremely low-maintenance, long-lasting house."

Tri-Steel Structures, Inc. (1400 Cresent, Denton, TX 76201), is another manufacturer of modern steel houses. Tri-Steel makes simulated tile out of galvanized steel for roofing and galvanized steel panels for exteriors at a cost of about $55 a square. (For more information about such steel structures, see *Steel Homes,* by Drs. Carl and Barbara Giles [TAB Books, 1981].)

House Siding: Steel versus Aluminum versus Vinyl

About the only thing I ever learn from going to home shows is that *everybody* has the best product. If you are looking for a siding for your home, be prepared to listen to a bewildering array of superlatives (topped only by the sellers of replacement windows). One thing seems certain to me: the vinyl-siding salespeople outperform the others, even if their product does not.

I staggered home from my last home show with my sackful of brochures and did what I should have done in the first place. I asked around for the name of a reliable siding company that installed a variety of different products. Don's Siding Company, Tiffin, Ohio, handles steel, aluminum, and vinyl, among other materials. When I asked the folks there how they ranked the three for low-maintenance value, there was no hesitation: steel was best, aluminum second, and vinyl third.

Vinyl's advantage is price. Aluminum costs about 15 percent more, and steel 30 percent more. Looking at about 100 homes the company had sided most recently, the average cost to the homeowner for steel was about $7,500; for aluminum, $6,200; and for vinyl, $5,300. Given the fact that all three sidings (if of good quality) now carry 50-year or lifetime-of-the-purchaser warranties, many people are going to choose vinyl.

In extremes of weather temperature changes, vinyl will expand and contract as much as 1 to 1½ inches per 12 feet of length. So it is very important that each nail be placed in the center of its slotted hole, or the vinyl will buckle when it expands. Aluminum will expand ⅜ inch per 12 feet, and if there is not room allowed for that expansion, I've seen it loosen, even break off nails, then work loose in the wind. Steel's expansion and contraction is negligible.

The coating is guaranteed not to fade on all three products. The aluminum gable ends on my house are a deep brown, and they did fade over time, however, which led to a minor argument between me and Don's Siding Company. They told me that my aluminum did not fade, but "chalked," and that if I had read my warranty closely and followed it, I would have washed the chalking off twice a year and prevented the "fading" effect. (There is—was—a chalk in the paint to make it stick to the aluminum better.) Obviously, washing off aluminum siding twice a year is not my idea of low maintenance, and if I had known then what I know now, I'd have chosen steel for those gable ends, not aluminum. The new baked-on enamels (like Du Pont's Tedlar) appear to be as permanent as vinyl's integrated colors. Only time will tell for both products.

Hail will dent aluminum sometimes, a flying stone or baseball will nearly always. In very cold weather, a blow to vinyl might crack it, but that would be unusual. Steel or aluminum might interfere with television reception if you had only a small inside aerial. Metal siding will usually ground itself in the event of electrical contact, but some people go to the precaution of attaching a regular ground anyway, not unlike a ground used for a lightning rod.

There is no insulative value in either metal, and very little in the vinyl. All three, being mere skins on the house, have no thermal storage capacity, either. (Although you can buy Styrofoam insulating panels that are sized to slip behind such siding when it's being installed.) Vinyl and aluminum add no strength to the house. This is my main objection to them. We build stud frames that are not exactly hefty in the first place, and then we hang layer after layer of "skins" inside and out. Stone, masonry, wood, even heavy-gauged steel, combine beauty and strength and make more sense even at higher prices.

The first reason the people at Don's Siding gave for putting steel ahead of aluminum and vinyl is that is looks better. Joints, edges, and seams overlap much more neatly, giving a quality look to the house. And no doubt, keep rain from ever seeping through.

Exterior Wood Siding

People generally think that wood is the least durable of all sidings, and some of what I've written would support that. However, certain woods known for moisture resistance will weather very well.

Walnut

A fable for today's homebuilder: Not far from my place stands a clapboard house whose exterior wood is entirely black walnut. Some of the interior framing is black walnut, too. The house has stood empty for many years, but it is still square, straight, and undecayed. If you know your woods, this will not surprise you. Black walnut is at least as resistant to decay in the weather as cedar and redwood (See R. Bruce Hoadley's book *Understanding Wood,* The Taunton Press, 1980, for a good grasp of the properties of various kinds of wood.) But who would be so stupid or rich to use such valuable wood for siding?

The answer is that black walnut was once common and plentiful in the Midwest, from Pennsylvania to Iowa, and could still be with a little foresight. We cut down most of the forest where black walnut likes to grow because that's where corn grows best, too. Now we have such a surplus of corn that the government pays billions of dollars in subsidies (read taxpayer money) to keep corn farmers from going broke, while the price of black walnut rises until some foresters refer to it as black gold. The tree will grow literally like a weed, if given half a chance. Where there is an old tree to produce seeds, the seedlings will spring up as if by magic in old pastures, as they are doing on land I am taking back to forest.

Recently I walked a wooded creek valley that just 16 years ago was clear pasture. To my amazement, the young woodland was studded with black walnut trees already 6 to 8 inches in diameter and 20 feet high or more to the first limb. Thousands and thousands of acres of such little valleys cultivated for corn every year (they flood out three out of four years) should be growing black walnut, enough even for beautiful, long-lasting house siding.

But what is that to a modern homebuyer who can only shed so many tears for the past while he worries about his present alternatives? Not much perhaps, but eventually the same tragedy will occur with cedar and redwood, about the only available woods left that will endure as house siding without regular painting. Secondly, a lucky few in the right place with the right knowledge might be able to buy black walnut logs too defective for the high veneer price or even the high-grade furniture market and buy them reasonably for random board siding or for shingles. Sounds fantastic, but I had a couple of logs that timber buyers wouldn't even pay firewood prices for. They would have made fine shingles.

Mesquite

In northern Mexico and some parts of our own Southwest, there are stone houses dating from the latter 1700s with *exposed* lintels over doors and windows made of mesquite—still solid. Mesquite is a very durable wood, as these lintels prove. And why is that of special note? Because in the Southwest, especially in west Texas, ranchers have been trying (unsuccessfully) to kill about 58 million acres of mesquite to make pasture for cattle whose red meat is not only in surplus but also now of questionable dietary value. In addition to its low-maintenance durability, mesquite machines well, takes a beautiful finish, and makes quality parquet floors. All it needs to become commercially valuable is to grow larger in size, which it has not been able to do in the last half century because of ranchers hell-bent on playing cowboy at the expense of the ecology of west Texas.

Black Locust

The best example I can give of a really durable low-maintenance wood is black locust, all but ignored in this country. Black locust will last in contact with moist soil for 30 or 40 years, no preservatives needed. Aboveground, it will outlast a human life, or two. Researchers have discovered it contains a natural fungicide. The wood is, in addition, very strong and very hard when dry. It makes excellent hardwood and parquet flooring. When it burns, it puts out a lot of British thermal units (Btu), so it makes good firewood. Black locust grows relatively fast; is a legume that enriches the soil it grows in; will tolerate a wide range of soil types and climates; and its prodigious blossoms produce a superior honey.

America, the native home of this tree, has nevertheless lost interest in it since the 1930s, when much work was done by the U.S. Department of Agriculture to develop superior strains. But in Europe and Asia, led by Hungary where today the main research efforts are underway, man-planted forests of black locust increased from 337,000 hectares to 1,890,000 hectares between 1958 and 1978. And that doesn't take into account huge afforestation projects with black locust in China.

What scientists are particularly excited about is the strain discovered in 1936 in the United States, referred to as "shipmast locust" because of its habit of growing a straight, tall trunk, excellent for commercial lumbering. Thousands of these trees have been planted in other countries and work continues. But not in the United States. I suppose when redwood and cedar finally become too expensive to use for home exteriors, we will import locust from Hungary.

Be that as it may, there is plenty of black locust around yet. If you are a do-it-yourselfer looking for a really long-lasting siding for your house, have some black locust sawed into planks and strips for board-and-batten siding. You'll have to go to local sawmills—commercial lumberyard dealers will stare strangely at you and tell you how hard it is to pound nails into locust. When I hear that, I stare back just as strangely and say it's hard to pound nails into masonry, too, but we have the nails to do it and it's done all the time.

Cedar and Redwood Sidings

Western red cedar and redwood are, for all practical purposes, the choices you have for a durable natural wood exterior that you don't have to spend lots of time painting or staining regularly. Redwood is better and more expensive, but both are good, so long as they come from big trees with lots of heartwood. Wood from the heart of a tree is more decay resistant, and wood from the heart of a *big* old tree is the most resistant of all as long as the tree is healthy. Thus, you will see many old barns with siding over a century old, weathered gray but solid. That wood came from the virgin forests, trees you will not see in our day unless you visit remnant old-growth forests protected by law. Second- and third-growth lumber, 50 to 70 years in the growing, or even 100 years, can't match wood from trees 200 to 300 years old or more.

In the dry West, redwood siding will easily last a lifetime without any treatment at all, and cedar-shingled houses in cold New England have resisted decay for over a century. Cedar shingles are especially adaptive to seaside environments, which is why you see so many cedar-shingled houses along the New England coast. All woods resist salt spray better than metal, but the salt actually *improves* the rot-resistance of unpainted cedar shingles. That's why they last 100 years along the coast of Maine.

But given that I live in a landlocked state, there is no salt air to help preserve the cedar siding I just bought for a new building. And because the siding has quite a few "tight knots," as they call them, I intend to put on an initial coating of a penetrating stain and preservative to make sure it lasts a lifetime.

Other Woods

Green rough-sawn board and batten from a local sawmill, a full inch thick, is strong, insulative, and durable. And a great buy. Expect to pay, right now, 70¢ to 80¢ a board foot, maybe less if you deal sharply. Of the commonly available woods, oak is best in my part of the country.

For whatever kind of siding you decide to use, the following list contains those woods that are very resistant to decay. If you are not using pressure-treated wood, these are the ones for low maintenance. Most of them, unfortunately, are not available for siding. Catalpa, for example, is becoming a rare wood, as all the old catalpa orchards, grown for fence posts a century ago, have mostly been bulldozed away for corn. Catalpa will last nearly as long as black locust, but has the added advantage of taking nails easily after it is dry. Wood-carvers love it. Chestnut, of course, is almost gone, and it would be difficult to find logs of some of these woods, like Pacific yew, large enough for siding possibilities.

Bald cypress (especially old growth)
Black locust
Black walnut
Black or wild cherry
Catalpa
Cedars (especially Atlantic white cedar, much used for shingles in the
        East; Northern white cedar, much used for log homes; and
        Western red cedar, the principal source for cedar shakes and
        shingles)
Chestnut
Junipers (Eastern red cedar is a juniper)
Mesquite
Mulberry (especially red mulberrry)
Osage orange
Pacific yew
Redwood
Sassafras
White oaks (including bur oak, chestnut oak, gambel oak, Oregon
        white oak, and post oak)

The following woods are *moderately* resistant to decay, requiring regular maintenance when used as house exteriors:

Bald cypress (young growth)
Douglas fir
Eastern white pine
Honey locust
Southern yellow pine (longleaf pine, slash pine)
Swamp chestnut oak
Tamarack
Western larch

Board and Batten

Board and batten came into vogue precisely because many hardwoods when dry are very hard to drive nails into. When the wood is green, however, nails can be driven in as easily as they can in pine. But green boards shrink as they dry, opening cracks wide enough to let a blizzard inside. So strips wide enough to cover any shrinkage cracks were nailed over the junctures between boards. The vertical boards and the diagonal boards so popular today also shed water better and resist rotting better than horizontally lapped boards, although with black locust as with other rot-resistant boards, lapped horizontal siding works nearly as well if put on green. The pattern of board and batten appealed to many people decoratively, and so a favorite American house style was born. The supreme compliment: it's imitated in metal and other man-made sidings now.

Board and batten is a very practical siding. Thinner boards that cover the gaps between wider boards allow the wood to expand and contract without cracking or leaving gaps exposed to the weather. This is a particularly good siding to use with green wood.

Board and batten is one of the most forgiving ways to build an exterior wall. Precise, professional fitting of boards is not necessary since the battens cover any slight misalignment between boards, and trim over the top plate covers slight mistakes in measurement made there. Varying thickness and width of boards sawed by the somewhat crude machinery of local sawmills does not much matter either. Board and batten is a good siding for a beginner. Just remember to nail the battens onto just *one side* of a crack or the shrinking boards will crack the batten in two. Always remember that wood moves—swells during humid weather, shrinks during dry. Board and batten is one of the simplest and cheapest solutions to this characteristic of wood. (The shrinkage is mostly lateral, through the width of a board. The lengthwise shrinkage is very small and negligible in board-and-batten construction.)

Penetrating Oils and Stains for Cedar, Redwood, and Other Sidings

The Red Cedar Shingle and Hand Split Shake Bureau (515 116th Avenue NE, Suite 275, Bellevue, WA 98004) says a penetrating oil alone will protect cedar. It would also protect other natural woods noted as very resistant to decay in the list on page 59 used in a dry climate, but an oil with a preservative fungicide is advisable in warm, damp climates like Florida. The Bureau recommends Wood Guard and Wood Life, available in most paint stores. A little checking will familiarize you with many other good products, especially Cuprinol and the Olympic Stain products.

Even if you aren't worried about decay or mildew problems, another reason for treating natural wood siding with a penetrating stain is to preserve the fresh appearance of the wood. I like the fresh-cut look of red cedar, not the weathered gray, and would use a stain that darkens it a bit toward brown. There are scores of colors to choose from.

Penetrating oils and stains can be brushed or sprayed on, but the best way on rough sidings like cedar is to spray *and* follow up immediately with a brush, working the liquid well into the wood. You want to get plenty on, as the raw wood will soak up the stain like a thirsty blotter. Each product has its own instructions to follow.

Since the basic ingredient is often linseed oil with pigment added, in theory, the more coats applied over the years the better. But several coats are not really necessary with wood siding. Once every five years is not a bad idea in humid climates, if you wish the siding to last indefinitely. But one good soaking coat that gets into all the cracks and crevices, coupled with a good job of sealing joints around windows and doors with caulking or putty, should suffice. In *very* humid climates, wood siding as I have tried to convey, is not a good low-maintenance alternative. People, especially younger people, don't like to hear that it's not a good choice if they are very fond of wood because to them 20 years seems like a long time. Ah, if only that were true.

If you do have to paint, or repaint, or restain, there's a product on the market to make that horrid job of scraping off loose old coatings a lot easier. Called Restore-X (Restech Industries, Inc., P.O. Box 2747, Eugene, OR 97402), it uses buffered, sodium hydroxide-based compounds to remove deteriorated paint, stain, and even the graying effects of weathering. It is biodegradable, water soluble, and environmentally safe. It will not remove well-bonded paint—just the loose stuff you normally have to scrape or sand off. It dissolves old loosened paint or stain on wood, stucco, brick, concrete, metal and aluminum, but doesn't work for epoxy, baked enamel, or urethane coatings. You can apply it with a synthetic bristle brush, mop, or roller. Apply in a thick coat and then wait for the liquid to work on the old paint. When the old paint is ready, simply hose it off.

The Rodale Technical Group has independently tested Restore-X with good results. "Both the paint remover and the wood renewer do the job," they reported. "The former is powerful but biodegradable; the latter keeps water from soaking into wood decks. Both make maintaining wood products easier." In applying Restore-X, use eye protection and wear rubber gloves for safety.

Between the lines, Restore-X is really high maintenance. It's what you use when exterior painted and stained surfaces start giving you a headache. Olympic's ads show peeling paint of its competitors beside its own unpeeling brand. Cuprinol shows a deteriorating stain on a wood siding in its ad with a question: "If all oil stains protect, what happened here?" The bottom line is that if you want the beauty of wood, high-maintenance is your inheritance.

Log Exteriors

Although log houses enjoy a mystique of durable low maintenance, those not made from woods very resistant to decay (see the list on page 59) will require regular maintenance, unless pressure treated deep into the wood. I am always amazed how books on log houses spend 20 chapters on building with logs and generally no more than two pages on maintenance. Generally speaking, a log exterior in the humid South will need a preservative applied nearly every year, and in the North it will need one about every three years to be safe. There are many such preservatives on the market.

Fungicidal preservatives are usually copper naphthenate or zinc naphthenate. Oil-based penetrating stains are mostly linseed oil with colors added if desired. Some log house devotees claim that plain linseed oil, regularly applied, serves the purpose except in very humid, warm regions where mildew is a constant threat. But all that sounds like high maintenance to me and so outside the purview of this book. Also remember that woodpeckers (the pileated woodpecker is most harmful) and boring insects love to make holes in logs.

Exterior Paint

If you must paint, or are one of those rare individuals who actually likes to spend weekends painting, there are enough different brands and formulas to keep you busy for several years just selecting one "best" for you. In an effort to guide you to the "best," attempts are routinely made to test various paints (see the table "Outdoor House Paint Performance Tests" from *Rodale's New Shelter*, now titled *Rodale's Practical Homeowner* magazine). But usually the results are not very helpful because there are so many different kinds of paint. Competition between paint companies is keen, and manufacturers are constantly coming up with new formulas that make tests pretty obsolete by the time consumers become aware of them. The bottom line is that, for the most part, paints within the same category and price range are about equal.

The carrier for latex or water-based paint is water. I doubt if it makes much difference if it is water from New York or water from New Mexico. The carrier for oil-based paints is petroleum distillates or paint thinner, and there's no significant differences in these. I have not heard any paint company touting the quality of their carrier yet. As for pigment, if one company has discovered a source of red with particularly good hiding characteristics or staying power, the other chemists will be on it quickly. That leaves the third ingredient of paint, the binder, which gives it adhesive power. In water-based paints, the binder is a latex resin. In oil-based paints it is usually linseed oil, and I have never heard anyone try to claim his linseed oil was better than someone else's. There can be differences in the resin binders, as new, stickier substances are concocted, but discerning that difference is beyond the ken of the layperson who must either rely on an honest paint dealer who knows (there are many honest paint dealers, but not so many who really know) or a chemist or experience. Generally speaking, higher-priced paints are more durable. If you buy cheap paint, expect to paint again. Soon.

Actually, the condition of the surface to be painted is more important than the paint. The surface has to be dry and reasonably clean. And the surface has to *stay* dry. Peeling paint is rarely the paint's fault. Rather, it is moisture oozing out of the walls, either because the wood or whatever was not dried out in the first place, or because the lack of a vapor barrier is allowing humid inside air into the outer wall where it condenses upon meeting cold air. Paint will almost always peel from soffits that are unventilated. In addition, many finishing paints must be primed before they will stick well. Using two coats of paint instead of a coat of primer and then

(continued on page 66)

Outdoor House Paint Performance Tests

Manufacturer	Type	Grade	Paint Color	Abrasion Resistance
Benjamin-Moore	Latex	High	White Ivory Red	Fair Fair Average
Dutch-Boy	Latex	High	White Ivory Red	Good Average Excellent
Glidden	Latex	High	White Ivory Red	Good Average Good
	Oil	High	White Ivory Red	Good Average Good
Kelly-Moore	Latex	High	White Ivory Red	Good Good Good
	Oil	High	White Red	Good Excellent
MAB Paints	Latex	High	White Ivory Red	Good Fair Good
Olympic	Latex	High	White Ivory Red	Fair Good Excellent
Pittsburgh	Latex	High	White Ivory Red	Fair Average Good

WEATHERIZATION		ACID RAIN	
Gloss Retention	Color Retention	Color Retention	Resistance to Cracking
Average	Good	Good	Average
Fair	Good	Excellent	Good
Fair	Good	Excellent	Good
Good	Good	Good	Excellent
Average	Good	Excellent	Excellent
Good	Excellent	Excellent	Good
Good	Good	Good	Excellent
Good	Good	Excellent	Excellent
Good	Excellent	Excellent	Good
Fair	Fair	Poor	Good
Poor	Fair	Good	Good
Poor	Fair	Excellent	Excellent
Good	Good	Average	Good
Good	Good	Good	Good
Good	Good	Excellent	Average
Fair	Average	Fair	Excellent
Poor	Poor	Excellent	Excellent
Average	Average	Average	Good
Average	Good	Good	Good
Good	Good	Excellent	Good
Good	Good	Average	Good
Good	Good	Excellent	Good
Good	Good	Excellent	Good
Good	Good	Average	Good
Average	Good	Excellent	Excellent
Excellent	Excellent	Excellent	Good

(continued)

Outdoor House Paint Performance Tests—Continued

Manufacturer	Type	Grade	Paint Color	Abrasion Resistance
Sears	Latex	High	White	Average
			Ivory	Poor
			Red	Average
	Latex	Medium	White	Fair
			Ivory	Average
			Red	Excellent
Sherwin-Williams	Latex	High	White	Average
			Ivory	Average
			Red	Good
	Latex	Medium	White	Average
			Ivory	Average
			Red	Excellent
United Coatings	Latex	High	White	Good
			Ivory	Fair
			Red	Good
	Latex	Medium	White	Average
			Ivory	Average
			Red	Good

Source: *Rodale's New Shelter*, May–June 1986.

a coat of paint is not the same thing. Directions on the label tell us all that kind of mundane information but we don't pay attention. We know we are supposed to scrape off all loose paint and dirt, but we often do so only carelessly. We just can't wait to start painting. So it is not a very long wait before we have to paint again.

I include the table "Outdoor House Paint Performance Tests" mostly for its data on the effect of acid rain on paint, a subject about which little solid information is yet available. These tests were run by Dhirendra C. Mehta of the Rodale Technical Group, under the direction of Mark Kern. Paint samples on pine blocks were sprayed in cycles with a sulfuric acid

WEATHERIZATION		ACID RAIN	
Gloss Retention	Color Retention	Color Retention	Resistance to Cracking
Poor	Average	Good	Average
Poor	Good	Good	Average
Good	Good	Excellent	Average
Good	Average	Average	Average
Good	Good	Average	Average
Good	Average	Excellent	Good
Poor	Average	Average	Good
Poor	Average	Good	Good
Average	Good	Excellent	Excellent
Poor	Average	Average	Good
Poor	Average	Good	Good
Average	Good	Excellent	Good
Good	Good	Good	Good
Good	Good	Excellent	Good
Good	Excellent	Excellent	Average
Good	Good	Good	Good
Good	Good	Good	Good
Good	Good	Excellent	Average

solution equivalent to about a year's worth of acid rain and chemical pollution. White oil-based paints suffered most, turning a pale pink. Dark oil-based paints like the high-grade reds from Glidden and Kelly-Moore resisted acid rain as did all the latex paints, especially high-grade ivories from Dutch-Boy, Glidden, and Pittsburgh, as well as high-grade red from Sherwin-Williams.

Of course, the proper response to acid rain, which can make a joke of the search for low maintenance, is not so much finding materials resistant to it, but demanding that the problem be addressed adequately. Call it low-maintenance politics.

CHAPTER 4

ROOFING

No doubt the most vulnerable part of the house is the roof over your head. So it pays the low-maintenance buff to consider most closely the durability of various roofing materials. Some of those you may have thought of as being the best are not necessarily so.

Metal Roofing

Having been raised in a society where the change from metal roofing to asphalt shingles was considered a sign of progress, I am surprised when every roofer I ask says that metal roofs today are the best buy for the money of *any* kind of roofing. This contention is supported in an article by J. Azevedo in *Fine Homebuilding* (December 1984/January 1985), who writes: "The important thing to remember about metal roofing is that front-end costs are not as telling as life-cycle costs. A properly installed and maintained metal roof can last the life of the house. Consequently, the average yearly cost of a metal roof is less than for any other . . . ."

The slate and clay-tile manufacturers will argue that point, especially since some of the less costly metal roofing does require periodic painting. But however that argument might be settled, obviously those of us who have believed that asphalt shingles are the last word in the low- to middle-priced roof probably ought to reconsider. The biggest objection I hear to metal is that it is ugly, a charge not as true now as it once was, and one that is too subjective to mean much anyway. The $350,000 condominiums I toured recently (not to buy!) are roofed in blue steel, evidently quite attractive to today's high-powered buyer. Even "old-fashioned" galvanized steel in its traditional standing-seam installation is only ugly if you associate it with cheap old farmhouses—which are now considered charming. The same phenomenon happened to standing-seam roofs as happened to the wood-fired stove. In 1950, heating with wood was considered backward; in 1980, it was avant-garde. So too with standing-seam metal roofs.

Also, cheap corrugated metal barn roofing gave metal a bad name. That creaky corrugated stuff loosened in the wind and rusted away, if it didn't blow away. The sound of rain drumming on a metal roof can lull you to sleep; the sound of hail on it can send you flying to your feet.

Choices in Metal Roofing Materials

Galvanized steel will not hold up well in the salty air of sea breezes. In such situations, a newer product, aluminum- and zinc-plated steel, Galvalume (Bethlehem Steel Corporation, Bethlehem, PA 18016-7699) is advisable. There is another kind of galvanized steel, more expensive and heavier than the standard kind, which is not painted. Called Cor-Ten (USX Corporation, 600 Grant Street, Pittsburgh, PA 15230), it is deliberately made to rust, the rust forming a protective coating that lasts for many years. The rusty red color is attractive. The only hitch is that runoff water carries some of that color with it and can stain trim or walls. Used with dark trim, this staining may not be so noticeable.

Zinc alloy, Microzinc (W. P. Hickman Company, P.O. Box 15005, Asheville, NC 28813), has a life expectancy of over 100 years without maintenance if installed right. But it expands and contracts more than aluminum and this must be taken into account when installing. It can crack if it is bent in temperatures below 50°F. But all things considered, it is a Cadillac of a roof, for those who can afford it.

Copper bends easily for easy installation, so it is a dream for roofers. Or so it would seem. But hobnobbing with roofers, I've learned even copper has its weaknesses. It will corrode other metals it comes into contact with. And used for flashing, which is a wise move for a low-maintenance home, it must be installed ever so carefully. If in bending it to fit into a valley, the roofer crimps it unduly (rather than fashioning a nice gentle curve), the copper will break in two at the crimp quicker than galvanized steel if there is seasonal structural movement between the two roof planes, as can be expected. Tin solders and bends easier than galvanized steel but will not last as long for flashing. Soldered tin roofs over small flattish areas are not as durable as galvanized, but any flat roof is asking for trouble.

Stainless steel stands halfway between copper and galvanized steel in price and durability. It will pit and spring leaks after a long time. If you are going to spend that kind of money, you might as well step up to Terne-coated stainless steel, which is nearly as forever as copper (Follansbee Steel, P.O. Box 610, Follansbee, WV 26037).

A roof of plain steel Terne might be the best compromise between cost and low maintenance. If you are a reader of Alex Wade's delightful books (see Appendix B), you know that this sometimes outspoken architect favors Terne, even though it is relatively expensive. In installation, he uses a slightly different design in the standing-seam panels than what I describe a bit later; it requires bending in a machine shop. On-site bending with hand tools using the traditional method I suggest would save considerable money for the do-it-yourselfer. Terne is lead-coated steel and there's no reason I know of why it couldn't be bent to shape on-site with traditional tools. As Wade points out, the original Terne roof on Jefferson's Monticello is still in good shape. And since no one seems to have been harmed by the lead in the coating in all the years that it was lived in, I doubt there's need to worry in that regard. However, one might not want to drink cistern water off a Terne roof. I am reminded of a farm family I once wrote about whose water supply came from the barn and house for nearly two centuries through lead pipe. The health department finally made them quit using the water in the dairy room, so in anger they quit milking cows instead. And they continue to drink the water as generations of the family always have, apparently unharmed. However, health authorities still insist that lead pipe is a definite hazard.

Some newer metal roofing panels are designed so that you can nail or screw right through them; snap-on clips cover the nails or screws and prevent the roof from leaking around them. At least one popular steel panel, Met-Tile (P.O. Box 4268, Ontario, CA 91761-4268), uses exposed screw fasteners, each with a grommet seal. Met-Tile looks attractively like clay tiles. Well, almost. The coating on the metal, available in several colors, is Glidden Nebelar, one of the premium flurocarbon resins that the company says will last a good 20 years.

Costs

Copper is now about $2 a square foot, but copper prices are apt to be volatile. For zinc alloy, I'd figure 30 percent more than copper as I write this in 1986. Stainless steel coated with Terne, an alloy of lead and tin, is third most expensive, being nearly the cost of copper. Plain stainless steel is fourth at about two-thirds the cost of copper; then regular Terne, at a little less than half the cost of copper; then aluminum; and finally galvanized steel at less than 20 percent the price of copper.

It is difficult to talk except in general terms about the cost of metal roofing. In most cases, the standing-seam panels will be shaped on site and so the labor costs will add considerably to the cost of the metal itself. If the roof is a very simple one, with few valleys or obstructions like dormers and chimneys, installation is easier and therefore much cheaper than for a complicated multilevel, multivalleyed roof. With galvanized steel at $65 a square (100 square feet), a roof installed can cost from $90 to $125 a square and up.

The only case where standing-seam metal is going to be cheaper than asphalt shingles is in reroofing. The metal can be put on *over* a couple layers of asphalt shingles. If you are reroofing with asphalt-fiberglass shingles, those two or three old layers of shingles have to come off first, which will cost as much as putting on the new. The lesson in low maintenance favoring metal is obvious.

Also, in the case of galvanized steel, which is by far the most common metal roofing installed, there is a broad range of quality and therefore price. You can buy galvanized in various thicknesses (gauges) but the word, gauge, is not used precisely in the industry, so it is better to use measurements in fractions of the inch, so that both you and the dealer know what you are talking about when it comes to quoting prices. A measurement of .015 inch may seem as but a hair different than .036, but the second is at least twice as durable a roof as the first. Also, the quality of the steel depends upon the amount of zinc in the plating. The more zinc, the more resistance to corrosion. A G90 rating means 1.25 ounce of zinc per square foot, while G60 means .83 ounces per square foot—a big difference in galvanized steel.

The table "Cost and Investment Analysis for Reroofing Pitched Roofs" compares various materials. The analysis was done in southern California in 1983, so the costs should be used as a comparison guide only. Costs will obviously vary from one city to another. As such, the table is interesting not only for the reroofer, but also for those interested in roof values in general.

This table is good background for what comes in the rest of this chapter, because I think it justifies the extra cost of using more durable roofing materials. Note that fire-retardant pressure-treated cedar shakes cost almost as much as clay tile initially, but far more in terms of life cycle yearly costs. Also note that even heavy-duty fiberglass shingles have a higher life cycle cost than the more expensive clay tile. Unfortunately, the more expensive metals aren't included in the study, nor are any standing seam, although I believe they would have scored quite well economically in life cycle costs.

Standing-Seam Roofs

Almost all metal roofing is applied by some version of what is called standing-seam design because so far this is the best way to avoid any exposed nails. There are now sophisticated machines to bend and crimp the flat metal into standing-seam panels, but many roofers still do the work with traditional hand tools.

The metal is usually shaped on site, as this is the better way to keep from wasting any. A roofer calls down the precise length of panel he needs,

(continued on page 74)

Cost and Investment Analysis for Reroofing Pitched Roofs

Product Type	INSTALLATION REQUIREMENTS		
	Framing	Decking	Underlayment
FIRE RETARDANT			
Class "A" (maximum fire hazard protection)			
Fiberglass shingles	Standard	Solid	Type 15 felt
Heavy fiberglass	Standard	Solid	Type 15 felt
Concrete tiles	Heavy	Spaced or solid	Type 30 felt or ½" gypsum board
Clay tiles	Heavy	Solid	Type 30 felt
Cal-Shake	Standard	Spaced or solid	None
Class "B" (moderate fire hazard protection)			
Pressure treated cedar shakes	Standard	Solid	Metal foil and asbestos felt*
Metal tiles	Standard	Spaced or solid	Metal foil or 72 lb. cap sheet*
NON FIRE RETARDANT			
Class "C" (light fire hazard protection only)			
Asphalt shingles	Standard	Solid	Type 15 felt
Pressure treated cedar shakes	Standard	Spaced or solid	None
UNCLASSIFIED			
Ordinary (no fire hazard protection)			
Cedar shakes (medium)	Standard	Spaced or solid	None
Cedar shakes (heavy)	Standard	Spaced or solid	None
Metal tiles	Standard	Spaced or solid	Type 30 felt*

Source: Committee for Firesafe Roofing, 675 Brea Canyon Road, Suite 2, Walnut, CA 91789.

*Most typical underlayment shown. Some manufacturers have different methods. Check specifications carefully.

COSTS	LIFE	LIFE CYCLE
Avg. for Reroof of 3,200 sq. ft. Roof	**Expected Warranteed**	**Costs per Year**
$3,968	20–25 yr.	$176
5,568	25–30 yr.	202
7,232	Life	145
7,424	40–50 yr.	165
8,992	Life	180
7,968	Life	159
$8,736	10–15 yr.	$699
7,104	40–50 yr.	158
$3,968	15–20 yr.	$227
7,232	10–15 yr.	579
$4,832	8–12 yr.	$483
5,152	10–15 yr.	412
6,848	40–50 yr.	152

Basis: Costs for reroofing of shake-roofed 1,900 sq. ft. single family residence with attached garage, 3,200 square feet. Southern California, May 1983. Figures include bracing up roof construction where needed and installation of solid sheathing where required.

Notes: *Figures to be used as a comparison only,* actual costs might be higher due to roof complexity and geographical location. Metal tiles and treated wood shakes can have different fire ratings depending on their installation; ask manufacturer for details. Life cycle costs per year: Total costs divided by average life expectancy (assumption: lifetime = 50 years). Obviously clay tile (and slate, not listed) would have a longer lifetime, and no life cycle costs as given here for tiles is too high.

Standing-seam metal roofs make a neat, sturdy roof that will last for years and years so long as it is painted periodically.

his helpers cut it from the roll, then the edges are bent up by hand or machine. The brainwork of the process was all done years and years ago, and actually learning how to do it now is mostly a matter of spending a couple of days working for a roofer, as I did. In this case, the teacher was my son, so we reversed the usual order—a young man passing on to an older one a traditional skill.

We used the old traditional hand tools, which are somewhat slower (but not much) than an expensive roll-forming machine. Nevertheless, a homeowner is likely to get the job done cheaper by the kind of people who use the traditional tools because they don't have expensive machinery to pay for and usually don't charge as much for their labor.

Alex Wade talks about making standing seams, and, better yet, has art and photos explaining it, in his book *A Design and Construction Handbook for Energy-Saving Houses* (Rodale Press, 1980).

Painting a Galvanized Steel Roof

If you buy galvanized steel already painted (a wise purchase in my opinion), it will cost about 30 percent more than unpainted galvanized. The advantages of prepainted galvanized are many: First, it will mean that all the metal is coated with paint, even the edges, which are bent and crimped into the standing seam where you can't paint once the roof is installed. Second, it saves you from clambering up and down a smooth, slippery roof after installation, painting it. Third, unpainted galvanized steel from the factory has an oily coating that must be removed before paint will stick. Factory-painting does a better job of removing that oily coating and applying paint. Once the roof is up, what most people do is wait about a year before painting these unpainted roofs so that the oil weathers off. This practice also applies to chromate coatings on imported galvanized steel, which must be brushed off or weathered off before paint can be applied.

(If you want to clean the oil off a new galvanized steel panel, scrub it vigorously with a strong, hot solution of trisodium phosphate and then rinse with vinegar. Scrubbing well is important. A friend of mine evidently didn't do a sufficient job of scrubbing hers, because the roof has had to be scraped with a wire brush and then patch-painted three times in five years in spots where the oil was not entirely removed.)

Improved paints for galvanized steel are now available. After the oil film has been cleaned or weathered away, put on a primer of zinc chromate, or the older treatment, red iron oxide. Then apply the finish coats in the color of your choice. This may be an enamel for metal, or better, a silicone-modified polyester, which should last 20 years, or better yet, a fluorocarbon resin. There are newer and more expensive coatings, one with ground copper particles suspended in the fluorocarbon resin, and another of acrylic film called Korad (Polymer Extruded Products, Inc., 297 Ferry Street, Newark, NJ 07105). For information on suspended copper coatings, check with Berridge Manufacturing (1720 Maury Street, Houston, TX 77026); and Architectural Engineering Products (7455 Carroll Road, San Diego, CA 92121). For fluorocarbon coatings, see Penwalt Corporation (Plastics Department, 3 Parkway, Philadelphia, PA 19102); and PPG Industries, Inc. (One PPG Place, Pittsburgh, PA 15272).

Slate Roofing

The way to prove the durability and low maintenance of various building materials in my rural area is to observe abandoned houses in the country, of which, sad to say, we have many. The ones that stand the longest without any care at all, until the bulldozer gets them or some loving restorer brings them back to life, are brick houses with slate roofs. If the slates are the gray kind, what we call Pennsylvania slate, they are most often rotten by the time they are 100 years old. If they are the red- or green-hued kinds, what we call Vermont slate, most of them are good for another 100 years at least. My son salvaged enough to cover the front half of our woodworking shop.

With a little practice, you can tell in an instant if they are reusable by tapping them with a hammer. A crisp ring means the slate is still good; a duller thud means it is rotten or cracked. Sunlight finally rots slate—

ultraviolet light eventually will get just about everything. But salvaging Vermont slate is a very profitable practice. Roofers usually charge about 50¢ for a good old slate of 12 by 24 inches. New pieces of Vermont slate cost up to $5 each. I have seen some new slate from Spain priced as low as $286 a square (100 square feet), but it is quite thin compared to the old (and new) Vermont slates. But even at $300 to $400 a square, slate is a good long-term investment.

Installing slate is much easier than I expected. The slates I have seen from Spain have predrilled holes for the nails, but what we use you can drive a nail through just like through a board. It is better, even, to hit the nail a good crack the first time to drive it in, rather than tapping on it gently in fear of cracking the slate. You really should use copper nails, at least 11 gauge. On many old slate roofs, if copper nails were not used, the nails gave out long before the slate, and the roof deteriorated on that

Slate makes a lovely, very durable roof and is a good choice. Learning to do the work yourself may be easier than finding someone with the skill to do the job. Laying a slate roof is, unfortunately, a dying art.

account. Slate cutters, which resemble and work about like paper cutters, make sizing a slate for any particular spot an easy operation.

Some roofers believe slate will last longer if it is nailed over thin battens that raise the slates off the sheeting a bit, allowing air to circulate between slate and underlayment. Others contend that just the way the slates lap each other provides enough air space for good circulation.

Manufacturer specifications I have seen do not require such battens, but only a "cant strip" under the first course to tilt the slates up so that subsequent layers will lap down tight over them. This is standard procedure for laying any kind of roof tile. With slate, the outer roof edges need to be covered—aluminum stripping is most often used now. (If you need general directions on how to install any roofing, read the manufacturer's specifications on the backs of the brochures that advertise their wares, and you will find a whole lot of valuable instruction, all for free.)

Slate roofs are extra heavy (and if they're loaded down with snow, even heavier). In fact, on some roofs you may need snow and ice arresters. Consult an architect or building engineer for your particular case.

I have seen old slate roofs painted, a horrid practice, but where money is short and the slates leaking, it is a stopgap measure that will buy some time. There are, in fact, all sorts of plasticized products marketed in recent years that will supposedly waterproof almost anything. Some of them are as expensive as putting on a new roof.

Vitrified Clay Roof Tiles

Fired clay roof tiles, like fired clay bricks, are one of the most durable and maintenance-free materials made by man. These products not only result in consummate beauty, durability, and low maintenance, but they also appeal to the best in humankind. Their very existence in our society bespeaks stability and art. Clay-tile manufacture, for example, has been in decline basically because the "throwaway house" has been fashionable. Throwaway houses are built by throwaway societies, made up of people with no sense of the wisdom of past knowledge, so laboriously learned, and little care for the future. Building with stone and baked clay does not really require money (although lots of money for them is what the times now demand), but to a commitment to a place and a mastery of traditional skill. I ate in a restaurant yesterday that was built of bricks handmade on the place 100 years ago. A month ago, I interviewed a farmer who lives in a brick home, the clay for which came from the garden—100 years ago. Anyone who can bake bricks can bake roofing tiles even easier, and for centuries in other parts of the world, roofing tile was "homebaked," along with the bricks.

Stone and clay demand craftsmanship. You couldn't even put a heavy clay-tile roof on a throwaway house; it might collapse. In a clay-tile factory, what you find, surprisingly, is still lots of handcrafting. That's one reason clay tiles are expensive.

At the Ludowici-Celadon clay-tile factory at New Lexington, Ohio (Ludowici-Celadon Company, 4757 Tile Plant Road, New Lexington, OH 43764), known worldwide for its work, I watched three people turning out one of the many styles of tile produced there—Americana. One operated a machine that pressed out the tiles in the wet clay. The other two workers took the individual tiles from the press and trimmed away the excess clay, punched in the holes for the roofing nails, and rubbed the surface smooth—all by hand. They could each work on 500 a day. In another part of the factory, a machine can press out, without help, 11,000 tiles of the Spanish style per day. Obviously, the machined tiles will cost considerably less. Ironically, because there is more demand for the Spanish than the Americana (the Americana is much more beautiful, I think, but the Spanish is better known), the factory can afford to automate for the Spanish, but not for the Americana. In other words, people don't buy Americana clay-tile roofing because it is too high priced, and it is too high priced because so few will buy it!

Colors and Styles in Tile

After viewing and reviewing all kinds of roofing, I went to the Ludowici-Celadon tile factory because it is the only one I know of and the only one within easy driving distance. When I saw the variety and beauty of clay tiles made there, I was, plainly speaking, overcome. No other materials I'd seen, including slate, which I like a lot, came close to equaling the beauty of the clay-tile designs I saw laid out there. Hitherto I, like most Americans, thought of clay tile in terms of what you see on Taco Bell fast-food restaurants, and that doesn't particularly appeal to me. Ludowici-Celadon's Spanish-style tile was, first of all, darker than what you see on Taco Bells, a definite improvement. But that was only one of a surprising variety of styles and colors available. I'm going to take the time to mention most of them because I'm sure most of us aren't aware of them.

Among the *standard* styles available are: Americana, French, Imperial, Lanai, Norman, Spanish, Straight Barrel Mission, and Williamsburg Classic. Here's a sampling of the colors available (not all colors are available in all styles): Aged Cedar, Barcelona Buff, Beach Brown, Brookville Green, Colonial Cedar, Coral, Earth Gray, Fine Machine Scored Red, Fireflash in three shades of brown, Forest Green, Hand Rough Aged Cedar, Hand Rough Colonial Gray, Hand Rough Forest Green, Hawaiian Gold, Lava Black, Mediterranean Blue, Norman Dark Black, Norman Light Black, Norman Medium Black, Pacific Blue, Red, Sunset Red.

Or, if you want to pay extravagantly, you can have a color custom-made. For example, Beaver Creek Lodge near Aspen, Colorado, wanted a blue roof like one the owners had seen in Andorra in northern Spain, but which they could not find the likeness of produced anywhere in Europe. It took Ludowici-Celadon six months to develop the color, which they now call Beaver Creek Blue.

Some of the tiles are terribly expensive because the individual tiles are smaller, and it takes more of them to cover the same amount of space. Norman is an example; it makes, in fact, the most beautifully textured roof I have ever seen. It costs, hold your breath, over $1,000 per square (100 square feet). Also, some of the color glazes, like Brookville Green and Mediterranean Blue, available on only a few styles, cost from $800 to nearly $1,000 a square. The Spanish style in red costs about $250 a square, which makes it reasonable for a good moderately priced home. Other styles in a good choice of colors sell in the $300-per-square range. Still other choices are available in the $400- to $500-per-square range.

Not all clay tile on the market is necessarily of high quality. If fired in the 2,050°F range, the tiles are strong and durable. If the top firing degree falls below that, the tiles will be weaker. Some clay tile, and American tile makers like to throw the adjective "imported" into that statement, is fired at lower temperatures. They may last a long time in mild, dry climates, but not necessarily in the extremes of northern North America. Ludowici-Celadon guarantees their tile for 50 years, and they have a life expectancy of well over 100 years.

Terra cotta and fire clay are not the same; the former is made from special shales with perhaps some fire clay added. In general, terra cotta is used for more massive architectural details—pillars, gargoyles, etc. On the other hand, fire clay, which is used for roof tile, has little or no shale in it— just clay and water and a little barium carbonate so the tile surface on the roof doesn't get scummy.

Clay roofing tiles make beautiful roofs. The ones shown here are being tested for durability. They're expensive but are usually just a one-time investment because they hold up so well.

Tile Manufacturing: A Fading Art

The area around New Lexington and Zanesville in east-central Ohio has long been noted for shales and clays perfect for all kinds of ceramic products, which explains why Ludowici-Celadon's last factory (originally there were five scattered across the country) is here. The shale and clay are plentiful and often available as a by-product of coal strip-mining, which then makes them cheaper yet. Labor and the fuel to heat the kilns are the two major expenses.

Some clay-tile manufacturers are very small—little more than cottage industries that contract a certain amount of work each year more as artisans than factories. In a declining market that attracts only the wealthy or the very tasteful, making roof tiles becomes each year more art than manufacture, just as it does at Ludowici-Celadon, whose work force is down to about 75 people now. As far as I know, there are few or no retail outlets for clay roof tiles. With Ludowici-Celadon, you deal directly with the company, through regional salespeople or with someone at the factory. (In case you're wondering, neither myself nor the publisher of this book has any connection with the company.)

Tile's Insulative Value

Like brick or concrete, clay-tile roofs have no insulative value to speak of, but they do act as a heat- or cold-storage sink. In the winter, they keep buildings warm by absorbing heat during the day and radiating it back at night. In summer, they cool off at night, helping to keep the building from getting too hot too soon during the day. They even out temperature variation and with a particularly heavy, bulky roof style like Norman, the effect can be quite significant.

Concrete Roof Tile

If you can't afford real clay tile, you may want to consider concrete ones that now come in a few colors and styles that make them look remarkably like clay tiles. The forerunners of these tiles were the asbestos concrete roof shingles, which were very popular 40 years ago, before asbestos got its bad reputation. Johns Manville sold them as a "lifetime roof," and plenty of them remain as good as they ever were, so long as no one carelessly walks on them. They crack very easily.

Actually, tests have not indicated any danger from old asbestos-concrete roofing shingles to builders or homeowners if manufacturers guidelines are followed. The concrete locks in the asbestos fibers, maintain the manufacturers, and can't be released into the atmosphere unless

Concrete can now be molded into several very attractive shapes that mimic in style and color traditional roofing materials. Once these tiles are up on the roof, most people cannot tell the difference between them and real clay tiles.

sanding, drilling, or scraping the shingle takes place—all of which are not recommended. As of 1986, some of these very long-lasting shingles were still being manufactured, all quite legally. If interested, one company to contact is Supradur Manufacturing Corporation (P.O. Box 908, Rye, NY 10580).

Most of today's concrete tile doesn't have asbestos in it and is certainly a thousand times more beautiful to look at. Why it has not enjoyed popularity so far except on the West Coast and the Southwest is hard to explain. Its low-maintenance advantage would seem to make it a good candidate for anywhere. The Marley Roof Tiles Corporation (1990 East Riverview Drive, San Bernardino, CA 92408 or 1901 San Felipe Road, Hollister, CA 95023) for example, offers concrete tiles in Spanish style in gray, charcoal, burgundy, clay red, brown, and alpine; an "Old English Slate" in gray, red, and brown; and a "Western Shake" in gray, alpine, and brown—all with 50-year limited warranties. The company also offers a new, lighter-weight concrete tile called Duralite, which weighs about half that of normal concrete. These tiles can sometimes be installed right over old roofing, too.

Detractors say that the colors in concrete tiles do fade after 15 years or so, despite manufacturers' claims, but a lot of the new materials haven't been around long enough to tell for sure. The only reason I am not thrilled with them is that I have had some experience with concrete drainage tile compared to fired clay drain tile. The latter will just about last forever in the ground. Concrete, in the same situation, tends to absorb moisture and rot, crack, and cave in after 15 or 20 years. But, as asbestos concrete shingles have proved, this isn't necessarily so on a roof.

Asphalt-Fiberglass Shingles

You learn the weaknesses of a product when its manufacturer describes it *after* another product is developed to take its place. For instance, asphalt shingles used to be described as having an "organic mat base." But now that asphalt-fiberglass shingles are being promoted in place of plain asphalt ones, the manufacturers tell us that the latter had "merely a cardboard base." A fiberglass mat, being inorganic, is not supposed to deteriorate as quickly as mere cardboard. The fiberglass, so the manufacturers say, also will hold more impregnated asphalt and ceramic-coated granules in the asphalt. So it will last longer—with up to 30-year prorated warranties.

None of that kind of talk tells the whole truth. But maybe the whole truth is not possible. Up into about the '60s, you could buy a good, heavy asphalt shingle with a "mere cardboard" base that would last 25 years, and I personally know of some that did. "Heavy" is the key word. On the other hand, the fiberglass on our roof, which is supposed to last 30 years, is not going to make it to 20, a roofer tells me.

One thing that happened on the way to "improve" asphalt roofing was to put a dab of tar on each shingle so that the overlapping shingle will stick to it when the sun burns hot on the roof. Once stuck down, the shingles will not flap in the wind. This is probably a good idea, except that it enables manufacturers to make thinner, lighter shingles because they figure that the shingles can depend upon the dabs of tar to hold them down instead of their weight. Now you have to worry about whether they will stick down before they blow away—no small worry if the roof is put on in cold weather. And either way, you still have a light shingle; I don't care what it is made out of. Light shingles equal high maintenance.

Your best alternative is to invest in the heaviest fiberglass shingles available—some have two layers of fiberglass mat. These thicker shingles are the more attractive—in line with today's fashion for a heavily textured roof surface. Top-of-the-line fiberglass shingles are not cheap by any means, but they are cheaper than wood shakes, clay tile, or good metal. And they have a class A fire rating.

If you refer to the table "Cost and Investment Analysis for Reroofing Pitched Roofs," you will note that in life cycle costs per year fiberglass and asphalt shingles are two of the most expensive roofs. The same old question rears its head and only you can decide. With roofs, you've got some of the same options you have when making other home-supply purchases. It is going to cost you so much to keep the rain off your head, no matter which you choose. You can spend it once and be done with it, or you can spend it three times and worry about it in between.

Where roof shingles (of any material, but perhaps most of all asphalt and fiberglass) are laid on a relatively low-pitched roof, leaks can occur when ice forms at the roof edge, stopping the flow of melt water off the roof and backing it up under the shingles. A layer of roofing felt over the plywood subroof deals with this problem fairly well. At the very least, this felt flashing strip should be placed down before the shingles are installed from the edge of the roof back to at least a foot inside the vertical wall line. There's a new type of roll waterproofing flashing made specifically for this purpose. It's called Ice and Water Shield (W. R. Grace & Company, 62 Whittemore Avenue, Cambridge, MA 02140). It is self-adhesive underlayment, and it bonds to both roof deck and shingles and seals around nails, making it almost impossible for water to seep back under or through it.

Wood Shakes

If you took a poll, cedar shakes would probably rate as America's favorite roofing, especially by those who don't have them. Beautiful they are, but beyond that there is little to praise them for. Untreated cedar shakes are somewhat cheaper than the pressure-treated ones, but they are rather short-lived. Even treated, cedar shakes need regular maintenance, and in humid climates the thinner ones are not any more durable than asphalt. Pressure treated, they become as expensive as some clay tile, though much shorter-lived. Therefore, their annual life cycle cost is very high.

One feels like a traitor, pointing out maintenance disadvantages in America's dream roof. What can I say? There are companies in the Northwest, where western red cedar comes from, that make an entire business of caring for cedar roofs and siding.

The cost of replacing a cedar roof, according to 1980 statistics, was about $3 a square foot, and probably a bit higher right now. If you protect it with something like Flood's Roof Grade protective clear wood finish for cedar shakes (The Flood Company, P.O. Box 399, Hudson, OH 44236), you will need to redo it about every five years, says the manufacturer. Crews usually spray on the treatments. With such high maintenance, the shakes could last a long time. The Flood Company has a shingle they like to show, which was treated with their products years ago and which remained in good condition under adverse weather conditions for over 40 years. They don't have a whole roof of them, however.

Standard handsplit and resawn shakes come in 18- and 24-inch lengths, in ½- and ¾-inch thicknesses. Treated, they weigh from 250 to 350 pounds per square (100 square feet). Pressure treatments are usually both fire retardant and weather resistant. Their fire rating is still only class C, although the Koppers Company, Inc. (436 Seventh Avenue, Pittsburgh, PA 15219), has a patented system whereby their cedar roofs have been upgraded from a C to a B rating. The shakes are mounted over Koppers' plastic-coated steel foil and a minimum ½-inch plywood deck or 2-inch nominal and thicker tongue-and-groove decking.

CHAPTER 5

DOORS AND WINDOWS

A glance at the table "What Price Renovation?" shows us that replacing doors and windows is one of the higher-priced home improvement projects, costing quite a bit more than reroofing and residing. This might tempt a home renovator to try to get by with cheap materials, but that's not a good idea from the standpoint of low maintenance. Better to buy good doors and windows and cut out frill improvements like solar greenhouses, wood decks, etc. By the same token, in order to save money, a new housebuilder might be tempted to install smaller windows than the architect thinks fit the proportions of the house. That's not a good idea, either. Doors and windows are very visible and influence the way your house looks perhaps more than any other feature. Windows, too small proportionately, look weird.

Glass

Glass, or glazing as the pros call it when referring to windows, is a marvelous material from the standpoint of low maintenance. It breaks fairly easily, but if you can avoid that, glass lasts nearly forever. Probably no one gets through house maintenance over a lifetime without experiencing at least one broken window.

Breakability

Actually, you can obtain glass panes that are just about unbreakable. But they are too expensive and too heavy to outfit a house. One of the cafés

What Price Renovation?

Improvement/ Average Cost	Description
1. Add a room $27,000	400 sq. ft. (15′ × 25′) addition with slab foundation, roofing, siding, gypsum-board interior, insulation in walls and ceiling, six insulated glass windows, two skylights, patio door, electrical work, and decorating.
2. Add a swimming pool $17,000	16′ × 32′ in-ground pool with aluminum walls, vinyl liner, accessories, and 3′ concrete surround.
3. Remodel kitchen (major) $15,000	New cabinets, paint, and appliances (dishwasher, stove, range hood, and sink), vinyl flooring (12′ × 14′), ceramic tile for backsplash, and new laminate countertop and molding.
4. Replace windows and doors $9,500	Replace 16 exterior windows with new aluminum, wood, or vinyl windows with insulated glass, replace two wood entry doors with energy-efficient doors, and add two storm doors.
5. Add a solar greenhouse $9,200	8′ × 13′ solar greenhouse installed against house, with double glazing, door, concrete foundation, and slab floor.
6. Add a full bath $6,000	Tub and shower, vanity, sink, cabinets, tile for wall, and flooring for 5′ × 7′ bath.
7. Add new siding with insulation board $5,500	New aluminum, vinyl, or steel siding for 1,600 sq. ft. house with ¼″ foam insulating board.
8. Remodel kitchen (minor) $5,200	Refinish cabinets, new vinyl flooring (12′ × 14′), paint, sink, range, and new laminate countertops.
9. Remodel a bath $4,400	Paint, new wall and floor tile, and complete new fixtures (sink, tub, and toilet) in 5′ × 7′ bathroom.
10. Add a wood deck $4,000	16′ × 20′ deck of cedar or preservative-treated wood with handrail and built-in bench, and concrete for posts.

(continued)

What Price Renovation?—Continued

Improvement/ Average Cost	Description
11. Add a fireplace $3,000	Energy-efficient, factory-built model with glass doors, floor-to-ceiling stone or brick face, 5′ × 5′ hearth, 6′ mantel, flue and fittings.
12. Add a two-car garage (shell, detached) $11,100	Frame construction on 20′ × 24′ concrete slab, fiberglass roof shingles, aluminum siding, two overhead doors, gutters, paint, window, and basic electrical service.
Add a two-car garage (shell, attached) $10,250	20′ × 24′, same as above.
13. Construct a dormer (shell) $2,200	8′ × 10′ shell with shed roof, 7′ ceiling, asphalt shingles, aluminum siding, and one window.
14. Reroofing $1,370	260 lb. fiberglass shingles installed over old roof or cleared deck on roof of 24′ × 40′ house. Roof of average pitch.
15. Add resilient flooring $1,130	Sheet vinyl (medium grade), with ¼″ underlayment and vinyl baseboard in 14′ × 20′ room.
16. Insulate attic floor $1,200	R-30 fiberglass or rock wool blown in between joists of 24′ × 40′ attic.
$770	R-30 fiberglass batts between joists of 24′ × 40′ attic.
17. Replace carpeting $980	Remove old carpeting. Interior carpeting priced at $12 per yard installed with padding in 14′ × 20′ room.
18. Add a skylight $510	Double-glazed skylights 25″ × 49″ aluminum frame on wood curb installed in asphalt-shingled roof.

Source: *Rodale's New Shelter*, March 1986.

Notes: Keep in mind that labor and materials costs vary widely in different parts of the country, so the figures listed here are only ballpark estimates. An extensive, detailed listing of costs for these and other home improvements can be found in *Means Home Improvement Cost Guide*, published by R. S. Means Company, Inc., 100 Construction Plaza, Kingston, MA 02364.

Cost figures 1 through 11 are average figures from a survey by *Remodeling World* magazine. Cost figures 12 through 18 are based on estimates for a typical metropolitan area in *Home-Tech Remodeling and Renovation Cost Estimator* (1985), compiled and edited by Henry Reynolds. All figures used by permission.

in our town has an entrance door with a large window that has cracked a time or two by an overexuberance emanating from the bar. Also in our town is a Guardian Glass factory. The café owner and the international glass company got together on the problem and installed an experimental new kind of glass that is almost unbreakable. Oh, you might be able to drive a bulldozer blade through it. But you can kick it as hard as you can wearing Green Beret boots, and the only thing that will happen is that you will come away with a bruised foot.

Improving Glass's Insulative Value

The problem with glass, beyond its breakability, is that heat and cold can pass through it almost as easily as light. It has hardly any insulative value. To solve that problem, first the storm window was invented, in effect providing two panes for the cold air to work its way through. Since air itself is not a bad insulator, it works pretty well, cutting down about 50 percent of heat loss through the window. A refinement upon that came next: double panes with a hermetically sealed air space about ½ inch wide between them. Then came triple panes, and even "quad panes." Who knows where that would have stopped were it not for another discovery: Special coatings on the panes, usually put on the air space surface of the room side of a double-glazed window, could give more insulative value than adding a third pane. Within a year, all the advertising hype about how great triple-pane windows were over double-pane windows quieted down in favor of hyping coated double-pane windows, which is where the progress in insulated glass now stands. (This is another example of how quickly "expert advice" can become obsolete in the housing industry, or at least how it can become beside the point. It should teach us, but probably won't, to be a bit more conservative in how fast we're ready to spend good money on the most current promising improvements.)

Using Andersen Window statistics, a Perma Shield Casement window with a double pane has a U-value of .52. With a triple pane, the same window has a U-value of .35. With High Performance coated, insulating double-pane glass, the U-value goes down to .30. And the latter window costs less than the triple pane one.

The first coatings developed to slow down the transfer of heat or cold through windows were plastic films sandwiched between two layers of glass. But the new coatings are metallic, bonded to the glass, and go by various names: low-e (for low emittance); High Performance (Andersen); Sungate (PPG Industries, Inc.); Sunglas (Ford Glass); and no doubt many more by the time you read this. The metallic coatings do not cut down the clarity of the glass noticeably. But they do slow down the movement of heat from the outside during summer and from the inside during winter. Also, there is less loss of interior cool air from air-conditioning in summer. But there is something of a trade-off with these coatings: The windows will

---

The Values of U-value and R-value

U-value is a designer calculation, arrived at by tests that rely on complicated scientific measurements. U-value expresses the total amount of heat transfer in Btu that 1 square foot of wall or ceiling or floor, etc., will transmit per hour for each degree Fahrenheit of temperature difference between the air on the warm and cool sides.

R-value is the measure of the resistance that a section of building, material, and air space or surface film offers to the flow of heat. The R-value is thus the reciprocal of the U-value.

In windows, R-value can be roughly calculated with this formula:

R-value = 1 divided by U-value

The lower the U-value, the better the insulation. Conversely, the higher the R-value, the better the insulation.

---

not let as much solar heat through in winter, either, when you could benefit from it.

(We are talking here of radiant heat—the transmission of energy by means of electromagnetic waves. These coatings cut down on the movement of such waves. Conduction is the transfer of heat through a solid medium, and conventional insulation over windows [like thermal shades and shutters] inhibits that. Convection is heat transfer by the movement of air; air barriers such as you find between layers of glass cut down on that.)

Condensation Problems

In addition to cutting down on heat loss in winter and the loss of cool air in summer, insulating windows with coated glass and double and triple panes has another advantage: condensation is minimized on the inside pane. This is a great boost to low maintenance.

Condensation runs down the window pane and the moisture soaking into the sash causes paint to peel, wood to swell, even possibly deteriorate. Not only that, but it is a little-known fact that wood is a good insulator (and therefore the reason it has been preferred for window frames). But it's only great when it's dry. When wood is wet, its insulative value decreases considerably. It may then "sweat" almost as badly as a metal sash that has no thermal barrier in it.

Condensation occurs when warm, humid air cools rapidly. Cool air can't hold as much moisture as warm air, and so when warm air cools as it comes in contact with a cooler window or any cooler surface, it releases the water in it. Obviously the closer to room temperature the inside pane of glass is kept, the less condensation.

However, the real cause of excessive condensation is not the window so much as it is the air: The window dripping with watery sweat is telling you that the air in your house is too humid. If you have good double-pane insulating windows and condensation is still bad, it may mean your family is taking too many showers without turning on the exhaust fan, or you have a clothes dryer and/or gas appliances without outside vents (water vapor is a by-product of gas combustion), or moist air is seeping through your basement walls, or your crawl spaces lack vapor barriers covering them, or your attic and/or crawl spaces lack good cross ventilation.

If condensation forms on the inside surface of a storm window, your regular window is not tight enough and your storm window is too tight. A storm window needs to have a bit of ventilation to the outside. If you get moisture between double- or triple-pane glass, the hermetic seal is broken or not sealed right in the first place. Good windows usually carry a guarantee against this happening.

Under certain conditions, you may get a flare-up of condensation. Do not lose your cool and start sweating yourself. Right after you have done some renovating (or when you first heat up a new house), you may get heavy temporary condensation on the windows. This is the moisture being driven out of the new concrete, plaster, and wood by your heating system—all perfectly natural. Also, over a humid summer your house will usually absorb considerable amounts of moisture, and when you first turn on the heat in the fall, you may experience window condensation for a week or so.

Another point to remember: If your windows are condensing more than they should, it is very possible that condensation is also forming

---

What's New in Window Glass Improvements?

Even with the best coatings available now, glass has an insulation value of no more than R-3.7, a mighty improvement over its unadorned state, but not much compared to what can be done with the rest of the house. (Walls typically have R-values of 12 to 18; ceilings have R-values of 20 and more.) The future holds great promise, however. Scientists (especially at the Solar Energy Research Institute in Golden, Colorado) have experimentally raised the R-value of glass windows to over 10 by using one or more coatings plus what is called "evacuated glazing." The air is removed from between a double pane of glass and the space filled with a gas or with tiny glass beads that keep the panes from collapsing due to the vacuum. Along with low-emittance coatings, this glass-honeycombed vacuum results in relatively high R-values, with good light transmission. The glass beads are so tiny they are not visible as such. The technology uses lasers to seal the glass. With improvements in laser technology, the process can become cost-effective, say scientists.

Another method involves the use of aerogel, a pure silica very much like glass. But it is porous, not solid like glass, and full of tiny air pockets that inhibit heat transfer. Sealed between two panes of glass, this material also increases the R-value of windows significantly. Much of the work on this project is being done by the Windows and Daylighting Group at the Lawrence Berkeley Lab, Berkeley, California.

inside your walls where you don't see it, just waiting to cause you all kinds of eventual maintenance problems.

Tinted (and Screened) Glass

Glassmakers are marketing tinted windows now to shield out sunlight and save on air-conditioning, particularly in warm climates. Such tints are especially effective if used with one of the coated glazings I just spoke about. These tints cut down on clarity but still allow a good view of the outdoors. Also available are tinted "solar screens," which fasten outside the regular window like a storm window and do away with the need for interior blinds. These screens, usually of vinyl-coated fiberglass, are often installed on tall office buildings where solar heat gain can be a special problem.

Coatings and tints do more than add to glass's insulative value. They also block out some of the sun's ultraviolet light, which, as we have seen, eventually deteriorates nearly everything, even slate roofs. Thus fading and deterioration of fabrics—drapes, carpets, furniture—inside the windows is reduced.

Decorative Glass

The ultimate in tinted windows, for very special places, is the decorative window of beveled, leaded, stained, patterned, or etched glass. We think of these products as being decorative only, however, like brick and stone, they can be marvelously functional, too. Not only can they be more insulative than ordinary glass and more shielding of ultraviolet rays, but they act as privacy screens while still admitting considerable amounts of light. That's why they work beautifully as entrance sidelights, tub enclosures, and room dividers, for example. Most decorative window glass is used for door windows where a homeowner can show off the elegance of beveled and leaded glass to best effect.

If you can't afford the cost of real leaded glass, inventive mankind has come to the rescue. There is a process now by which the lead channels or "came" is bonded onto laminated glass, giving the appearance of leaded glass patiently pieced together by handcrafting. No, it doesn't look as good as well-made leaded glass, at least not to the craftsperson, but on the other hand, it doesn't look as bad as poorly made leaded glass, either. The laminated "real-fake" stuff usually carries a 10-year guarantee against separation of the laminations. The price, of course, is much less than for real leaded glass (although not cheap by any means) and is a better compromise than the out-and-out simulated leaded glass. Beveled, sand-etched, and patterned glass can all be manufactured mostly by machine (rather than handcrafted) and so, for a comparatively low price, can be satisfactory for most homeowners.

But I would urge anyone interested in a door window, or entrance sidelights, or in an overhead transom window to search out a stained glass craftsperson in your area and commission a custom-made real McCoy. A smallish piece will not break you, and it will be a source of joy forever. As much as anything, the cost of the glass itself will govern price. Some of the exceedingly beautiful art glass available is expensive. And worth it, at least for a small window.

Window Frames and Sash

With home improvement projects so much more popular now than "trading up" to a new home (a trend that could change soon with interest rates going down as I write), the replacement window business is sweeping through the marketplace like wildfire. Which replacement window is best? The confused customer becomes only more confused when he tries to find out.

Wood, Vinyl, Aluminum, or Steel?

You've got a choice of wood, vinyl-clad wood, aluminum-clad wood, vinyl, aluminum, vinyl-clad aluminum, steel, and I suppose eventually fiberglass, though I know of none right now. Every manufacturer has a bible full of statistics and facts to show why its product is better for the price than the others.

Solid vinyl replacement windows appear at the moment to be the best buy for low maintenance, and I say that grudgingly since I confess to a built-in bias against vinyl. But before I get ahead of my story, let's examine some statistics accepted by all the replacement window proponents. According to official standard testing procedures, heat loss in British Thermal Units (Btu) per hour through the various materials was found to be:

> Wood 1.2
> Vinyl 1.3
> Steel 312.0
> Aluminum......1,416.0

Vinyl is not good insulation itself, but it obviously conducts a little more heat through it than wood, and both are far better than metal. But perhaps the most significant part of this set of statistics is how much less conductive steel is than aluminum. The difference is so great that one

Special Care for Vinyl

In some cases, paints and stains can cause damage to vinyl. Do not paint vinyl-covered foam weather stripping. Creosote-based stains can be particularly harmful. Check the information and cautions that come with your windows or talk over any painting or staining with your window dealer.

should no longer compare wood versus metal, but more specifically, wood versus steel, or wood versus aluminum. Steel, with a baked-on enamel, might be a practical compromise between aluminum and wood or vinyl in that it is stronger than any of them and far more low maintenance than wood. Wood's advantages are several. It has greater tensile strength than vinyl; it can be shaped into a window with home shop tools if necessary (no small consideration in this era of high window prices); and it is considered by most people to be the most beautiful.

But wood means high maintenance, whereas vinyl is extremely low maintenance. In fact, some vinyl windows now come with a lifetime guarantee against fading, cracking, peeling, etc.—all the ills that climate can visit upon wood. Cladding the exterior side of the wood window with aluminum or vinyl reduces maintenance but is no guarantee that moisture will not get into the wood and eventually deteriorate it.

The only clear disadvantage I can find to solid vinyl (and I've hunted hard) is that *some* kinds will not take paint. Since they come in only a very limited number of colors (a situation surely to be remedied as the windows grow in popularity), they may not fit the color of your house, or, more importantly, of your interior decor. Vinyl's other disadvantage is purely subjective. To some of us, it is ugly. It need not be ugly, but I suspect if the plastics industry started making really gorgeous vinyl colors, patterns, or textures, it would cost as much as good wood or enameled steel.

Aluminum supporters insist their product is stronger and more enduring than vinyl, but it may turn out that aluminum's wonderful combination of lightness and strength cannot be adequately utilized or appreciated in a window. Time will tell.

Solid vinyl windows are too new at any rate for a final decision as to endurance. But right now, a good vinyl window, molded for strength with lots of little air pockets inside for insulation, looks like the best buy for low maintenance. A good steel frame with a built-in thermal barrier for insulation is a close second. Wood, with exterior vinyl cladding, is best for insulation and beauty by the standards of today's fashion.

Finally, all the talk about how insulative various frames and glass are amounts to little if there are cracks and leaks around the window. A window is only going to be as good as its fit into the wall, and that means a careful carpenter and a good caulking job.

Double Hung, Sliding, or Casement?

Whether you buy double-hung, sliding, or casement windows is a matter of choice, I suppose. Used to be, sliding and casement windows had the edge for ease of cleaning. But now you can get double-hung windows that tilt inward, so you can clean both sides from inside the house. There are places where a casement window, swinging in or out on hinges, will be in the way or unhandy, but they are much to be preferred otherwise, if you want my biased opinion. Casement windows fit tighter. The other two kinds slide in grooves, and if there is any law that holds true today, yesterday, and (I will bet) tomorrow, it is this: any window that can stick will stick. (A great cure for a slightly sticking window is petroleum jelly, by the way.)

Have great respect for those little cranks on casement windows that allow you to open and close the windows from inside. Even on the best windows, the cranks are fairly fragile; their little worm-type gears are not really quite large enough for the job they are asked to do. Learn and memorize which way turns the window *out* and which way turns it back *in*. The threads on those cranks are often stripped by people trying to turn them the wrong way. High maintenance from sheer carelessness.

The outside of double-hung windows used to be difficult to clean. But not anymore. Many new models tilt in for easy cleaning.

Comparing Window Frame Construction Materials

Although the table here is overly prejudiced toward vinyl, it will help you get a quick grasp of the maintenance problems involved with windows. The table appears to me to be unfair to both wood and steel. Wood frames treated with preservative will need maintenance but "very often" is overdoing it. Steel with the baked-on enamels now being used can hardly be said to rust unless the paint chips off, which is unlikely. To say that vinyl will *never* deteriorate or require maintenance is to walk boldly into the future indeed. Never is a long, long word. Solid vinyl windows are scarcely five years old. And you will notice there is no comparison of structural or tensile strength in the table. And heat or cold *does* transmit through vinyl even though as a material it is a poor conductor of heat or cold. What's more, there is no allowance made in the Btu statistics for a thermal barrier in a metal frame, which increases metal's insulative value considerably.

Considerations When Selecting Frame Materials for Windows:

Will it remain structurally strong for years of trouble-free service?

Does heat or cold transmit through the material?

How many Btu per hour are lost?

Is it warm to touch even when it is winter outside?

Will it require painting or other regular maintenance?

Will scratches show a different color material under the paint?

Does it pit, rust, rot, or warp in inclement weather conditions or by natural aging?

Does soap and water cleaning make the material look new again?

*These are the judgments I consider unfair.

Shutters, Shades, and Insulating Covers

It may be a decade or more before products made from things like gas, glass beads, and aerogel are practical for the residential market. In the meantime, you can greatly increase a window's insulative value by the use of various kinds of shutters, blinds, shades, etc., that were publicized so much during the years of high fuel prices. Now that oil prices are tumbling, you need to punch new figures into your calculator to see if the expense of more insulation really pays. But just as sure as night follows day, there will be more fuel shortages down the road, be they real or contrived.

Many, many kinds of interior window shades and shutters have come and sometimes gone in the last decade. The only real drawback to the less

| 100% Rigid Vinyl | OTHER FRAME MATERIALS | | | | |
	Aluminum	Wood	Steel	Vinyl-clad Wood	Vinyl-clad Aluminum
Yes	Yes	Yes	Yes	Yes	Yes
No	Yes	No	Yes	Not if wood is kept dry	Yes
1.3	1,416*	1.2	312*	1.3	250–600
Yes	No	Yes	No	Yes, if wood is kept dry	Only the vinyl is warm
Never*	Yes, if scratched	Very often	Often*	Wood must be painted often*	Yes, if scratched
No	Yes	Yes	Yes	Yes, on the wood	Yes, on the aluminum
Never	Yes	Yes	Yes	Wood will rot and warp	Aluminum will pit
Yes	No	No	No	Yes, on vinyl No, on wood	Yes, on vinyl No, on aluminum

expensive ones is that, try as hard as you can to think positive, they still aren't very attractive. As homeowners improved or replaced leaky old windows, these more or less stopgap (literally) methods of keeping heat in and cold out have declined in popularity. But the more attractive, relatively expensive, interior folding shutters, some with movable louvers, are still available (see your lumber and home supply dealer).

There are also some good interior storm windows available. They're much easier to put up than exterior storms, but most, if not all, make it impossible to open the window once they're in place, so they're best put only on those windows you plan to keep closed all winter. The tightest are shrink-wrap plastics, but they are usually used one season and then thrown away.

EXTERIOR WINDOW SHADES AND COVERINGS

Exteriorly, a really excellent low-maintenance solution for keeping out unwanted summer sunlight is to build a house with a roof that extends out far enough to shade windows in summer while still allowing lower winter sun in. The overhang also adds years of life to window frames and siding. Building low maintenance directly into the house design is the most economical way to do it. If your house does not have an overhang, window awnings, on the south side at least, are a low-cost alternative.

Exterior shutters are a good idea, and the proof is that they keep coming back in new form. Shutters on the outside are more effective than on the inside in keeping cold out of the house. They provide good storm protection, muffle noise, insulate during the night when windows lose so much heat, and provide privacy, especially over those large glass patio doors where drapes aren't practical. The new rolling shutters, which can be operated by hand or electrically from inside, also are fairly effective deterrents to burglars. And they are good for fine-tuning the amount of sunlight you want to allow through glass walls in a passive solar heated home. The interlocking slats of vinyl unroll from an aluminum housing

Popular in Europe for many years, rolling exterior vinyl window shutters are becoming more commonplace here. They provide window security, and the ones that have insulated vinyl slats add cold weather protection as well.

tucked up under the roofline, and in many models the bottom slat locks automatically in the lower sill. No regular maintenance is necessary. Two manufacturers are Perfecta (Reflexa Werke in West Germany, distributed by American Reflexa, 31843 West 8 Mile Road, Livonia, MI 48152), and Security Shutters (Security Shutters Corporation, 109 James Street, Venice, FL 33595). Other brands are available through local lumberyards and housing suppliers.

Automatic rolling shutters are quite expensive. For a 3-by-4-foot window shutter installed, Perfecta quotes a price of $292 (1986). And for one 6-by-7-foot glass patio door, $565 fully installed. The shutters come in a selection of colors, and they are, while not beautiful, not unattractive. At their high price, though, I wonder if some enterprising builder might not start marketing a modern version of the old wood shutters that would probably be less expensive, look better, and perform the same job. They were once so popular and in a way, still are (although now we use them just to frame our windows).

Exterior shutters have another potential advantage rarely mentioned. Because today's double-pane windows reflect the exterior landscape almost like a mirror, birds fly into them and die of broken necks, especially where houses are surrounded by trees. Closing the shutters partially, especially during mating and nesting seasons, would save many birds.

Skylights and Roof Windows

All the climatic problems that ordinary windows must deal with are compounded in skylights. Where an ordinary window loses some heat at night, a skylight is prone to lose more. Where sun glare through an ordinary window can be a problem, it will be worse through a skylight. The chances of a skylight leak are much greater than an ordinary window leak. To quote David Bullen, of the American Institute of Architects, from an article in *Rodale's New Shelter* (November/December, 1983): "A skylight will make an energy contribution in a northern climate if it: 1. faces south; 2. is pitched steeply to catch the low winter sun; 3. is somehow shaded to keep out summer sun; 4. can be opened to vent hot air; 5. is at least double glazed and ideally equipped with insulation; and 6. is sized correctly—not so big that it overheats the room it lights." In the South, the skylight should be shaded and face north, says Bullen, to minimize air-conditioning costs.

Obviously, that's a tall order and from the low-maintenance point of view, a homeowner might wonder if the effort is worth it. Most architects say yes, not just because skylights and roof windows add a dramatic touch to the interior of the house, but because, engineered correctly, they really can take the place of daytime electric lighting. Imagine a light fixture in your ceiling that never burns out, never needs maintenance once properly installed except for cleaning, and adds nothing to your electric bill.

Shading on skylights is imperative to save on air-conditioning and glare. Some skylights come with optional shutters—miniature versions of the roller shutters I described earlier. Others have a metal screen on the exterior of the glazing to deflect strong sun. Still others have tinted glass or plastic. In hot climates, the skylights should open to let out excessive heat. For cold climates, double panes should be the rule, but some manufacturers sell a triple and even a quadruple thermal insulated skylight made of Lexan. It is rated at a U-value of .16 in a 15 mph wind, and has an R-value of 6.35, which the company says is 400 percent more energy efficient than conventional, aluminum-framed models. Velux skylights are also quality products (Velux-America, Inc., P.O. Box 3208, Greenwood, SC 29648). The firm has been a pacesetter in the skylight business for years, and their prefabricated flashings all but solve the perennial leak problem in roof openings.

Because of the diffusiveness of light, researchers and inventors are finding that the roof opening need not be large at all; in fact, it can be quite small. Entering light, with proper reflective surfaces in the ceiling, spreads out to bathe the room below. Light entering the room through a vertical shaft on the roof is diffused by reflective plastic glazing, then spread out inside the room by the flared ceiling on either side of the opening.

When choosing a skylight, remember that they will get dirty quicker than windows. The roof windows that open so that you can clean both sides from below may be worth the extra cost.

Despite all the good news about improvements in skylights, clerestory windows, serving the same purpose as skylights, are a better choice strictly from the standpoint of low maintenance. Though we are inclined to think of them as something new, clerestories go back at least to the Romanesque architecture of the early Middle Ages. Being vertical, such

Clerestory windows let in a good deal of light but don't bring with them many of the problems that skylights are prone to, like leaking and over-heating the room below with direct sun.

windows are less likely to leak and can be more easily opened for ventilation, or shaded against the glare of sunshine. Clerestories are of course less adaptable; they have to be designed into the house, or rather, the house designed for them. Remodeling a roof to take clerestory windows may be economically impractical, despite low-maintenance advantages.

Glass Patio Doors

When glass doors first became popular, people were forever running into them, or through them, with subsequent ghastly injuries. Now tempered safety glass is almost always used. If your patio door does not have safety glass in it, replacing it should be a high priority. Low maintenance extends to you and your children, too.

The old patio doors were also unsatisfactory in other ways. Usually made of uninsulated glass framed in aluminum, they had little or no insulative value. Now you can get clad wooden frames or insulated metal ones as well as tinted glass that cuts down on glare and on heat transmission. Old patio doors leaked water and in winter, frost built up on the inner surface of the glass. Insulated glass and all kinds of magnetic or vinyl or compression sealed weather stripping are standard on patio doors now. In addition, old sliders tended to balk and stick, inspiring new and wonderful combinations of cusswords. Nor were they very secure against intruders, which led to some amazing high-tech security devices utilizing, among other things, broom handles. Special locks and strike plates make patio doors securer now. In addition, Bilt Best Windows (175 10th Street, Sainte Genevieve, MO 63670) and no doubt others, supply a footbolt with their windows that is supposed to keep out that most unwanted of intruders, the bug. (A footbolt is a little sliding bolt at the base of the door, operated by the foot, of course. Close the door and wedge the bolt against the side of the channel that the door slides in.) Rollers equipped with ball-bearing wheels now allow sliding doors to move easily and much more quietly.

Patio doors that swing open like casement windows or ordinary doors are now coming into vogue. They generally close tighter than sliders. Such doors are usually installed in two sections—one fixed, one movable. But triple sections, with two fixed and one movable section, are available, as are other combinations, if you want to special order. Patio doors are made in the same choice of materials as entry doors (see below).

Entry Doors

When it comes to choosing an entry door, people that are otherwise very practical throw the logic of low maintenance to the wind in favor of what they consider beautiful. If this is foolish, I nonetheless find satisfaction in it since it proves once more that human beings are still, well, human. The true-blue American, especially when she is my wife, will have a varnished wooden door, no matter what. Period. End of discussion. Don't bother me with facts about low maintenance.

The only way to build low maintenance into a wooden entry door is to build an ample overhang over it, or an entryway in front of it and add a storm door—in effect making the exterior door an interior one. Obviously adding a storm door hides the glory one has spent so much money to achieve at the entrance. Considering the increase in burglars and door-to-door salespeople (I can't swear that statistics show an increase, but it seems to me that both are more common these days), I wonder why people want an inviting front door anyway. My secret desire is to have an artist paint a very realistic likeness of a cannon on mine.

But it was not until Mrs. True-Blue American refinished her lovely wood door the third time (in 12 years) that she even consented to a storm door. This addition alone dropped our winter fuel bill by $50. It stopped most of the hurricane that had whistled through the cracks that appeared when the door warped in cold weather. (It wasn't the cold weather that actually warped the door, but rather the fact that the outside face of the door was a frigid 0°F and the inside face was a warm 80°F.)

I'm overmaligning wood doors a little, since you can buy good ones that are guaranteed not to warp more than 3/16 inch—like the solid oak doors sold by mail nationwide by Kirby Mill Works (Box 898, Ignacio, CO 81137). But by the time you get such a door installed, complete with hinges, hardware, jambsets, etc., you are talking in the neighborhood of $1,000. And even Kirby says, at the end of its limited warranty statement: "We do not recommend *any* type of wood door in areas that get heavy exposure to sun, snow, or rain."

The sun causes the worst damage. Ultraviolet rays will get you, sooner or later, and in the case of wood, sooner more often than later. Here is where, if ever, woods naturally resistant to rot, like walnut, should be used. But a solid walnut door would be an extravagance of the highest order. Oak is the best we can afford, it seems. Oak is okay if it is good old-growth oak, which is scarcer than walnut.

If you insist on having a wood door at the entrance, you should treat it with a penetrating oil that will make it water-repellent, and then put on a minimum of three coats of good, hard ultraviolet-inhibiting exterior varnish. I recommend the best grade marine (boat) varnish you can buy, even if it is rather too shiny for a door. Paints, which shield out the sun, hold up better than any clear finish, but of course, if you are going to paint over the wood's beautiful grain, you have eliminated the only reason for using wood in an entry door.

As an alternative, there are insulated steel doors that look like wood, which are almost twice as insulative as standard wood doors. They have a polystyrene or some other insulative core, and thermal breaks that keep cold from crawling through and frosting the inside, as can otherwise happen with steel. These doors are not beautiful to the traditional eye, I grant, and they can warp a wee bit in the same strained situation I put my wooden door through, but they require far and away much lower maintenance than wood. They are attractive, too (for a factory product), and in some cases you can hardly tell by looking that they are not wood. (I often wonder about our penchant for tradition. Wood grain is beautiful and I love it. But metals have their own beauty, too. Why make steel look like wood? Burnished steel can be as beautiful as varnished wood.) Steel doors, like wood doors, have been spruced up with all kinds of decorative moldings (called plants): real and fake leaded glass lights, beveled glass lights—whatever you desire. With all kinds of new magnetic seals and vinyl weather stripping, why not a steel exterior door? It is much more secure against breaking and entering, or can be, and of course it is also fireproof.

Every door has weaknesses. Many steel doors have plastic plants on them. With the sun glaring down through a storm window, so much heat can be generated that the plastic will melt and distort, if it is painted a dark color. Steel doors are not maintenance-free. Rust will get to them eventually, requiring repainting perhaps. Also the wood lock blocks in steel doors are often smaller and weaker than in good wood doors.

You can attempt the best of both worlds by choosing an aluminum or a vinyl-clad wood door. The advantages and disadvantages are the same as for clad windows: aluminum adds strength, is more durable, but has no insulative value. Vinyl has a little, but tends to get brittle in cold temperatures. Either way you get better low maintenance for the money than from a midpriced, all-wood door.

The latest addition to the replacement door market is a fiberglass model from Therma-Tru Corporation (P.O. Box 7404, Toledo, OH 43615). The door is made of two sheets of compression-molded fiberglass with a core of insulating polyurethane. There's a 5-year limited warranty against splitting, cracking, warping, or rotting. Notice I do not use the word "fading." You can plane, stain, or paint fiberglass like wood, although I imagine your plane will dull quicker. A primer before painting is a must. Fiberglass doors, according to tests, have greater insulative value than either wood or insulated steel. Therma-Tru claims insulation values for their doors up to R-15.

Locks

You should equip your entry door with a dead-bolt lock. Such a lock can't be opened with a plastic card the way the detectives do on television. Hacksawing a dead bolt is difficult, especially if it's a 2-incher. A single cylinder dead bolt with a thumb turn on the inside is handiest, but a burglar can often break the glass of the sidelight, reach in, and flip the thumb turn. Dead bolts that open only with a key on both sides are not legal in all states because you may not find the key if you need to escape quickly in case of fire.

Having a storm door also equipped with a dead bolt adds to security. Becoming popular now are ornamental iron storm doors with double dead-bolt locking systems. These storm doors are attractive, and an intruder almost needs a welding torch to get through. But they hide the beauty of the entry door.

Garage Doors

Let a person who is without bias correct me, but isn't the garage door about the ugliest part of the modern home? Typically it is also the door for highest maintenance. And depending on where the garage is attached to the house, it can be the source of a lot of cold air working its way into your fuel bill.

The typical garage door is a flush door with sectional panels of exterior "hardboard." Hardboard might be any number of kinds of regurgitated wood—flakes, sawdust, whatever, and lots of glue. But don't look down your nose too much. The panels are fairly durable and won't warp as much as wood in its original state. They will need repainting occasionally, but so will other materials.

If you want to spend a little more money, manufacturers are offering better-insulated garage doors that are more attractive, too. Some manufacturers offer raised panel doors in real wood or in insulated steel. The steel ones require less maintenance—the better ones are prepainted with baked-on epoxy primer and polyester finish coats that last a long time with minimal or no rust. The insulation is a polyurethane core bonded between the exterior and interior steel skins. Watertight seals between the panel sections and self-draining water channels are two more features to look for in an overhead garage door. On the cheapest doors, or in some cases not-so-cheap doors, the hardware is of low quality. Even the handles will break after several years for no apparent reason.

Rollers need to be oiled regularly. It is amazing what oil will in fact achieve in ease of operation. Other than that though, overhead sectional doors are surprisingly durable. If you install an automatic garage-door opener, then you will begin to experience maintenance problems. The only guaranteed low-maintenance automatic garage-door opener is your arms and legs. Good low maintenance for your body, too.

Weather Stripping

Caulking is still a good way to seal out weather around doors and windows, but it's high maintenance. So are other "quick fixes" like duct tape, plastic inserts for windows, and other easily applied seals. But a little more time and money spent on weather stripping the first time gives you a much longer period of low maintenance or no maintenance.

CHAPTER 6
DECKS, PORCHES, AND PATIOS

The porch is a good example of that ancient adage: the more things change, the more they stay the same. The migration to the suburbs in the '50s left the porch behind, it being symbolic of a lifestyle the new suburbanites thought they wanted to escape from. Even the old neighborhood habit of evening porch sitting was ridiculed in the suburbs as "hickish," in the same tone used by city porch sitters years earlier to refer to neighbors who still kept chickens in the backyard.

Television and air-conditioning almost made the porch obsolete anyway. Compared to the view from the front porch, the tube was a whole universe more exciting, or so it seemed. And with the air conditioner at open throttle, you didn't have to wait on the porch for the house to cool down before going to bed.

But humans still wanted some extension of the house's living space into the out-of-doors. The patio replaced the porch. Where a patio was not practical, as for a second-story extension or over unlevel terrain, the deck became popular. By and by, however, the absence of rain protection for patio and deck parties became a pain. Why not roof over the patio, or part of it? That done, patio lovers decided to take care of the mosquito menace once and for all. Up went a border partition along the edge of the roofed part of the patio that looked suspiciously like the kneewall of yesterday's porch, with posts extending up to the roof between which screens could be inserted in the summer. If it wasn't a porch, it was only because the floor was masonry embedded in the ground rather than a raised wood floor with latticework around the sides.

In such a roundabout way, the porch's practicality has been vindicated. Modern homeowners have rediscovered what Victorians and antebellum Southerners all took for granted: No matter how hot the day, there's always a breeze on the porch, especially if it wraps around more than one side of the house, like the ageless veranda. Why porches draw breezes an engineer could probably demonstrate easily. Porch sitters only know that it is so.

You get the same phenomenon from what we have named the "breezeway," which is itself an adaptation of the traditional "dogtrot" or "possum trot"—the open hall between the two halves of a traditional Southern log cabin. We are relearning almost accidentally that the breeze that finds its way softly to the porch brings a much more soothing, staying coolness than the heavy, all-too-insulating cold of air-conditioning. Not to mention that the former is free. Moreover, we now realize that television is simply unable to provide enough really satisfying programs to draw the attention of *all* our leisure time. Porch sitting, jawing with passing neighbors, or simply counting fireflies isn't so boring after all.

Decks

The open, slat-floored deck so popular today is the cheapest way to extend living space into the out-of-doors. It is also, in one sense, a high-maintenance alternative. That decks are practical at all depends entirely on the use of pressure-treated woods or woods like redwood, which are naturally resistant to rot. Nevertheless, wood exposed to the elements, no matter how it is treated, requires fairly continual maintenance or replacement. In selecting treated wood, stick with established, proven products with 30- to 40-year warranties—and read the warranties closely. Wolmanized Lumber (Koppers Company, Inc., 436 Seventh Avenue, Pittsburgh, PA 15219) and Osmose Sunwood (Osmose Wood Preserving, Inc., 980 Ellicott Street, Buffalo, NY 14209) are two brands offering 30- and 40-year guarantees respectively. Generally speaking, even the best material will need waterproofing protection periodically.

Deck nomenclature.

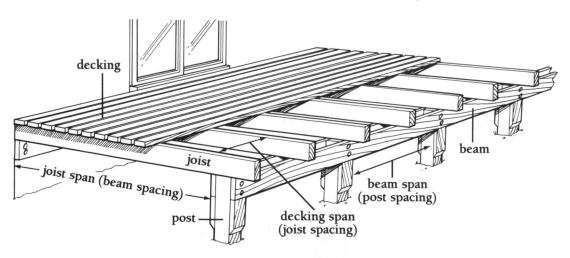

decking

joist

joist span (beam spacing)

post

decking span
(joist spacing)

beam span
(post spacing)

beam

Here are some other tips to keep deck maintenance at a minimum:

1. Use rustproof nails and screws; hot-dipped galvanized ones are the most economical. Use ring-shank or spiral-shank nails; they hold better and help reduce warping. If nails cause splitting, blunt the points slightly. If that doesn't work, drill holes for the nails slightly smaller than the nail shank.

2. Nail 2 × 4 deck boards flat on the joists with two nails at each joist. Nail 2 × 6s with three nails at each joist.

3. Space between deck boards should be no less than ¼ inch, no more than about ½ inch.

4. When connecting framing with bolts or lag screws, use flat washers under bolt heads and nuts to prevent heads and nuts from pulling into the wood and opening a passageway for water into the wood.

5. Bevel the tops of posts exposed to the weather about 45 degrees so that water runs off rapidly. Even treated wood can and will check and split on the end grain, and a beveled top will encourage water to drain away rather than into the cracks.

6. When nailing down deck boards, lay the boards on the joists with the curve of the grain *down*, as seen on the end of the boards. Any warpage will then cause the board to rise in the middle rather than cup up on the edges and hold water.

7. Joists should be spaced 16 inches apart for deck boards of 2 × 4s laid flat. Space the joists 24 inches apart for 2 × 6 deck boards laid flat.

8. If 2 × 6 joists are used, they should span no more than 9¾ feet at 24-inch spacings, or 8 feet at 16-inch spacings. If using 2 × 8 joists, the span at 24-inch spacings should be no more than 12 feet 10 inches, or 10 feet 8 inches at 16-inch spacings. The span limit is 16½ feet for 16-inch spacings and 13 feet 4 inches at 24-inch spacings. You can usually cheat an inch or two on these dimensions, but where heavy snow loads or big parties are expected on your deck, they ought to be adhered to rather closely. A group of teenagers trying out a new dance step in unison could unleash awesome vibrations not entirely connected with the music. Hot tubs could require extra strong bracing; consult directions or an experienced carpenter.

9. Upright posts should usually be 6 × 6s. You can use 4 × 4s where the deck is small and posts less than 6 feet tall.

10. Beams that attach to the posts for the joists to sit on vary in size depending on how far apart the posts are set and how much space there is between beams. A very rough rule of thumb says that an 8-foot spacing requires at least 2 × 8 beams; a 10-foot spacing, 2 × 10 beams; and 12-foot spacing, 2 × 12 beams. Often, the outer beam is doubled, either laminated together to make a 4 × 8 (or 4 × 10 or 4 × 12) or more often, one 2 × 8 beam is nailed on the outside of the posts and one on the inside.

Our deck, however, is not nearly that strongly built, and it has stood the test of time. Consult a carpenter if you are in doubt. It is always better to overbrace than underbrace.

The correct way to lay boards on joists.

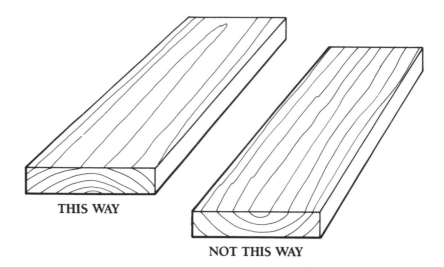

THIS WAY

NOT THIS WAY

11. Treated wood posts can be set directly in the ground—at least 2 feet deep or to below frost line—and tamped with earth and gravel, or with a concrete collar. A flat rock in the bottom of the hole to act as a footer plate might add stability in sandy soil. In heavy clay, that wouldn't be necessary—and certainly not if you are pouring concrete around the post.

Actually, it is seldom necessary to anchor deck posts so irretrievably solid in concrete. The post isn't going anywhere. It is held firmly by the deck bracing to the house and to the other posts. All you need to worry about is that it sits deep enough in the ground so frost won't heave it up. Our deck posts sit on a concrete slab, which is the lower patio floor, not in the ground at all. In fact, they sit on little squares of insulation board rather than on the concrete itself—the builder's way of shielding the posts from moisture that much more. Sure, treated wood *resists* moisture, but it will resist better, the less it has to resist.

12. If you want your deck to last, give it a coat or two of a recommended water repellent. Also, you may wish to stain it a more woodlike color. I still think plain old linseed oil is an effective, cheap preservative and stain for outdoor wood, but manufacturers of treated wood are recommending stains that are alkyd-based over linseed-oil formulations. They say the former dry faster (true) and retain color better (maybe). At any rate, the wood must be dry before applying any of these protectants or stains.

Precautions for Preservatives

Whenever man "triumphs over nature" there are always trade-offs that make one wonder about the victory. So too with treated wood, which turns about any cheap wood into a product that resists decay and termites for years. But such wood will twist, warp, crack, and splinter occasionally. Also, any opening in the wood that goes deeper than the penetration of the preservative treatment will provide an entrance for decay.

The copper or zinc formulations that give treated wood its decay resistance are considered to be safe for normal use around humans and animals. Treated wood with guaranteed resistance to termites usually contains inorganic arsenic. Thus certain sensible precautions should be observed when using these woods.

Such wood should never be used as food containers, cutting boards, etc. Nor should it be used for animal food containers, either. It is arguable whether any treated wood should be used in animal pens, where animals get bored and hungry and start chewing or licking on wood, horses particularly. Don't make parts of beehives that come in contact with the honey out of treated wood. Avoid prolonged inhalation of sawdust from treated wood. If you are sawing or sanding a lot of it, wear a dust mask. Don't burn treated wood in stoves or fireplaces, or even in an open fire outdoors. The wood (or ashes) may give off toxic fumes. Acquaint yourself with any other safety recommendations that come with the brand of treated wood you decide to use.

After reading the label, you may, instead, decide to spend the extra money on a natural wood that resists decay, like redwood.

Porches

A porch at first glance translates into high maintenance. But in some respects, it can mean better low maintenance than a deck, even though you have the roof to tend to. The roof will at least mean less maintenance for the porch floor and walls and the wall of the house it extends over, and especially the door into the house. All of these components are protected from the weather by the porch roof. The old-fashioned front porch actually served the purpose of the modern portico and foyer combined.

Whether you intend to save an old porch or add a new one, the main concerns are the foundation, crawl space, and any exposed wood. Foundations on old porches settle, mainly because they were not dug in deeply enough in the first place. When they sink, the roof starts coming loose from the wall. If that has occurred, jack up the roof and pour a new foundation or strengthen the old one considerably. Then reattach the roof to the wall, using new lumber if necessary. Rotting usually occurs at the junction of wall and sagging porch, where water leaks in. Replace flashing.

Outer pillars may be rotten, too, on an old porch, even, or especially, if the posts are embedded in concrete. Some think that setting a wood post in concrete protects it from moisture when quite the opposite is true.

The crawl space under raised porch floors should be well ventilated. Skirts should have ventings or latticework, not be solid. The soil surface under the porch can be covered with plastic film to stop some of the rising moisture. The porch floor should slope slightly away from the house so water drains away. Make sure roof spouting directs water away from the crawl space, not into it.

If adding a porch to the front of the house, check your zoning to make sure the porch will not bring your house out too close to the front of your property. You may need a zoning variance if this is the case, but be prepared to be persistant.

Ceiling fans, or large floor or window fans have been found to create enough breeze to discourage mosquitoes. Letting little pieces of punky wood smolder and smoke like incense will also drive mosquitoes away.

Screening

Screening a porch requires some wall framing. The usual method is to build a low kneewall around the perimeter of the porch if one does not already exist. Then build up framing to the ceiling with openings for the screens to fit into.

With the age of air-conditioning upon us, not much attention is paid to screens anymore, although there are more days in the year when a bit of a breeze from outdoors would refresh a house economically than there are days hot enough for air-conditioning. But at least porches, where we retreat from the closed confinement of the house, can be much improved if screened against bugs.

Copper screening is still available, but aluminum cloth is cheaper and quite rust resistant, too. Fiberglass, nylon, and other nonmetallic materials used for screening over the years are not as effective as metal. They are not stiff enough and in some cases melt easily—lit cigarettes quickly melt holes in them. As far as frames for the screens are concerned, aluminum ones are light and low maintenance, while wood ones are stouter.

The lack of screening stiffness is especially critical in full-length screens for screen doors and storm doors. Even aluminum and steel will, in time, sag in this situation, especially where children frequently use the door. They tend to push or kick against screening rather than against the metal or wood panels that support the screen. Pet cats, begging to be let back indoors, climb such screens, making them sag all the more. If you have cats, I advise you to buy the kind of door that is solid wood or metal in the bottom third or half.

Refrain from buying screen doors with metal decorative borders that reach out over the screening. My family and I learned the hard way that especially with nonmetallic screening, pushing even slightly against it (as when washing it, which should be done once a year), the screening rubs on the sharp metal edge of the decorative border, and in a few years breaks at critical stress points.

If you glass in a porch, it is hardly a porch anymore. You will then have to build walls strong enough to support windows—hence, like the rest of the house.

Patios

Patio floors are usually masonry or stone, and if there are kneewalls around the perimeter, they are also of such durable material, making patios the lowest maintenance of all outdoorsy house additions. Patios, especially smaller ones, provide a good place to use imaginative low-maintenance materials. Embed flagstones, quarry tiles, or slate slabs in your concrete, or lay the slabs on top of the concrete and mortar between them. There are neat new ways to make a concrete slab look like an expensive stone floor. Plastic pattern forms are available to imprint hexagonal, cobblestone, or brick-shaped patterns in a wet concrete slab. They cost about $70. One source for them is the Masonry Specialty Catalog (4430 Gibsonia Road, Gibsonia, PA 15044). At least one company, the Bowmanite Corporation (81 Encina Avenue, Palo Alto, CA 94301), has developed this idea to the ultimate—attractive floors that appear to be brick, slate, or beautifully colored flagstones, but which are in reality less expensive special concretes, cast in place, using an almost limitless number of designs, textures, and integral colors to achieve their effects.

For low maintenance, patio floors should be mortared. That way there's no chance that weed and grass seeds can be blown into the spaces between slate or masonry, necessitating lots of bending over and pulling them out. You also won't have to worry about shifting slate or masonry, due to settling of sand, stones, or soil underneath, or heaving during periods of freezing and thawing.

Patio Furniture

Patio and deck lovers need to consider furniture. Picnic benches, chairs, and tables can be built permanently into the deck arrangement, when the deck is being built, or later. For table tops that come into contact with food, you might rather use untreated wood. Whether you are doing the work yourself, or hiring a carpenter, furniture of this kind will prove to be cheaper and more durable than most of the cheaper aluminum and plastic patio furniture you can buy.

Cheap outdoor furniture requires no more care than more expensive kinds—it just needs to be brought in out of the weather if you wish it to last any length of time. Sunlight deteriorates plastic and it cracks or breaks; moisture rusts steel, aluminum eventually pits and corrodes from moisture, too; conventional wood rots unless periodically painted or varnished or treated to resist moisture. Rattan and wicker are too expensive to leave

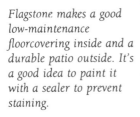

Flagstone makes a good low-maintenance floorcovering inside and a durable patio outside. It's a good idea to paint it with a sealer to prevent staining.

out in the weather, and they ought to have their lacquer finishes renewed periodically.

Wrought-iron furniture is still probably the best for low maintenance, for the money. It is heavy and sturdy and resists rust for years if painted, or better, if covered with baked-on enamel. Touch-ups are a fact of life with wrought iron, though, because it's bound to chip here and there, providing openings for rust to intrude. New enameled cast-aluminum furniture is long lasting and can be left outdoors with little adverse effect. Woodward wrought-iron furniture, sold by many stores and catalogs like the Speigel catalog (1113 West 22 Street, Oak Brook, IL 60609) has a good selection of quality outdoor furniture of all kinds. Woodward gives you a choice of light fine designs, too, if the heavy traditional wrought-iron furniture is not to your liking.

Perhaps the best, and certainly the most expensive, outdoor furniture is made of teakwood with mortise-and-tenon joinery. Teak doesn't rot and needs no protective paint or varnish. It can sit out in humid weather for a century and the only change is the weathering of the wood to a silvery

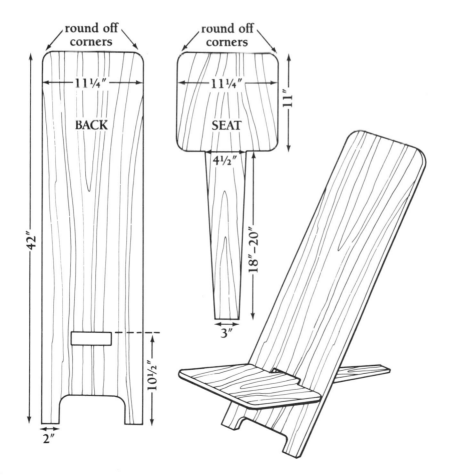

A very simple wooden lawn-chair design, by the Koppers Company.

gray. A good source is Smith & Hawken Ltd. (25 Corte Madera, Mill Valley, CA 94941).

For a chair that you can carry around with you easily—from one patio conversation to another—there is an old simple design now being popularized by the Wolmanized treated-lumber folks, which you can make entirely from one 2-by-12-inch piece of lumber, 8 feet long. Saw the board into two 42-inch pieces, then shape them as shown in the illustration on the preceding page.

Part 2
The Low-Maintenance Landscape

CHAPTER *7*

THE LAWN

Researchers at the national lawn care service headquartered in Worthington, Ohio, tell about a strain of zoysia grass, discovered in an Asian cemetery, that doesn't need mowing. Certain strains of zoysia, vigorously promoted these last ten years, stay presentable with only two mowings per year, or so proponents claim. Meanwhile, work continues on using hormones to control grass growth, hopefully to cut down on the homeowner's mowing chores. All this sounds like good news except to lawn mower manufacturers. But if I were selling mowers, I wouldn't be too worried. The evidence suggests that more people like to mow than hate the job, and the best proof of that is the way homeowners continue to mow much more than necessary, both in area and frequency.

My mother's favorite job was mowing—after she got a riding mower. In the midst of raising a large family, she said that the time on her mower was peaceful and meditative, the noise of the motor insulating her from the world. Many other people tell me the same thing. Or demonstrate it by their actions. The retired farmer down the road keeps his lawn carpet neat, but that is not enough. About three years ago, he began to mow the roadside ditch in front of his property. Little by little, he extended the mowed area along the road in both directions. By the end of last summer he was mowing a quarter mile in both directions. With the call of the open road beckoning him on, he may push his mowing frontier this year as far as a tank of gas will take him. Maybe he will carry gas and refuel along the way, eventually crossing the country with the first transcontinental swath of mow grass. Cutting grass in America provides the same outlet that the motorcycle does for the Easy Rider. What people want is not a low-maintenance lawn, but a no-maintenance mower.

Another common mowing personality might be called Superneat. Superneat says he hates mowing and would rather be golfing, but his actions belie his words. He mows even when it is almost impossible to tell the cut portion from the uncut. So long as one dandelion sticks its fuzzy head above the ruglike surface of his lawn, Superneat will not rest.

113

Low-maintenance lawn care provides no comfort either for those people fixated by the Lord-of-the-Manor tradition rooted in eighteenth-century Europe: as the size of one's castle increases, so must the size of the lawn roundabout. And the real proof of your medieval wealth was that you didn't have to graze livestock on that grass, either. This may be a fine status symbol for the rich, who can pay others to do the work, but pity the rest of us who wish to appear equally as successful but must keep up the appearances by the sweat of our own brows. It is nice to be Lord-of-the-Manor only if you do not have to be Peasant-of-the-Manor, also.

Meadow Lawns

If you want a low-maintenance lawn the first thing you should do is keep it small—or at least keep small that portion that you regularly mow. On a larger lawn, consider maintaining some of it in a meadow, about 6 inches high, to be clipped twice or thrice a year the way a farmer does a pasture field. (A sickle-bar mower attachment works better for this operation than a rotary blade.) You will open up a whole world of nature to your eyes, in addition to cutting down on your work. The meadow provides a habitat for ground-nesting birds—chipping sparrow, field sparrow, meadowlark, bobolink, and quail to name a few—and a safe harbor for many beneficial animals like toads. Moles can tunnel there in pursuit of Japanese beetle larvae and no one will ever know. The taller grass will hide their tunnels.

You can call your meadow a wildflower garden or a butterfly garden since it will become both. You can either let nature provide you with an assortment of weedy wildflowers or plant the ones you like best. One favorite is a milkweed with bright orange blossoms, often called butterfly weed (*Asclepias tuberosa*). (In this chapter, as well as chapters 8 and 9, I give botanical names only for those plants that I want to distinguish from others similar to it, or for plants that are quite uncommon. Those plants not followed by a botanical name are the common plants most all of us have heard of.) All the milkweeds draw butterflies, the monarch particularly, and many other interesting insects, but the other kinds tend to spread too fast.

One of our neighbors decided there had to be a better way than twice-a-week mowing. She hired a farmer to tear up half her lawn with a disc. This takes some nerve, since the Superneats will disapprove, but we still live in a free part of America where there is no stupid law to keep us from planting our yards to something besides grass. (However, some towns and cities prohibit the growing of anything but neat ground covers and grasses in the front yard, and others have ordinances that require homeowners to mow regularly, which makes wildflower lawns virtually impossible; flowers never have a chance to bloom and reseed themselves.)

This neighbor of ours scattered wildflower seeds over the torn-up sod and waited. By summer, the former lawn was a riot of color and became a showplace of sorts, as people from all over the county drove by to see what That-Lady-Who-Won't-Mow was going to do next. "It's worked so well," she says after two years, "that I wish I had torn up the whole lawn." Then she laughs. "One day I looked out the window and there was a stranger picking the flowers. I rushed out and explained that she was trespassing on my *lawn*. The woman looked at me in great astonishment. 'But it isn't *mowed*,' she said." It could only happen in America.

Wildflower lawns will not necessarily keep an ideal balance between the various desirable grasses and wildflowers. Our neighbor pulls thistles and wild carrot (Queen Anne's lace) and such weedy flowers that will overwhelm the others if given a chance. "But it takes less time than mowing," she says, "is cheaper, and is something I can do with my children. You can't mow with them, that's for sure."

A natural meadow can be clipped to control unwanted weeds and tree seedlings the way a farmer clips pastures two or three times a year. You have little control over what grows or doesn't grow, except by the timing of the mowing. The idea is to let those plants you wish to grow mature before clipping and clip those you wish to keep from spreading before they go to seed. This is not easily done since the desirable and undesirable often go to seed at the same time.

Patch mowing—clipping a clump here and a clump there as necessary—is one alternative, but a high-maintenance one. Rotating the natural meadow with a conventional lawn is an easier way. The meadow is allowed to grow as it will for three to five years, with a clipping in July and another in August. Then for two years, the meadow is mowed as a conventional lawn. There are no set rules for the length of the rotation since very little experimentation has been done with this kind of landscaping. You have to proceed by trial and error. Climate can greatly affect the methodology. For example, in drier parts of the West, where there are prairie grasses instead of forest, tree seedlings would not be a problem, so that the prairie lawn need not be clipped or rotated with conventional lawn to stabilize it. If you are familiar with the Flint Hills of Kansas, you know what I mean.

Ground Covers

A more practical way to cut down on mowing, or at least one that is more socially acceptable, is to replace lawn with low-maintenance ground covers. Three of the better ones are creeping euonymus for sunny places, and pachysandra and myrtle for shady spots. These ground covers, once established, grow thickly enough to shade out weeds (except for an occasional intruder or tree seedling), and they need pruning only rarely, if ever. They are particularly practical in areas difficult to mow—under trees where grass won't grow very well anyway, or on hillsides where mowing can be hazardous.

Lane Palmer, the editor of *Farm Journal* magazine, a man who knows his way around plants, has been maintaining an euonymus lawn since 1956 at his suburban Philadelphia home. The Palmers' lot breaks away steeply to the street on two sides, creating an area that is dangerous to mow. With some clippings he was given by a grounds keeper pruning in Independence Square, Palmer started rooting *Euonymus radicans coloratus* in flats. At the rate of about 50 to 75 square feet per year, he transplanted the rooted cuttings to the problem hillside. The reason for doing only a little bit at a time was that for the first two years the new plantings had to be hand-weeded. After that time, they grew thick enough to shade out the competition on their own.

Propagating

Ground covers root easily, so you can propagate your own if you want to save money by not buying plants. Cut healthy sprigs about 6 inches long off the ends of growing vines. Pinch off all but the top three or four leaves. Stick the cuttings in a bedding mixture—about half peat and half sand works fine. The mixture should be thoroughly soaked. Dip the base of each cutting in a rooting hormone before inserting it in the soil. (Rootone is a commonly available brand.) Cover the flat of cuttings with plastic film to keep the environment moist around the cuttings. Most of the cuttings will grow roots and will be ready to transplant in about a month.

Planting

Before setting out the ground cover, the sod should be killed. Palmer used a chemical, but cultivation or a thick blanket of leaves put down well before setting out the transplants will suffice. Palmer says he had his best luck planting the ground cover in September after a good soaking rain, so the sod killing should be carried out in summer. The easiest way to plant the cuttings is to open a slit in the soil with a trowel, slip a cutting in behind the blade, remove the trowel, and tamp the soil firmly against the cutting's roots. Set cuttings 6 inches apart in both directions to ensure good coverage in one year. At 12-inch spacings, you save on cuttings but have to hand weed for two years.

Euonymus is subject to a scale that can usually be controlled with a dormant oil spray in early spring. Occasionally, Palmer has followed up with a malathion spray in May. If you don't want to use such chemicals, you can prune the old infected plants close to the ground with a power hedge trimmer. Scale affects only old wood. The new growth will come up healthy and will cover the ground effectively in a month.

"If that all sounds like a lot of work," says Palmer, "I can assure you it is only a fraction of the work of mowing and grass care. And the euonymus looks attractive all winter long."

He grows pachysandra (*Pachysandra terminalis*) the same way, but only in shady areas where it grows best. Palmer says pachysandra requires even less maintenance than euonymus. He likes to plant it under and around trees where it grows much better than grass and where it relieves him of the necessity of mowing close to trees, which carries the risk of scraping the bark of the trunks and getting a twig in the eye. Pachysandra is not very hardy from the colder parts of zone 5 on north. (See the zone map in chapter 8.)

As an alternative in the Midwest, myrtle (*Vinca minor*) with its purple-blue flowers is a traditional choice. English ivy works okay too. Don't let it have free reign up the side of your house or trees. It can eventually kill a tree, weaken the mortar between stones and bricks, and pull the shingles off your roof.

Mulches

Bark, wood chips, gravel, rocks, and other inert materials make excellent low-maintenance ground covers for small areas. Grass and weeds will eventually work through, but a layer of black plastic film with holes punched in for drainage, laid down before the ground-cover mulch is applied, will considerably lessen the grass- and weed-pulling work. Around tree trunks and along ornamental borders, such ground covers not only shorten mowing time, but also save the inevitable wounds to plants that mowers cause. One of the most attractive and inexpensive ground covers is pine cones. At a residence I was visiting recently, a corner nook along the house beside the entrance door was covered with various sizes of cones raked from the yard, with dwarf flowers set into the mulch, underlaid with black plastic. The cones will last several years—if the squirrels don't carry them away.

Pine needles also make an attractive mulch. They are abundant under larger white pine trees. In addition to old standbys like buckwheat hulls, bagasse, salt hay, peat moss, and shredded bark, you may find you have access to corncobs, rice hulls, shavings from power wood planers, shredded cornstalks, ground seashells, or oyster shells (in the South), peanut hulls, or broken shards of brick or pottery or clay tile (around factories).

Wood chips are a classic ground cover, but corncobs, rice hulls, chipped bark, and buckwheat hulls also work well in smothering weeds, holding in water, and providing a neat appearance—common goals of all low-maintenance gardeners.

All kinds of possibilities offer themselves in crushed stone and gravel. I've seen smooth stones up to the size of a fist piled up attractively around big trees to avoid mowing over exposed roots.

The disadvantage of using much larger rocks is that they can become even more hazardous to the mower than the gnarled roots they cover. Ordinarily, the purpose of gravel or any inert ground cover is to provide what landscapers call mowing strips, meaning nonmowing strips actually. The ground cover is put down about a foot out from trees, plants, walls, fences, etc., so that you can dream away as you mow and not have to worry about collision courses with your landscape. But obviously, the ground cover must be down even with the mowing surface. Sidewalks and flower borders raised above lawn level are a menace to mowers and a hindrance to low-maintenance mowing, forcing you to make continuous use of an edger.

*Large and small stones
provide a lasting border
for these garden plants.*

Combining Live Ground Covers
and Inert Mulches

Sometimes live and inert ground covers can be used in combination
with excellent low-maintenance results. A gravel or shredded bark mulch
will hold back weeds a long time while ground-cover plants are getting
established. Ground-cover plants spread mostly by underground stolons
and send up stout new shoots that will penetrate up through the inert
ground cover much more readily than weeds. By the time a weed has even
thought about rearing its ugly head above the mulch, the ground cover has
spread to cover all. This can work well not only for the ground covers
already mentioned, but for some you might not have considered. Lily of
the valley (*Convallaria majalis*), for example, spreads thickly by underground roots and, with the help of a permanent mulch, will outcompete

weeds most of the time. This works especially well in a partially shaded area where lily of the valley is at home, but many weeds are not.

Another slick way to combine two kinds of ground covers for low maintenance is with flagstones and creeping thyme *(Thymus serpyllum)*. In this case, the larger the flagstones, the more effective the low maintenance. The stones are laid as for a terrace right on the ground; no underlayment is necessary. And the spaces between the stones are planted to creeping thyme. This plant has one advantage over other ground covers: it will stand heavy human traffic. It is very low growing and will spread out a little over the outer perimeters of the flagstones and eventually keep weeds from growing up between the stones. The effect is one of stepping stones in a "pool" of thyme.

As with other ground-cover plants, this one is obviously high maintenance at first, with years of low maintenance to follow.

Creeping thyme, here in all its flowering glory, softens the harsh edges of these stepping stones. Because it spreads so easily and quickly, it's a good low-care ground cover.

Other Ground-Cover Suggestions

There are other ground-cover plants to consider for special situations. Bearberry *(Arctostaphylos uva-ursi)* is good for cold climates or barren soil high in acidity. Crown vetch *(Coronilla varia)* serves fairly well on steep and similar problem areas but always appears oversized for small landscapes. Various heaths *(Erica carnea,* for example) and heathers *(Calluna vulgaris)* are good for sandy, acid conditions on both coasts. For dry, hot areas like the Southwest, ice plant *(Mesembryanthemum crystallinum)* is a popular choice.

Finally, a caution. Some low-maintenance ground covers turn out to be very high-maintenance weeds. Honeysuckle *(Lonicera japonica)* is a great mistake, and if you aren't choking with it already, don't plant it. Beware, too, of one of the speedwells *(Veronica officinalis),* which I have heard referred to as "creeping Charlie" but more often around here as "creeping #$%"&"!"—and you can't interpret that too foully. This low-growing plant with little bluish flowers is not meant to be a ground cover, but in a lawn it can become that. Speedwell is a good name for it because it will speed well over your whole lawn in a year's time. Almost all lawns I see in the northeast quarter of the country are overrun with it. If you don't have it yet, be very careful about transplants taken from a friend's garden; you may unknowingly bring along a bit of speedwell, too. Actually, it is fairly harmless and remains green no matter how often or low you mow it. But it will force out bluegrass in partly shady areas, if not sunny areas, and run rampant there. Only herbicides can kill it. You can't get rid of it by tearing up the sod, unless you tear at it for several years. Even then, if one little bit of root remains alive (and it will), within a few years it will take over again.

Other Low-Maintenance Alternatives to Lawns

Grass itself can be a low-maintenance plant, as we shall see later in this chapter—certainly better than a rock garden or a peach orchard. But some alternate uses of the yard are less work and expense.

A Daisy Field

Long before "flower lawns" became popular, Ivan Hill of Tiffin, Ohio, discovered quite by accident that he could maintain his lawn as a "daisy field" as he calls it, with much less mowing. When Shasta daisies *(Chrysan-*

themum maximum) first appeared in his yard years ago, he didn't have the heart to mow them. Each year the clump grew in size until finally the whole lawn along the street was a waving sea of daisies every May and June. "All I do is just not mow until late in June," he explains. "I've started to plant the whole backyard to daisies, too." To do so, all he does is sprinkle some mature seed heads on the ground. Nature does the rest.

Apparently, daisies have some way (perhaps by a natural herbicide like the oat plant produces) of keeping competition from other weeds at bay because Hill's "daisy field" is remarkably free of other weedy growth, even though it has been established for years. "And you can't hurt the daisies by tramping through them. They spring right back up. The neighbors' kids play ball on that lot." He pauses, smiles. "They spend most of their time hunting for the ball, though."

The Hills have given away many bouquets for church and wedding decorations and to passersby who stop to ask. And they have cut mowing time nearly in half.

"Tree Lawns"

Normally, a good low-maintenance lawn practice is to plant trees and ornamentals in clumps to free up lawn space in one relatively easy area to mow instead of dotting trees and bushes all over the landscape. But Bob and Judy Gucker near McCutchenville, Ohio, are finding freedom from mowing in the opposite ploy. They planted their very large hillside lawn completely to evergreen trees at 10-by-10-foot spacings. That was 11 years ago. For the first couple of years, mowing around the little trees was a difficult job, but the Guckers were young and able. (We're talking about over 400 trees, counting the side yard.) Now the trees have filled in most of the lawn space, with only quiet, lush hallways of grass remaining. Within 2 or 3 more years what had once been a large, tedious mowing job will be no mowing job at all.

There have been other advantages. Bird life has increased remarkably, to the delight of the Guckers who are avid bird-watchers. The "tree lawn" has become a very effective windbreaker for their hilltop house and also acts as natural air-conditioning, thanks to the breezes that filter through. The Guckers have never needed to buy an air conditioner. "And the tree lawn makes a marvelous place for children to play," says Judy. "We always had a hard time with parties, getting the kids to come in the house. They wanted to play hide-and-seek out there all night."

Low-Maintenance Grass

You can make a mistake by ruling out grass entirely from your yard. It is possible to do that with a house in the woods, letting the yard be just a continuation of the forest floor. But that gambit has drawbacks, too (this is the voice of experience speaking). To make it work demands that trees cluster around the house, throwing fairly heavy shade on the ground to inhibit brush, grass, and weedy growth. The subsequent leaf-mold floor is free of weeds and grass, true, and if you have superior botanical knowledge, you can coax it to support some ferns, a moss garden, and a few shade-loving plants. But it will not stand much traffic, and mud and other shoe-clinging debris will find its way into the house. In this situation, lots of decks and walks are necessary, and so one trades one kind of high maintenance (lawns) for another (care of wood decks, etc.). Not to mention that you have to worry about trees falling on the house. What's more, such woodland houses will invariably have problems with mildew because of minimum sunlight and poor air circulation. The house will smell the way a vacation cabin does that has been closed up too long. A dehumidifier roaring away will only partially solve the problem.

Nor is replacing all grass with gravel or (horrors) green cement an advisable alternative. An architect in Chicago once told me that owners of downtown office and apartment buildings had discovered that although pools and fountains and concrete landscaping cost considerably more than grass to install, over the long haul maintenance was cheaper! But this conclusion would hardly ever apply to a residential home. First of all, in the latter case, the space around the house is a part of the living area in a way that is not true of an office building. But more importantly, homeowners in the dry, hot West who gravel or concrete over their entire lawn area have seen their air-conditioning costs rise dramatically. Grass absorbs heat; masonry gets hot and throws it back in your face.

The search for the perfect grass will never end, because as scientists develop better ones, human expectations rise still higher. The perfect grass must be a rich dark green. No other color, such as the rich browns of a Texas Bermuda-grass lawn in January, will do, even if it goes better with the color of the house. When nature will not cooperate, you can buy green dyes to spray the lawn (or your Christmas tree), but dyeing the grass has not caught on, even in the South, there being limits to the excesses of even the fussiest homeowner. The perfect grass will, of course, never yellow with any disease; will be drought resistant; will smother out all other plants; will not wear thin under the pounding footsteps of the entire fourth grade playing football on it every day; will give off a harmless odor undetectable to humans, but which drives stray dogs, moles, and mosquitoes into the neighbor's yard; and will cut easily with a dull mower blade.

Drainage

In the realm of practicality, the type of grass you choose is not nearly as important as the condition of the soil you wish to grow it in. The absolutely essential ingredient for success is well-drained soil. Grass will not grow well in poorly drained soil. Fertilizer will not become available to grass in poorly drained soil. Diseases can't be prevented in poorly drained soil.

Grading properly lets excess water run off the lawn most of the time, but level lawns, or lawns with even a slight depression or low spots, especially if the soil is a heavy clay, may need to be helped out with drainage tiles. Established city lawns seldom have a drainage problem—or the problem was taken care of years ago. But if you live in the new suburbs, especially in areas with larger lawns underlaid with heavy clay, be fore-warned. And you'll only exacerbate the problem if you let water from the roof and walls of your house spill off into such problem low spots.

A line of drainage tile 1 to 2 feet deep through a problem area can usually be hooked to the drain tile that carries water away from the footers of the house foundation. Sometimes the soil surface can be raised with hauled-in topsoil to provide enough surface drainage to alleviate the problem, but this is no good if the new soil only levels the depression or, worse, backslopes the water towards the house. There are contractors in every community now equipped with the small rotating wheel ditchers, which do a much neater job than a backhoe at a reasonable price.

Good Soil

Once drainage problems have been solved, next give attention to the pH of your soil—its balance between acidity and alkalinity. Like most plants, grass likes a slightly acid to neutral soil, a pH of 6.0 to 7.0. If the pH is lower (i.e., more acidic), you can raise it with agricultural limestone. If it is higher (i.e., more alkaline), as it might be in the western Plains area, you can lower it with gypsum. Garden stores and farm service businesses in your area have these materials, and lawn service companies are only too eager to advise you and/or test your soil. Do-it-yourself soil testing kits have a litmus paper test you can perform yourself to tell if your soil is very acid or not. If blueberries, rhododendrons, azaleas, and such acid-loving plants grow well in your yard, the soil is no doubt a bit too acid for a good bluegrass lawn. Keep lime away from your blueberries, rhododendrons, and azaleas. It can kill them, as I found out the hard way.

Low-Maintenance Lawn Maintenance

With drainage and pH taken care of, low-maintenance fertility programs are a snap or would be if homeowners would follow them. But low-maintenance methods make all the sacred cows of Superneat lawn management bellow in protest. You may need an initial application of some purchased fertilizer, especially where the bulldozer has left a new house with only subsoil to work with, but after the grass is established, none will be needed in most cases, if you follow a simple procedure:

Throw away that bagger on your mower. At least throw it away after that first flush of heavy grass growth in spring. Let the grass clippings fall back into the lawn, there to rot away and return to the soil the nutrients that they consumed while growing. Or if you are bound and determined to play Superneat, carry your penchant for hard work one step further. Instead of putting the grass clippings out for the garbage man to haul to the dump (compounding the problem of waste disposal), compost them and then sprinkle the compost back on the lawn.

Removing clippings is usually ridiculous from the standpoint of low maintenance. Superneat pumps fertilizer on his lawn and the lawn pumps it right back out again in excessive grass growth. The extra lushness of all that expensive nitrogen attracts various fungal diseases. Statistics say that there would be more than 16 million acres of grass clippings clogging our dumps if we were all as fastidious as the Superneats. Is that sane? John Howard Falk in his study "The Energetics of a Suburban Lawn," says the energy inputs in water, fertilizer, pesticides, gasoline, and human labor on a typical California lawn amount to 573 kilocalories per square meter. That is more energy than what is expended on a commercial corn crop! Other studies indicate that in some urban areas, there is more chemical residue runoff from lawn acreage than from farm acreage.

There may be times when picking up the grass clippings is necessary, primarily on a new lawn just getting established. Excessive clippings could smother new shoot growth, although I hasten to add this could happen only if the soil has been heavily fertilized and watered. Otherwise, *some* clippings on the new growth actually shade it and protect it in the start-up period, which is why a light straw mulch on a new lawn seeding is a good idea. Also, in dry parts of the nation, clippings will not rot back into the soil nearly as fast as they do in the humid East or South, and so sometimes excess clippings might need to be removed. But here again, the buildup of clippings is most often due to excessive growth instigated by fertilizers and irrigation.

People who bag clippings (and especially people who sell baggers) protest that the clippings will contribute to a thatch problem. Actually, clippings are a very minor part of thatch and are not the cause of the problem, if a problem does indeed exist. Thatch consists mainly of incompletely decayed grass roots, stems, and lower leaf sheaths—the ligneous or more woody parts of the grass plants. Thatch problems are the worst with grasses that spread by a thick layer of stoloniferous growth—vinelike shoots that grow more on the soil surface than in the ground. Zoysia is very prone to thatch problems for this reason. Without good contact with dirt, which would speed decay, old stolon and stem growth build up to where the "thatch" acts just like thatch on a roof—on zoysia it can actually shed water rather than absorb it. On such thick grasses (Bermuda grass and bent grass can sometimes be problematic, too), picking up clippings may become an aid to thatch control. Because the grass is so thick, the clippings can't work their way down to the soil quickly to hasten decay.

But there are other reasons why thatch is sometimes a problem today but was not years ago—all of them the fault of human fastidiousness, not nature. Having planted very vigorous, dense modern cultivars, which might be advantageous in some respects, the homeowner compounds the disadvantages of these cultivars by fertilizing and watering heavily. Then, quoting from *10,000 Garden Questions Answered by 20 Experts* (Doubleday, 1974) "Tissue decomposition can't keep up with production, especially on stoloniferous turfs where the thatch hardly contacts soil."

Pesticides also can slow down decomposition. Earthworms are an enormous help in thatch control because they actually eat it and at the same time bring soil and thatch in closer contact with each other. The minute piles of earthworm droppings on the lawn surface, which for mysterious reasons are so repulsive to Superneat, are a godsend to the grass. Again I quote from the volume cited above: "When earthworms are eliminated, as with chlordane treatments, thatching generally increases."

Although not very practical for home lawns (it used to be a method used on golf courses), an effective control for thatch is simply to sift weed-free dirt or compost over the grass, which does the same thing that earthworms do better. Instead, Superneat resorts to high technology. He rents a "dethatcher" which tears the hell out of the sod, and of course will only solve the problem temporarily. Or he buys a big spiked drum to pull behind his lawn tractor, which supposedly aerates his soil by punching holes through the thatch. These aerators are miniature versions of the soil compactors used in roadway construction and compact your lawn soil at least as much as they aerate it. Earthworms aerate your soil free of charge and bring up minerals from the subsoil that your grass needs to grow well.

A good earthworm population means you will eventually have moles, which are themselves terrific soil aerators. But Superneat, who abhors a mole tunnel, embraces a dethatching machine that renders his lawn twice as ugly as a whole colony of moles. To get rid of moles, his handy-dandy lawn service expert has a standard sales line. Moles eat grubs (another ugh creature) and so to get rid of moles he poisons the grubs. Good logic. Except that he poisons the earthworms, too, and heaven only knows how many other beneficial soil microbes and insects. It is one thing to spray herbicides, which by comparison are not known to be as harmful to humans, but soil insecticides are strong medicine. Recently (1986), a golfer playing a course that had just been sprayed with insecticides, became ill and died, his skin coming off in layers. The insecticide to which the cause of death was traced was one of the supposedly milder ones. You can imagine the lawsuit that will develop over this strange occurrence. Why risk anything like it on your lawn for what amounts to nothing?

IN DEFENSE OF THE POOR MOLE

Moles are in fact very beneficial animals. I know of no case where they have ever harmed a human being. Moles eat soil insects. They do not eat your flower bulbs, carrots, and other plants you prize. A mouse running in a mole hole will eat bulbs, but the mouse doesn't need the mole hole to do it. He can dig his own. A mole tunnel running down your carrot row should be a reason to rejoice. If there are any carrot maggots down there, the mole will be eating them. And his raised tunnel will hardly ever harm the carrots, as I have learned innumerable times.

The mole tunnel rising slightly above the lawn is visible because we shave off the grass there with the mower. Of its own accord, the tunnel would settle back after a few rains, and the grass would grow better there than previously. Furthermore, moles are fairly transient. They move through an area eating earthworms, white grubs, webworms (which can damage the sod more than moles), and Japanese beetle grubs, among others. Then they move on, leaving a generally healthier sod that will quickly rejuvenate itself while the moles work on another part of the lawn. Beats a dethatcher hands down.

Having gone through this argument a hundred times, I know that the American homeowner in general is not going to listen. But if you want to save money, achieve low maintenance, and work far less, leave the moles and earthworms alone. You and your lawn really will survive. And either way, the moles will.

Another common practice that increases the chance of a mole "crisis" is the incessant watering of lawns, even in the humid East. Moles work where the earthworms linger. The earthworms linger where there's moisture. In the drier parts of the summer, they descend deeper as the moisture decreases. The moles you think have disappeared after you poisoned them in the spring are usually only working farther down in the ground and so their tunnels aren't visible. When you sprinkle the lawn in dry weather, you draw worms and moles back up.

Since cool-weather grasses, like bluegrass, naturally go dormant in late summer, you are probably wasting water anyway. If you do manage to keep the lawn green, you will also make it more vulnerable to a host of fungal diseases. Hot-weather grasses, like zoysia, will stay green anyway with little watering until the weather cools, and then they will begin to turn brown no matter how much you water them. As one courageous lawn expert said recently in the Sunday paper garden section, the best low-maintenance practice to ensure a green lawn in August in the eastern half of the country is to allow "weeds" to grow in the lawn that will endure mowing (like white clover). In late summer, these "weeds" might be all the green a typical homeowner has going for him and what really is so bad about that?

FIND SOMETHING MORE PRODUCTIVE TO BE FUSSY ABOUT

The first rule of low-maintenance lawn care is to not be so fussy about grass—and not let fussy people draw you into competing with them. Fussiness is probably therapeutic for the Superneats—a way to calm their feelings of insecurity—but it should be understood as that, not the standard by which civilization should be judged.

I have a close acquaintance who is a Superneat *par excellence*. He has qualities I admire, and anyway, what would we do without a few Superneats to maintain some kind of order in a chaotic world. He thinks I am crazy because I have occasionally let my front yard grow up and taken a hay crop from it. I think he is crazy because he manicures, and I do mean manicures, about 5 acres of lawn. The extent he will go to in pursuit of the perfect lawn boggles Neatless Souls like me.

WHITE CLOVER, VIOLETS, AND OTHER LAWN FLOWERS

There is hardly any plant more beneficial to the low-maintenance lawn than white clover, sometimes called Dutch or Little Dutch clover (*Trifolium repens*). It is such a common and ubiquitous plant that in many areas of the United States it will come up of its own accord on any plot of ground that is mowed frequently. It seems to like being mowed and will keep a lawn green except in extreme dry weather. With grass, especially bluegrass, it has worked out an extremely efficient low-maintenance symbiotic partnership. Like all legumes, white clover, with the help of rhizobium bacteria, draws nitrogen from the air and "fixes" it in the soil. The grass, in turn feeds on this nitrogen, grows vigorously, and crowds out most of the clover. Then when the supply of nitrogen has been used up, the grass diminishes and the white clover comes back to flourish again.

Unfortunately, Superneat considers white clover to be a lawn evil and he attempts, without much success, to exterminate it. Why he hates white clover is not clear. It is not that white clover draws honeybees (which should be considered a blessing anyway, unless one is seriously allergic to stings). For some reason, the little white blossoms dotting his otherwise immaculately green sward are terribly upsetting to his eye, like pimples are to a teenager. He fights every year the good fight against white clover, damn the cost, damn the herbicidal runoff.

From where I was working in a village once, I watched an old lady laboriously patrol her lawn every day with a butcher knife, attacking dandelions. At the end of the week, I congratulated her on her persistance. But she was not happy.

"Now I have to start all over again, on the violets," she moaned.

If she ever were unlucky enough to get rid of them, too, there wouldn't be anything much left growing in her lawn. There is one kind of violet that makes a most delightful lawn flower because it grows very low to the ground and does not compete with grass at all. The bloom is deep purple and very aromatic, but its main advantage is that it blooms very early in spring, about the same time that crocuses do, and has for all practical purposes disappeared by the time you get the lawn mower out. I have found no species listed in the garden encyclopedias that has a description matching this violet, but I have found it both in Pennsylvania and Ohio, growing either in older lawns or along roadsides in very early spring. It transplants very easily into the lawn and then spreads slowly of its own accord.

Another inoffensive low-growing flower for lawns, especially shady, moist areas is moneywort (*Lysimachia nummularia*). This viny plant that grows flat on the ground blooms yellow in early summer. It's really a ground cover, but does not grow strongly enough to smother out other plants, and it can be mowed regularly.

It is a homeowner's privilege, I guess, to curse dandelions and plantain and hurl at them the full force of chemical technology. Neatless Souls rather enjoy a few dandelions, and mowing provides enough control to hold them in check. The same with quack grass, which is what keeps part of my lawn green in a dry August. But of course, for the Superneats, such behavior is uncivilized. My experience is that no matter which road one follows, we arrive at the same point: more dandelions, more quack grass.

The Best and Worst Grasses for Low Maintenance

There are seven kinds of grasses conventionally used in lawns, and many, many strains and varieties of each. Dr. Reed Funk, a professor and turf scientist at Rutgers University in New Brunswick, New Jersey, has developed 50 new grasses in the last 25 years—and he is only one of many involved in this work. Thus it would be presumptuous if not arrogant for any writer, let alone a Neatless Soul like me, to pretend to know which varieties or strains provide the least maintenance work for any particular lawn. However, I am going to be arrogant and presumptuous and state a general rule of thumb few lawn experts will quarrel with: Choose bluegrass as your primary grass wherever it will grow well and rely on other grasses only where it won't. A brief review of the seven grasses used in lawns will, I think, bear this out.

PERENNIAL RYES

Perennial rye probably should be rated high on the list of low-maintenance lawn grasses. Rye has always been used in cheap grass mixtures, because it pops up quickly and provides some footing while slower germinating grasses get established. But conventional ryegrasses are annuals, short-lived and coarse. When Dr. Funk, mentioned above, developed the first perennial rye (which he called Manhattan because he discovered it in Central Park), it was a sensation. Even better varieties have been developed since then. They start quickly and are not as aggressive as conventional annual ryegrasses. This makes them a good addition to any grass mixture, especially when planted in the fall, when you want to get the ground covered quickly. Perennial rye is a low cost, no-frills grass and will take fairly heavy human traffic. So it sounds like just the thing for low maintenance, and as varieties continue to improve, it may indeed become No. 1 in this category. But right now, keeping perennial rye perennial takes almost as much care as caring for bluegrass—maybe more in some instances—and even then it will not endure as long as bluegrass. Moreover, it does not make as tight a sod as bluegrass for the same amount of maintenance expended and thus is something of an open invitation to excessive weed growth. But definitely this is the grass for a quick lawn. Used alone, sow 6 pounds per 1,000 square feet.

FINE FESCUES

Of the two very different kinds of fescue planted in lawns, fine fescues of the creeping red or chewings varieties are used in with bluegrass, mainly because they will grow quite well in moderate shade. They will even dominate most bluegrasses there. Since it is fine textured, however, that is no disadvantage. It does not require as much general care as bluegrass, either, doing better with less fertilizer on poorer ground. If planted alone, the rate is about 4 pounds per 1,000 square feet. If planted with bluegrass, make the mix 30 percent fine fescue to approximately 70 percent bluegrass, increasing the portion of fescue for shadier lawns to perhaps 50–50.

COARSE FESCUES

The coarser, broad-leaved fescues have only recently begun to receive attention in lawn mixtures. They are tough and stand wear and tear better than bluegrass. Used in mixtures with bluegrass, they make a lawn hold up better against the constant tramping of feet. They stay green better in late summer than bluegrass, but at this date, they are not nearly ready to replace bluegrasses, if they ever do. Seeding is about 2 pounds per 1,000 square feet.

BERMUDA GRASSES

Bermuda grass is popular for the hot South. Improved varieties continue to come out. All of them should be mowed frequently to preserve the green color, but they turn brown in winter. The brown lawns I have looked at in Dallas in January seem quite attractive to me—better than the drifted snow lawns I normally have to look at in January back home in Ohio. I have already mentioned the biggest low-maintenance objection to Bermuda grass—its invasiveness into adjacent gardens.

In California, homeowners sometimes plant Merion bluegrass and Bermuda grass together to get a year-round green lawn. To each his own. If Merion bluegrass does well there, I say a gardener would be foolish to plant Bermuda grass, too. Better a half year with a dormant bluegrass than a whole year fighting Bermuda grass in the garden.

ZOYSIAS

No grass has been merchandised in recent years as vigorously as zoysia. It is rather easily planted with plugs spotted around an existing lawn. It then spreads slowly to cover all—an indication that it too, like Bermuda grass, can be invasive and difficult to keep out of adjacent ornamental plantings, flower borders, and gardens. Zoysia (even the hardier varieties) is generally not too hardy in the colder parts of the North but excellent for heat and drought resistance in the mid-South. Zoysia smothers out much undesirable weed growth without the help of herbicides, but on the other hand, it is sometimes prone to thatch problems. It turns brown with the advent of cool fall weather and greens up late in spring. But brown or green, it makes a soft, resilient footing and does not require as much mowing as other grasses. It's a good low-maintenance grass where invasiveness is not a problem. Plant plugs about one per every square foot for fast coverage.

BLUEGRASSES

Despite all the latest discoveries of other grass varieties, where cool-season grasses grow well, bluegrass is still best for low maintenance, all things considered. You can, of course, manage a bluegrass lawn with very high maintenance—using the bluegrass varieties that need to be coddled with lots of fertilizer, frequent watering, and exacting pH. And then you must endeavor to keep out all other plants. But a mixture of the newer bluegrasses (namely Citation, Glade, Merion, Newport, Park) and old reliable native bluegrasses—even the wild ones that grow unbidden in many parts of the North—together with white clover for fertility and creeping red fescues for the shadier parts of the lawn, will in the long run require the least amount of maintenance.

It's better to plant bluegrass mixtures than planting just one variety. With two or more, if one is not acclimated to your soil or not resistant to disease in your particular microclimate, the others probably will be. That is why native Kentucky bluegrass is usually added to fine bluegrass mixtures for a typical lawn. It doesn't need to be coddled. For low maintenance, the volunteer bluegrass of your region may be even more acclimated than what you buy as Kentucky bluegrass.

Bluegrass and acid soil do not mix. The soil pH should be above 6 at least, and closer to 7 for the finer varieties. Bluegrass is sown at about 2 to 3 pounds per 100 square feet—more for Kentucky bluegrass, less for Merion and the finer-seeded varieties. Directions always come with the package. White clover has a very fine seed and 4 to 5 ounces per 1,000 square feet will suffice. Since such a small amount is hard to spread evenly, it's best to mix it with the grass seed. In the North, plant grass in the early fall after rains have moistened the soil well. Southern lawns are best planted in early spring. Ideally, the clover should be planted in very early spring, broadcast over the new lawn, even though white clover will survive fall sowing. It will generally come up as a volunteer whether you sow it or not after the lawn is mowed a couple of years.

BENT GRASSES

The bents are at the very low end of the low-maintenance measuring stick. They make probably the finest lawns of all, very nice for golf greens and croquet courts. But they require much care, pampering, mowing, etc., and do not like dry weather. There are two types, usually referred to as Colonial, and Creeping or Velvet. Both are used in mixtures where a very fine lawn is desired, but neither is recommended for low maintenance.

Mowing

Among the Superneats, mowing has been raised to a high art. As a general rule, grass should be kept 1½ inches high, they say, bent grasses and Bermuda grass shorter than that, coarse fescues a little taller. But if low maintenance is your goal, 2 to 3 inches will suffice for bluegrasses, zoysias, and fescues, bent grass should be avoided, and so only Bermuda grass needs to be mowed short. Most people scalp their lawns too close, leaving the grass weak and prone to disease, drought injury, and overly reliant on added fertilizer. Blades of grass are the grass's leaves, and the amount of leaf exposed to sunlight determines how much chlorophyll and other life-supporting substances the plants produce. According to the experts, if you raise the height of the cut just ⅛ inch, you increase the leaf surface 300 square feet per 1,000 square feet of lawn. Lowering it ⅛ inch has the opposite effect. Clipping most grasses below 1½ inches has an effect not unlike trying to grow grass in the shade. Obviously if you clip routinely at 2½ inches, the grass will be that much more vigorous to withstand drought, shade, weed encroachment, and the need for additional fertilizer.

If maintaining grass height at 2½ to 3 inches offends your sense of a carpet lawn (how about thinking in terms of a shag rug?), then at least you should vary cutting height by season. In early spring, when conditions for growth are most favorable, cut at the minimum height for the variety of grass you have. In hot, dry midsummer, cut higher. In the early fall when moister weather returns, switch back to the minimum, and then clip high in the late fall.

A more important number to watch in low-maintenance management is not cutting height, but frequency of mowings. No matter what height you choose, the old rule of thumb is not to let grass grow more than 100 percent of that height before mowing again. If you maintain at 3 inches, you can let it grow another 3 inches before mowing and not weaken the plants. If you maintain at 1½ inches, you will obviously mow twice as often. There won't be much difference on the wear and tear of the mower between mowing off 3 inches and mowing off 1½, but you operate your mower twice as much and spend twice as much time at it. The mower will wear out in half the time. The difference in the appearance of the two lawns will not be great except in the eyes of the Superneats.

Another advantage of mowing only half as much as the Superneats is that the mower blade will stay sharp twice as long. Dull blades injure the grass and shorten the life of the mower. Even Superneats resist getting down under the mower, removing the blade, and sharpening it. Turf scientists test new grasses with dull mowers because, unfortunately, most mower blades are dull most of the time.

Low-Maintenance Mowers

It is almost ridiculous to try to compare lawn mowers anymore. The leading mowers often have components made by the same factory or another just like it. I bought a riding mower this spring, my first (and for my wife who does not approve of walking tractors the way I do). The Bolens I almost bought has a body from Denmark and a motor from Briggs-Stratton. In fact, about the only part of it that was Bolens originally was the name, which in reality stood for the place where all the parts were put together. The same is true of most every manufacturer. All those little tractors with such American names on them like Ford and John Deere are made in foreign countries. And motors? Well, someone makes the spark plugs, and someone else makes the blocks, and someone else the clutch belts or gears, and likely as not, the same manufacturer supplies competing brands.

Within any line of lawn mowers, however, some are made better than others, and the price reflects that difference. The difference between a riding lawn mower and a lawn tractor is about six more years of trouble-free operation. The tractor is built a little heavier and has a motor built to run a little longer. In buying, the most important aspect to pay attention to is the motor. If they are all Briggs-Stratton, or Kohler, with here and there a Tecumseh, how do you judge them?

Some of these motors are cast iron or have a cast-iron piston sleeve, and the ones that do not will not last as long, and you will not pay quite as much for them. It pays to buy motor quality. If you have to economize, cut down on accessories or convenient designs. Thus, on the Bolens I liked (it had the mower up front and a steering system designed for easy trimming around trees), the motor was an 8-horsepower (HP) Briggs. The price, as I recall, was something like $2,300. The same dealer handled Snapper. A Snapper of slightly smaller mowing width, with the mower deck between the front and back wheels, had an 11-HP Briggs motor. Its price was $1,500. There was another mower there that appeared to be quite similar to the Snapper with an 11-HP Briggs on it, too, but it was cheaper yet. The difference? The 11-HP motor on the Snapper was an I/C 11 HP, which is to say a heavy-duty industrial/commercial model, and what that means principally is that it had cast iron in the engine block where cast iron is still necessary for long life, especially in the piston sleeve. It was worth every cent more than the other 11-HP Briggs that was not I/C. And it was a much better motor than the 8-HP regular Briggs on the Bolens mower. What I would have paid about $800 more for in the Bolens was easier operation and a more comfortable seat and only a few inches more capacity. For me, the Snapper was a better buy.

Actually, for low-maintenance purposes, a walk-behind tractor like the old Gravely I have operated for 18 years now, is even more practical. You pay less if you are willing to walk rather than ride (and thereby also keep your weight down, hopefully). You also get more use out of them because such tractors double as trimmers and because with other attachments you can cultivate the garden with them.

There is an even more economical way to handle mowing chores, but one not popular in America. The walking tractors, especially those made in Europe and Japan—Mainline, Ferrari, Pasquali, and others used mostly as rotary tillers—all can be equipped with what is called a mulching sickle-bar mower. (There are American models made specifically to run a sickle-bar mower and take cultivating shovels.) Write to Kinco (1669 Grand Avenue, Saint Paul, MN 55105) for a description of their models.

In any case, the advantages are several. For the same mowing width, you need less horsepower to run a sickle bar than a rotary mower. The mulching cutter bar will cut grass almost as low as a rotary and drop it immediately behind the bar, rather than send it in great slugs and globs out the side or rear where it piles up and is slow to decay into the grass. Unlike regular sickle-bar mowers for hay, the little mulching bars cut better; they do not plug up on wavy grass like the hay cutters tend to do. Although the sickle-bar blade is more difficult to sharpen, it does not dull as fast as a rotary blade. Last but not least, the sickle bar is a hundred times safer. You

Increasing Mower Life

Keeping your mower in good running order is not a low-maintenance proposition, but *regular* maintenance can prevent costly high maintenance. At the International Lawn, Garden, and Power Equipment Expo in 1985, a survey of mower repairmen revealed that the number one cause of mower malfunctioning was not adding motor oil when necessary. So check your oil regularly, as specified in your owner's manual. The second leading cause of motor damage came from not cleaning the air filter regularly (see your owner's manual for instructions). Striking rocks and other objects with the blade was the third most common cause. Fourth was not changing the oil as often as required, which really should be part of number one, making poor motor lubrication the all-time-high gremlin of mower failure.

The last significant cause of short mower life was overheating, caused by clogged cooling fins. Clean the dirt out of the fins on the motor block every spring when you haul the mower out of storage. Those fins are designed into the block very purposely, but they can't keep the motor cool if they are full of debris. The easiest way to clean them is to run a wire through every groove between the fins to push out the dirt. Use an air compressor to blow the remaining dirt away, if you have one. Lung power is sufficient as an alternative. Some folks blast away with a stream of water when the engine is cool, but water could do more harm than good.

can cut a finger or toe off in them if you are so foolish as to put a finger or toe between the guards, but the sickle bar does not throw rocks and sticks into your flesh or your windows, nor can you gash the blade on sidewalks or tree roots. Trimming is easy and much safer. There are sickle-bar attachments for riding garden tractors, too, but they are not as handy nor do they cut as well as the little (3 to 4 feet) mulching bars.

The one I have tried is made in Italy and sold by Mainline, whose advertisements appear regularly in garden magazines. When I last checked, the cost for the mower ran from about $800 to $1,200 and the attachment was about $400. If you have tall weeds to mow, this mower will perform that task much more easily than any rotary mower. The mulching sickle bar does not mow as neatly as a rotary mower does, so I don't expect it to ever become popular in the world of Superneat, but you should at least be aware of it.

CHAPTER 8

TREES AND SHRUBS

As with lawns, the search for the perfect landscaping tree goes on forever. Strangely enough though, while we insist that grass be green, we strive hard to establish trees of every novel color possible: Blue Spruce, Copper Beech, Crimson Maple, Sunburst Locust. If a tree cannot have some weird color during summer, it must at least turn to gorgeous colors in the fall, and then the leaves should disappear into thin air. The perfect tree does not have roots to rear up on the soil surface and lunge at the mower blade, nor tunnel down into the ground and clog sewer systems. It should bloom prodigiously, but make no fruit to fall squishy-squashy on the ground. No bug or disease should ever molest it. In short, the perfect shade tree would be an artificial tree, possibly of plastic, and if you've got the money, I imagine Neiman-Marcus will find someone to make it for you.

Searching for That Perfect Tree

Leaves are the biggest hindrance to the low-maintenance yard. The easiest way to get rid of them is to mulch them in place. Run over them as they fall with a rotary mower that you have plugged or partially plugged so the leaves can't squirt out the normal way. The whirling blade then shatters them to powder and they drop harmlessly on the grass to make fertilizer. Some mowers have a mulching attachment that narrows the slot that grass usually exhausts from under the deck, and so accomplishes the same purpose—at least my Gravely does. This method does not leave the lawn perfectly spotless green in the fall, so it is spurned by the Superneats, who use baggers instead.

Trees and Shrubs for the Seashore

Trees and ornamentals that will grow along the seashore without too much fret and worry from you must withstand wind damage and salt spray. Bayberry, beach plum, privet, and rosa rugosa are at home in this environment. American and English hornbeams, English hawthorn, honey locust, red maple, red oak, sassafras, and sycamore are other good choices, especially against strong winds. Among evergreens, creeping juniper, Japanese black pine, pitch pine, red cedar, and Swiss stone pine, resist both wind and salt.

The improvements in baggers and/or vacuum units to suck up leaves make them the next best alternative, although you then still have the bagged leaves to contend with. If you garden, this is great, because you can use them for mulch or compost.

But the best road to low maintenance in leaf removal is to grow mostly evergreens in your yard. Conifer needles hardly ever need to be raked up. Even when they accumulate, as under large white pines, they seem somehow appropriate. If I may make a suggestion or plead a strong case, the blue spruce (or green if the specimens you buy do not turn out to be as blue as you desired) is one of the very best in terms of low maintenance. It never needs trimming. Neither insect nor disease is a big problem with it. It does not grow so almighty fast. It is easy to mow around and grows thick and low to the ground so that mowing *under* it is not usually necessary. It makes no leaves or needles that need to be cleaned up. It is beautiful. It adapts well to a wide variety of soils. It is immensely hardy and seldom damaged by heavy snows.

Another excellent choice is the Japanese umbrella pine (*Sciadopitys verticillata*), the favorite low-maintenance tree of Lane Palmer, of whom I spoke about in my discussion of ground covers in chapter 7. (In this chapter, as in chapter 7, I will give botanical names only for those plants that are not so common, or in instances when I want to distinguish one plant genus or species or variety from another.) Palmer, who's planted and ripped out many trees in search of the perfect low-maintenance species, gives the nod to this oriental pine because it has no pest or disease enemies; grows slowly; lives to at least 100 years; never gets beyond about 25 to 30 feet tall in that length of time; is hardy even in Maine; does not winterburn and needs no protection against it; and when the needles do fall, they are inconspicuous and do not need to be raked up. He started with seedlings he bought for 50¢ each and his specimens some 30 years later are about 20 feet tall, beautiful, and worth over $500 apiece.

Both this tree and the Colorado blue spruce (*Picea pungens*) are exceptions to a general low-maintenance rule. Normally, you should lean toward planting the native trees of your region, which are better acclimated to your climate, local diseases, and pests. Trees not native should be grown only if their endurance is proven in your climate. A walk through any older suburb in your area or older residential city street will quickly acquaint you with such proven trees.

In the case of evergreens, you will find for example that balsam fir (*Abies balsamea*) thrives in the cool, moist climate of the Northeast, even in wet places, but tends to be short-lived in the Midwest or any area with hot, dry summers. White fir (*Abies alba*), on the other hand, is drought-hardy, will even grow on poor, dry shallow sites, and is a fine selection for the western Plains. Red and Austrian pines (*Pinus resinosa and P. nigra,* respectively) are beset by sawfly larvae and tend to blow over in windy locations in early spring when the ground is soft, at least here in Ohio where there are no native conifers. White pine (*Picea alba*) tends to grow scraggily if not pruned and is also subject to diseases. Arborvitae, once the darling of landscapes for foundation plantings, is really a tree of wide-open spaces and moist soils. It requires high maintenance if planted next to the house. Heavy wet snows break down the limbs, too. Hemlock (*Tsuga canadensis*) is good for shady, moist areas, bad for dry, windy places. Junipers (*Juniperus* sp.) winterburn and become infested with red spider mite.

Of the smaller evergreens, yews (*Taxus* spp.) are one of the best low-maintenance trees, although in the shrubbier hybrids and strains, it needs to be pruned yearly to keep it within limits, especially when trained as a hedge. But Japanese yew, which is hardier than English, is nearly pest-free. In 20 years of growing both upright and spreading varieties, I've never had any problems, even in this harsh northern Ohio climate. Yews prefer a neutral soil, but will endure a rather acid one. They need fairly good drainage, but will stand shade better than any foundation plant I've tried. They endure dry sites fairly well, but try not to position one at the corner of the house where the downspout dumps the roof water. Neither snowdrift nor ice storm has ever harmed mine.

Deciduous Shade Trees

If you want a deciduous tree (one that sheds leaves every year) in your yard, you can still avoid much leaf collection by choosing species with less leaf bulk. Unfortunately, such a selection excludes the large maples that otherwise make magnificent shade trees and provide delightful fall color. Nothing shades like a maple, and very little grows under them as a result. If you put a shade-loving ground cover under a maple, you can't rake up the thickly falling leaves. And maples are notorious for roots that hump up out of the ground to make mowing hazardous.

If you wish to avoid heavy leaf raking but still enjoy large shade trees, select one of the finer-leaved oaks, especially pin oak (*Quercus palustris*), willow oak (*Q. phellos*), or shingle oak (*Q. imbricaria*), which is often called northern live oak. These oaks cast considerable shade, but if lower limbs are pruned off as the tree grows large, enough sun passes through for shade-tolerant grasses to grow under them. The leaves tend to shrivel when they fall and do not mat down as badly as maple leaves to smother grass if you don't get them cleaned up right away. Even the leaves of the white oak (*Q. alba*) make far less bulk than maple and, if you mow over them when dry, they shred enough to prevent a heavy mat forming on the grass. White oaks, especially when young (under 25 years of age) share another advantage with pin oak and shingle oak: Many of the leaves do not fall in the autumn but hang on the tree through winter, coming off only gradually up into early spring when the new buds begin to swell. Holding their leaves, the trees soften the winter landscape and greatly reduce leaf collection chores. Unless you are a really neurotic Superneat, you hardly notice them when they do fall in late winter, and they are not then a threat to the lawn grass.

Other good large shade trees with light leaf bulk are honey locust, which does well even in the dry Plains regions, black walnut, and the willows. Older weeping willows are a bit messy because they shed twigs regularly, but picking them up is a lot easier than raking leaves. Most of the willows thrive in a wet situation, and weeping willow and related species green up very early in spring and hold their green to very late in fall. Black walnut is an excellent choice where you want grass under a shade tree. You have the job of cleaning up the nuts that fall, but if you like black walnut cake and fudge as much as I do, you don't call that maintenance work. Bluegrass seems to grow well under the lacy shade of black walnut trees, not only because of sufficient sunshine, but because the natural herbicide that the tree's roots emit, called juglone, apparently keeps down competition from other plants while affecting the grass not at all. Black walnuts should not be grown near a garden. Tomatoes especially are susceptible to juglone.

Locusts are good for grass, too, since they are legumes and draw nitrogen from the air into the soil. The several varieties of thornless honey locust are favorites today in areas where mimosa webworm damage is not severe. A century ago, the black locust (*Robinia pseudoacacia*) was a favorite yard tree in addition to being planted in groves, its wood being almost impervious to decay and used extensively for fence posts and lumber. Its thorns are rather inconspicuous and it blooms beautifully in spring. It will grow on the poorest soil if it is fairly well drained.

At the present time, Dutch elm disease makes elms a poor choice for a large shade tree. Ash trees produce much seed, which sprout seedlings everywhere—under hedges, in ground covers, in the garden, etc. These seedlings can become as bad a nuisance as any weed. Beeches cast very heavy shade. Old ones become hollow, perhaps with no noticeable indication, and then wind blows them over easily on your house, or worse, on your neighbor's house. "Old shade" makes a home sell better, but if the old shade is close to the house, it will become a high-maintenance factor sooner or later, and generally sooner. As a rule of thumb, do not plant trees that grow large any closer than 30 feet from the house and farther than that on the side of the house from which storm winds usually blow—which is southwest to west throughout most of the United States. Or plant some trees closer and some farther away. Then, when the close ones become tall enough or old enough to present a hazard, take them out and rely on the ones farther away for shade.

There is another way to look at the problem, probably more sensible. An oak or any large shade tree known for its longevity in your climate is going to be a pretty safe risk even 20 feet from the house for at least its first 50 years unless a tornado happens by, in which case nothing is safe. Big trees that fall over and damage houses severely are usually very old, 75 years or more. The trees to worry about are fast-growing, *short*-lived ones, like Lombardy poplars (*Populus nigra* var. *italica*), which grow large enough before they keel over (in about 15 years) to do harm to the roof. Avoid anything advertised as fast growing, especially when low mainte-nance is your goal. Slow growing is much better. As a matter of fact, slow growing is often a matter of "compared to what?" Some supposedly slow-growing trees like white oak and blue spruce actually grow quite fast, especially in good soil. Black walnut will grow fast in a rich loam, slow in a poorer clay. Some trees appear to grow fast when young, then slower in middle age, although the opposite is actually the case. A tree with a diameter of 9 inches might put on an inch of trunk diameter in a year. A similar tree with an 18-inch diameter might add ½ inch in the same year. But the larger tree is adding a whole lot more circumference, a whole lot more board feet, and has a whole lot more leaves to make that growth possible.

Large versus Small Deciduous Trees

In deciding whether to plant large trees or small trees, you make trade-offs. Houses under a heavy shade of maple or even oak, or in one instance I know well, English walnut (*Juglans regia,* which casts a very heavy shade), are cool in summer, sometimes without air-conditioning at all, thus cutting down on that kind of maintenance. The owners feel that having to take down a tree or two in a lifetime in return for that shade is small payment indeed. In one case, the tree was a huge tulip poplar (*Liriodendron tulipifera*), which had stood for at least 60 years right next to the house. It was sawed up on the spot and the wood used to make furniture. This kind of arrangement is becoming common now that mobile band-saw sawmills have been invented. Nearly every community has someone offering this service. Formerly, sawmills would not take a yard tree for fear hardware in it would ruin costly blades. But a band-saw sawmill blade costs only about $20.

I think the real reason homeowners choose small trees rather than large ones is for variety in their landscape. A lot 50 by 100 feet will support two large shade trees or five small trees, without crowding. Close to the house, the small trees are practical not so much from a safety standpoint, but because they do not so quickly crowd against the house or obscure it from view or fill the gutters with leaves. (The high maintenance I endure from my white oaks around the house is cleaning out gutters. In spring, the gutters plug with catkins and in fall with leaves.) But small trees do not necessarily mean less maintenance, since it is possible to make much ado with planting, fertilizing, spraying, and pruning a small tree as much as with a large one. And you have in any event more trunks to dodge when you mow and more to trim around.

Small Tree Choices

In selecting small trees, the first rule is the same as for large ones. Choose trees native to your area or those with proven acclimatization. Take a walk along a wooded area or down an old grown-up fence row or roadside or simply down the street of an older suburb or city residential area. Excellent choices throughout the heartland of America are dogwood and redbud. Both stay relatively small, both bloom beautifully, both are relatively free of pest problems. They both prefer a woodsy soil, especially redbud, and rarely survive on subsoil left from bulldozed building sites or on beat-out farm soil.

Sassafras is a good choice for the eastern half of the country because it too has no serious disease or pest problems. Though it seldom receives much praise, sassafras is one of the most interesting trees horticulturally. The leaves are not all the same but of varying design. Hardly any tree turns a more gorgeous gold in the fall. The flowers are yellow and fragrant in spring. The fruits are blue, about the size of a large pea, and the fleshy stems that hold them a bright red. The wood is orange-yellow and interesting to use in woodworking. The root bark is used, of course, for sassafras tea and the making of delicious old-fashioned root beers. Sassafras can grow quite large, as is true of many of our native trees that we customarily see in only small size. The wood is somewhat brittle and should not be allowed to grow old close to a house. Sassafras spreads by shoots coming from the mother root, and if you cut down an established tree, a new sprout will invariably come up to take its place—a handy characteristic where you wish to keep a tree small to medium size.

Among non-native plants, mountain ash, with its bright orange berries that attract the cedar waxwings, is hardy and trouble-free. Japanese maple is trouble-free but not so hardy above zone 5 and sometimes freezes back in zone 5. (See the zone map later in this chapter.) Japanese snowbell (*Styrax japonica*) is very hardy, small, beautiful, and is given an A rating for yards by all landscapers.

Avoid white birch trees, as they are high maintenance. Their fragile trunk form, beautiful white bark, and absence of heavy leaf fall make them favorites around the house, but pests and diseases almost always take their toll before the tree is 12 years old, unless you spray routinely. The golden chain tree (*Laburnum ×watereri*) is small and beautiful with its panicles of yellow flowers. It doesn't require spraying but usually dies anyway in about 12 years.

Fruit Trees

Most domestic fruit trees are high maintenance, especially in humid regions. The closest thing we have to a trouble-free apple are the scab-immune varieties recently developed: Liberty and Freedom are the two latest and most highly touted. They can be grown successfully without any fungicidal sprays. This does not mean they will be free of insect damage, but in my experience, apples immune or highly resistant to scab, fire blight, cedar rust, and powdery mildew will produce enough good apples for family eating without any spraying. It is fungal diseases that are the big problem. You can make pies out of wormy apples, but nothing out of rotten ones.

Sour cherry trees are relatively low maintenance, but until they grow to at least medium size, the robins get all the fruit. You can screen small trees, but in my experience, it is easier to grow the larger, standard-size trees and let the birds have half the crop. You'll get enough, and the birds clean up the rest, which controls the cherry fruit worm problems better than any spraying.

Most dwarfed fruit trees on dwarfing rootstock are high maintenance because the roots are weak and not well acclimated to many American soils. If you must have dwarfed trees, buy those that have standard rootstocks and a dwarfing interstem grafted between rootstock trunk below and varietal trunk above. Most nurseries now offer most varieties this way, or will custom-graft such trees for you.

The Seckle pear, an old variety with small juicy fruits, is a good low-maintenance tree, being somewhat resistant to fire blight, the biggest problem with pears. Kieffer pear is another very old and very hardy pear that requires little care, if you don't mind cleaning up the fallen fruits. The fruit is very hard until early winter and is best used for canning. As with apples, I prefer standard pear trees to dwarfed, because in my experience, in typical yard situations, dwarfed fruit trees do not grow with good vigor. I'd rather prune a standard tree to a smaller size if I have only several to care for.

But by far the best solution to high-maintenance fruit trees in the home orchard is to propagate trees from wild specimens found in your climate—trees that are producing good fruit without any care at all. You find these trees, particularly apple trees, along country roads, fence rows, woods, abandoned homesteads, or old orchards no longer cared for. I have written elsewhere and often about these trees, and as I gain in experience, my enthusiasm increases. If a tree has lived in the wild for many years, it has demonstrated proof of some immunity to scab and to insect problems. If the fruit tastes good (often it does not) you have found a treasure. Members of the North American Fruit Explorers (see address a bit later or in Appendix C) make a lifetime hobby of hunting wild fruit trees for good quality.

After all this has been said, I must add that a fruit tree that flourishes in a wild environment may not necessarily do well in a conventional orchard alongside disease-susceptible trees, where sprays kill beneficial bugs and fungi as well as harmful ones. The trick is to mimic the wild environment from which the wild tree comes as much as you can. A typical backyard with only one or two species of each fruit tree, mixed in with other trees, and where little or no spraying of toxic chemicals is done, and little or no heavy fertilizing practiced, mimics pretty satisfactorily that wild environment. (And of course lowers your maintenance work.) You will not get 100 percent perfect fruit like the conventional orchardist must strive for to stay solvent at the bank, but you will get plenty. My transplanted fence row trees produce about 70 percent undamaged fruit with no spraying. Yellow apples, Grimes Golden and Golden Delicious, do about 60 percent so long as there are no red cedar trees within a couple hundred yards. (The red cedar is a host for cedar rust, which infests apples, too, particularly yellow varieties.) A late apple like a Winesap does best of all—about 80 percent undamaged fruit.

For years I did spray my trees once—with dormant oil in early spring, since light petroleum oil is not dangerous to humans. But I could not see where this spray application was cutting down on insect damage. Scab, a fungal disease, seemed to be more virulent than ever. I formulated my own theory, which has no support from science as far as I know, but which seems to be true in my experience. Perhaps the oil spray was killing as many (or more) beneficial bugs than pest bugs, and perhaps it was killing natural fungal enemies of the scab fungus. So I quit spraying altogether and at the same time tore out the varieties most susceptible to scab: Red Delicious, MacIntosh, and the varieties developed from them. I also quit manuring heavily around the trees, which prompted them to grow too lushly from the influx of all that extra nitrogen. By the second year of such low-maintenance or no-maintenance practices, I began to harvest more apples than I ever had before, and scab subsided even though the weather was wetter than it had been in the preceding years.

The homeowner wishing fruit that need not be sprayed can grow persimmons, papaws, and mulberries. Selected, named, grafted varieties are better when available, but you have to search through nursery catalogs assiduously to find them. The best way is to subscribe to *Pomona,* the quarterly journal of the North American Fruit Explorers (write Robert Kurle, 10 South 055 Madison Street, Hinsdale, IL 60521), in which information continually appears on the availability of select varieties of these rather esoteric fruit trees, and many others.

In warm climates, citrus *in the backyard environment* is a fairly low-maintenance fruit to grow. But of course only where it is acclimated. Not even birds bother citrus very much.

Horticultural varieties developed from the native American hawthorn make excellent small low-maintenance yard trees, the fruit (usually red) hanging on into late fall and not messy like mulberries. Avoid ginkgo trees unless you are sure they are male (staminate). The fruit of the female ginkgo is messy where it drops and smells exactly like dog manure. Male ginkgoes are good no-maintenance trees because they are not bothered by pests or disease and endure city pollution well.

Native crab apples make decorative small yard trees. If the birds don't eat all the little apples, or you don't make sauce out of the rest, the fruit may have to be cleaned up, though this is not a hard job and if you are not a Superneat, not absolutely essential. The problem with crab apples is that those developed from European or Japanese origin, rather than native American, are apt to be susceptible to the same scab that affects apples. The leaves discolor in wet humid weather, wrinkle, turn brown-black and fall off. The tree, if very susceptible, will eventually die; spraying is not always a remedy. I have not been able to find a list of crabs, among the numerous hybrids, strains, and varieties, that are resistant to scab, and both trees I have grown succumbed to it. Serviceberry or shadbush (*Amelanchier* sp.) are trouble-free smallish trees *in their native habitat.* They have fruit good for pies and for birds. There is one species native to the mid-Appalachian region, and a bushier one in Canada south into Minnesota and Wisconsin, which has become known as the saskatoon or Juneberry and is now grown commercially. Where winters are mild, the franklinia tree (*Gordonia alatamaha*) and the sourwood (*Oxydendrum arboreum*) are small, beautiful, white-flowered trees good for yards.

Nut Trees

Wild nut trees by and large are low-maintenance trees in their range. Hickories, black walnuts, and hazelnuts in the North, native pecans (not paper-shelled, commercial pecans) in the South and in central areas, and pine nuts in the West can be particularly rewarding with little maintenance work. If you are not interested in these trees for food, however, you will still have to clean up nuts from the ground occasionally.

Low-Maintenance Shrubs

A good way to determine the best low-maintenance bushes for your yard is the way I've already recommended for discovering the best low-maintenance trees: to drive through the countryside and learn what grows well where you live. Study especially abandoned farmsteads you pass or farmsteads that have been neglected or rented to people who have little interest in their landscape beyond mowing the lawn. What shrubs are still growing there? In our area, you would find lilac, a flowering red quince, perhaps a trumpet vine cascading its orange blossoms over an old post, a rose bush with small yellow blossoms, a rose of Sharon, a mock orange, maybe a weigela bush, sometimes an ancient wisteria vine climbing the windmill, surely a forsythia, and often a spirea.

These old-fashioned, common shrubs are old-fashioned and common because they endure without much maintenance, which should endear them to landscapers. But what appears common to the eye appears less desirable and is therefore shunned by those who wish to establish themselves as top gardeners, or who simply suffer from the common human desire to have "something different."

Objectively speaking, old-fashioned shrubs bloom or grow just as prettily as the New! Sensational! ones. If they were rare, they would be standards of beauty. That old yellow rose bush in the abandoned yard looks delightful after you have become jaded looking at fancy roses in an arboretum all day. And the rewards are great for being content with the commonplace. A fancy rose grower showed me through his collection one day, impressing me not only with the beauty of the flowers, but with the amount of work he did to keep them pretty. In addition to a spray schedule and a soil fertility program that would boggle Burbank, he painstakingly filled tar paper cylinders around each plant with peat moss every fall to guard against winterkill. And still some of the roses died back. "But look at this old red rambler," he said at the end of the tour. "It blooms nice every year and I never do a thing to it."

The same gentleman nodded towards his flowering crab and remarked that it was a "real bother" to keep it from growing too tall for his small yard and to keep suckers from growing thickly on the limbs. "But that mock orange gets about 7 feet tall and stays there without pruning, and it blooms just as nice as the crab."

Lilac will eventually grow too tall for most yards without pruning. But growth of that size takes a long time, and pruning is not necessary every year.

Zone map. These zones are approximations based on USDA and Agriculture Canada maps. Ask your extension agent or the horticulture department of a local university for the length of your frost-free period and match it with the appropriate number.

Both upright and low-growing forms of yew make excellent low-care bushes (see discussion of same under small trees). They make good foundation plants on the shady side of the house, although in this situation they will need periodic pruning.

Korean boxwood, being much hardier than American or English boxwood is another evergreen bush that requires little work except an occasional pruning if you wish it to look formal.

In their natural range, laurel, rhododendron, and even azaleas require little care *if* the soil acidity meets their requirements, a pH of 5 to 5.5. Rhododendron and azaleas will sometimes grow in more neutral soil, but only with much maintenance. Although it is never mentioned as such, elderberry makes a nice landscaping bush with very fragrant blossoms in June. Its fruit is beloved by many bird species and makes distinctive jelly and pie. Elderberry spreads by suckering, but you can maintain a bush a long time with the lawn mower. Let it sucker out on one side and mow

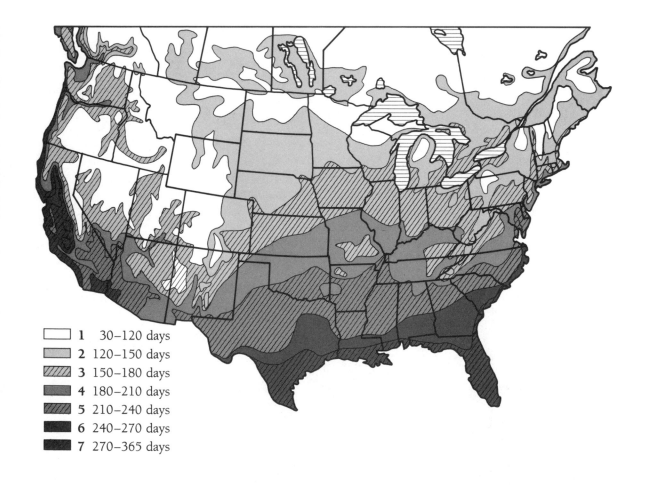

1 30–120 days
2 120–150 days
3 150–180 days
4 180–210 days
5 210–240 days
6 240–270 days
7 270–365 days

down the old plant after three to five years. Then when the new group of suckers has aged three to five years, let new suckers grow at the original site and mow down the aged group, moving back and forth indefinitely.

Skimmia (*Skimmia japonica*) is a very nice shrub for southern and coastal areas up to about as far north as New York City. It grows about 4 feet tall and stays there without pruning. It has fragrant white blooms and showy red berries.

In addition to the shrubs already mentioned, the following thrive without care and even under neglect:

- American hazelnut (*Corylus americana*). Hardy to zone 4 and parts of zone 3. No problems and good nuts to eat, too.
- Chokeberry (*Aronia arbutifolia*). Sports dense white to pink flowers. It has red fruit and stays 6 to 9 feet tall. It's hardy to zone 5.
- Privet (*Ligustrum* sp.). Some privets are hardy only in the South or where winters are mild. But California privet is hardy in zone 4 and will survive freezing to the ground in zone 3. The privets, each in their range, are an excellent choice for low-maintenance hedges. Hedges, by definition, are not low maintenance, in that they require clipping periodically, but privet hedges are otherwise easy to keep growing.
- Saint-John's-wort (the shrub, *Hypericum aureum* or *H. frondosum*). A small shrub to 3 feet, with interesting reddish bark.
- Spicebush (*Lindera benzoin*). Also called benjamin bush, has good autumn color. It draws birds and butterflies and is very hardy.
- Sweet gale (*Myrica* sp.). Pungently fragrant. Grows only to 4 feet. Very hardy. Caution: it suckers rather vigorously.
- Sweet pepper bush (*Clethra alnifolia*). Hardy to zone 4 but doesn't like overly dry conditions. Fragrant white blossoms in midsummer.
- Viburnum—almost all species. Some tend to grow too tall for small lots.
- Witch hazel (*Hamamelis virginiana*). Good for shady places. It blooms very early in spring. To zone 5.

The other two plants that make fairly carefree hedges are yew in the upright bush hybrids, particularly *Taxus ×media*, var. *hicksii*, and buckthorn (*Rhamnus* sp.) The former I've already described in this chapter. In hedges this yew does better than most plants because as the branches crowd each other, they do not kill each other because of lack of sunlight, as do many hedge plants that otherwise take shearing well. Buckthorn hedge plants are tall, slender bushes that grow densely enough so that clipping is not necessary. No disease or insect has harmed mine in years. The bushes tend to grow up too tall for hedging a small lot but are fine in the countryside. American holly also makes a low-care hedge where the soil is fairly acid and the winters fairly mild.

Pruning: Do as Little as You Can Get by With

Shearing or clipping a hedge is similar to giving a young man a butch haircut. (The idea is to get a smooth, dense surface.) But pruning shrubs is, or should be, another matter. Most of them are not meant to be clipped like a formal hedge, that is, all the branches cut off at the same height. Rather, older branches should be cut back *at the base,* to allow room for newer ones to grow vigorously. Don't give your shrubs butch haircuts. Bushes that blossom on new growth in late spring or early summer should be pruned in very early spring or in late winter. Bushes that blossom on the preceding years growth should be pruned soon after blooming *if* the fruit or seeds are not desired. If desired, prune after harvest—late fall or winter, the idea being to prune off the branches that have borne fruit—*if* any pruning really is necessary.

From the standpoint of low maintenance, be assured that pruning *a la* the experts, is usually overdone, or done for reasons that need not concern a busy homeowner. Observe an old practical saying: "When there is no clear need to prune, don't."

I know of three instances when there is this clear need: (1) In transplanting, top growth should be cut back to match approximately the root growth. (2) Dead wood or branches can be pruned out for appearance's sake, if nothing else. (3) Where a bush is definitely overcrowed with branches, older ones can be pruned out to rejuvenate the plant. But be aware that on a vigorous plant tending toward dense growth, pruning will encourage more lush water-sprout growth, so that by pruning a lot, you will make it necessary to prune still more.

The following shrubs are low growing by nature and so require little pruning to keep them within prescribed bounds.

- Cotoneaster (*Cotoneaster horizontalis* and *C. adpressa*). Hardy to zone 4.
- Deutzia (*D. gracilis*). Lots of flowers. Hardy to zone 5.
- Inkberry. This is a holly, *Ilex glabra.* This is a lovely old-fashioned shrub. Hardy to zone 3.
- Japanese holly. The variety *Ilex crenata* var. *microphylla,* especially. Hardy to zone 4.
- Juniper (the low-growing forms). Hardy to zone 4 and warmer parts of zone 3.
- Kerria (*Kerria japonica*). Will sometimes be frozen back in zone 5.
- Mahonia or Oregon holly grape (*Mahonia aquifolium*). Hardy to zone 5.
- Prostrate yews, e.g., *Taxus baccata* var. *repandens.*
- Snowberry (*Symphoricarpos racemosus*). Hardy to zone 3.
- Stephanandra (*Stephanandra flexuosa* or *S. incisa*). Related to spirea but does not grow as tall.
- *Viburnum opulus* var. *nanum.* A very dwarfed form of viburnum growing hardly 2 feet tall. I hesitate to advocate dwarfed forms of plants,

even though they mean less pruning chores. In my experience, dwarf plants are not particularly vigorous and must be fussed with to keep them growing—not low maintenance. This one, which I have never seen nor grown, appears to be an exception. Hardy to zone 3.

• Winter jasmine (*Jasminum nudiflorum*). Called winter jasmine because in the South it may bloom all year. Hardy to zone 4. In colder zones, flower buds may winter-kill, but the plant itself remains unharmed.

You can plant any of these in front of your picture window and not have to prune continually to keep them from blocking the view.

CHAPTER 9

FLOWERS AND VEGETABLES

Garden catalogs, artfully designed to get you to buy lots of seeds, tempt you with big, splashly pictures of gorgeous flowers and delicious vegetables. I should know; I've succumbed to their allure many times myself. But despite the glory those full-color photos promise, not all of the seeds you buy and plant will reward you with such specimens, unless perhaps you're willing to devote the kind of time and attention that professional gardeners can to get such results. On the other hand, there are certain flowers and vegetables that demand very little, and give much in return.

Flowers That Give You More Hammock Time

Popular fashions in flowers reveal the same human foibles as fashions in flowering shrubs and other ornamental plants. Those that best withstand nature's hazards endure to become common. Becoming common, they become uninteresting to the homeowner's bent for "something different." When "something different" requires hard work and attention to keep it alive, the old reliables are rediscovered and become popular until another generation forgets. Then the pendulum swings again.

Perennials

Perennials—flowers that once planted, come up and bloom year after year—are the first choice for low maintenance. But selection should be done carefully. Some perennials are more perennial than others; that is, some will last for many years without care, while others need to be dug up and the roots divided regularly. Some have special problems with insects or diseases that require regular maintenance. And the classic perennial border, popular in Victorian times and now enjoying a rebirth, is a high-maintenance project that should be undertaken only by those for whom flower growing is a major hobby. In a perennial border, plants are arranged artfully from low-growing varieties in front to tall ones in the rear, and chosen so that something is coming into bloom from spring to fall. One is constantly weeding, cutting off old blossoms, tying up, setting out, and taking in.

But some perennials, handled in less demanding ways, can give you flowers throughout your growing season with no work at all. For starters, here's a list that has grown out of my experience. (Note that I mention botanical names only when I think it necessary to distinguish one specific genus or species or variety from another. If no botanical name appears,

Peonies.

then you can assume that I'm referring to the flower that everybody—or most everybody—knows by its common name.)

PEONIES

This flower ranks number one with me. I'm sure there is *something* you should do to peonies in the way of care, but in all the years we've grown them, we did exactly nothing. Peonies make large gorgeous flowers in varying shades of red, pink, and white. They bloom for much of the spring. No insect harms them much. Don't spray them as one gardener I know did. He got rid of the ants, sure enough, but the flower buds would not open. Why? The ants suck a nectar that otherwise seals in the bud. Without the ant performing this operation, the buds won't open properly.

Treat a peony as an ornamental bush. The shoots in spring grow into a tight clump and are easy to mow around, making the bush a good choice for an isolated lawn location or as a row along a drive or walk.

Daylilies.

THE COMMON DAYLILY

Hemerocallis fulva and *H. flava,* especially the former, are the best varieties on my list. Many, many hybrids and varieties of daylily are available, all of them fairly low maintenance, but none beat these old originals in that respect. You find *H. fulva* growing along roadsides in tight clumps that defy weeds to come up among them. They endure mowings, herbicides, and farm equipment driving over them along our country roads and come back the next year as luxuriant as ever. Extremely hardy and pest-free, a bed of them in the yard or by the house requires no work and remains attractive even after blooming in summer. Daylilies are supposed to be dug up every few years and the roots divided, but *H. fulva* will go on forever without this work. *H. flava,* the lemon daylily, is nearly as low care, the blossom smaller and yellow rather than orange.

Tiger lilies look somewhat like old-fashioned daylilies but are spotted. Many, many new varieties are available from most garden catalogs. Colors range from red, pink, white, yellow, and cream to gold in addition to the old traditional orange. They are all hardy and enduring and good for low maintenance, although some do not grow in the tight clumps that so successfully keep out weeds.

LILY OF THE VALLEY

Especially for a shady spot by the house, a bed of these tiny lilies (*Convallaria majalis* or *C. montana*) will last forever with a little weeding. The roots spread out and send up new shoots until a solid bed is formed.

Lilies of the valley.

The new shoots arise from pips, as they are called, on the roots, which can be rather easily removed to start new beds or to force for winter blooms indoors. The flowers are small but very fragrant.

WINTER ACONITE

This member of the buttercup family (*Eranthis hyemalis*) is especially desirable because it blooms extremely early in the year—as early as late February even in my cold climate of northern Ohio. It takes only the slightest thaw to awaken it, and once blooming, will withstand temperatures falling into the teens with ease. If biotechnology could transfer this kind of cold hardiness to vegetables, northerners would be eating sweet corn in April. The other advantage of these dainty yellow flowers is that you can plant them right in the lawn, and if you are just a bit patient with the lawn mower, they will mature before the real mowing season begins. You can then mow right over them. Zero maintenance. And the seeds will spread the plant over the lawn very delightfully. The flowers even do very well in shady places (largely because they put on most of their yearly growth before leaves appear elsewhere).

There are other small early spring flowers that can be handled like winter aconite, although they need a bit more time to mature before they can be mowed off without weakening them for next year's growth; snow-drop (*Galanthus* spp.) and grape hyacinth (*Muscari* spp.) are two of these.

ADAM'S NEEDLE

This is a type of yucca (*Yucca filamentosa*) that is also called Spanish bayonet. It is hardy to zone 5 (see the zone map in chapter 8), and is an extremely low-care flower for dry, sandy, sunny areas. It will grow in good soil, too, have no fear, and come up year after year with a shower of white blooms in summer. It reaches a height of about 6 feet in zone 5 and will grow taller farther south. The sharp bayonetlike leaves make it somewhat undesirable in a child's play area. By the same token, it is much less likely to be harmed by frisky cats and dogs than some other flowers are.

DAFFODILS

The daffodils (*Narcissus* sp.) I'm talking about are the ones naturalized in a woodland or meadow setting; they go on nearly forever. There is a solitary one in our woods, planted by who knows who, that blooms every spring and then spends the rest of the summer in deep shade, dreaming about its few brief days of glory. It is a low-care flower to grow along a fence. When summer comes and the weeds and grass want to take over, just mow. Next spring the daffodils will be back. So will crocuses planted with them.

THE LITTLE SEMIWILD IRISES

These flowers (*Iris versicolor* and *I. cristata*) are not as showy as their bigger cousins, but they get along on their own far better and do not need to be lifted and divided so often or protected from weeds, slugs, and iris borers as much. They adapt to almost any site except those that are very dry, and they are particularly good for a wet, marshy place.

ASTERS

For a late fall bloom, the hardy asters are the least bother. But they ought to be lifted and divided about every third year.

There are other good perennials, of course, but the ones we think of first usually have some maintenance chore that prevents them from being included in my list of easy-care favorites. Delphiniums should be staked;

Asters.

mums should be pinched back; daisies, sweet Williams, and hollyhocks are not long lasting without replanting; dahlias should be lifted every fall. Daisies will often replant themselves and so will hollyhocks, but as such they probably should be dealt with more accurately as annuals.

WILDFLOWERS

The group of perennials requiring the least work of all are what we commonly call wildflowers. The trick to growing them with low maintenance is to grow them in the same kind of habitat they are accustomed to. In most cases, this means a woodsy or meadow environment, not in cultivated rows, borders, or beds. Thus bloodroot, dogtooth violet, Dutchman's-breeches, trillium, Virginia bluebell, wild geranium, wild phlox,

Black-eyed Susans.

Yarrow.

and wood anemone like a woodland environment, or more accurately, open glades in a woods. Black-eyed Susan, blue-eyed grass, columbine, evening primrose, poppy, spring beauty, and yarrow, to name a few, grow from the edge of the woods out into sunny fields. Some need very specific soil requirements: it is almost always useless to try to grow wild lady's slippers outside their natural range. Digging them up should be a crime and in some places is.

Meadow wildflowers endure in lawns if mowing is curtailed until the particular plant has matured, as I mentioned in chapter 7. In a typical yard, the woodsy wildflowers will not compete well with grass and need a place more or less to themselves near or under trees, where a moist leaf-mold soil can be maintained. My backyard is a compromise between grass and flowers, made possible because it is too shady for vigorous grass growth, and because I let falling oak leaves lie (like sleeping dogs) much of

Poppies.

The more casual and "wilder" perennials look best when they are allowed to grow informally and close together, crowding out weeds and providing a natural mulch for one another—low maintenance at its best.

the time. Thus I am able to let many wildflowers grow and bloom in spring. Columbine, dandelion, fire pink, Jacob's ladder, shooting star, spring beauty, trillium, trout lily, violet, Virginia bluebell, wild geranium, wild phlox, winter aconite (not technically a wildflower), and wood anemone grow until about July 1, when I mow the area into a reasonably neat lawn for the rest of the year. Moneywort crawls low on the ground and blooms yellow most of the summer. I will let clumps of this or that grow; for instance, an occasional pokeberry or blue-eyed grass that strikes my fancy. My maintenance in all this is a vigilant eye and a quick hand on the mower's steering mechanism, nothing more. Some of the wildflowers spread from roots, others reseed themselves, sometimes dying out in one area and appearing in another. The blazing red fire pinks move every year, and I must be alert to their dark green leaf clumps that grow in late summer or early spring and from which the June blooms will grow. With a wildflower lawn, never has laziness been so rewarded.

Annuals Can Be Carefree, Too

The simple difference between an annual and a perennial (although often the difference isn't that simple) is that the former needs to be planted or set out every year. This may seem like high maintenance compared to perennials, but that's not necessarily the case. My mother had a saying about flowers that bears repeating: "When in doubt, plant zinnias." She meant that no matter how ignorant or busy a person was, or how questionable the soil, zinnias would grow and bloom profusely.

ZINNIAS

Zinnia seeds will germinate faster than anything except maybe radishes. They will grow in most regions, ignored by pest insects and rabbits ornery enough to eat pansies right beside them. Mildew can be a problem, but because zinnias grow and bear in the dry, hottest part of the summer, this is rarely cause for concern. If you water them (usually not necessary but it makes certain insecure types of gardeners feel better), water only the soil, not the leaves. Zinnias make excellent cut flowers, and for that purpose are often grown in the garden in rows and weeded with the tiller as you would corn. They're very easy to care for that way. They are available from most mail-order seed houses.

MARIGOLDS

Zinnias generally bloom all summer, and about the time they begin to fail, the low-maintenance flower gardener will have marigolds coming into

Zinnias (center back);
marigolds (center front).

bloom in full force until hard frost. Marigolds came originally from ancient Mexico and to this day remain fairly immune to the vicissitudes of dry weather. Bugs do not bother marigolds, which some believe have their own insect-repellent powers. They are often planted next to beans to keep bean beetles at bay. Those who say they have success with this practice use the old-fashioned marigolds with the pungent odor. Both these and the French marigolds will rid the soil of nematodes, as has been demonstrated by scientific experiment. Some gardeners say marigolds will discourage rabbits, too, but in my experience, a hungry rabbit can be discouraged only by a large dog, a fence, or a bullet.

Garden Food
with Much Less Sweat

In my many years of vegetable gardening, I've tried all kinds of weird vegetables, sometimes just out of curiosity, sometimes for the challenge of it, and sometimes just for the sake of trying something different. But I always go back to the tried and true, because they are so reliable and they are so undemanding.

A Is for Asparagus

The low-maintenance vegetable garden begins with asparagus. Like other low-maintenance perennials, an asparagus bed, once planted, will last 15 years and longer. Because asparagus is grown commercially in light or sandy soil (in New Jersey, Michigan, and California), many people believe it won't grow in heavier soils, but nothing could be further from the truth. Asparagus grows well in any fertile, neutral soil, and when grown in clays and loams, it's not sandy when you eat it. Sand is only advantageous if fertilized heavily because it usually guarantees a well-drained soil, which asparagus must have, and allows you to cultivate weeds over the bed without hurting the roots in early spring before the shoots begin to grow. Heavier soils don't dry out soon enough to do that.

Weeding is the only maintenance necessary on vigorously growing asparagus, and that need not take much time on a bed about 20 feet long and about 2 feet wide—plenty big for a family. The asparagus beetle is seldom very harmful after a bed is established. For the lowest maintenance, proceed in this manner:

Plant seeds or roots—the latter means asparagus on the table a year sooner, but roots cost more. Dig a trench about 8 inches deep and 4 inches wide and plant the seed or roots in the bottom, covering the seed just barely, or covering the roots with about 2 inches of dirt. As the little plant grows, fill in with dirt gradually. This takes more or less all summer but the operation is at the same time also burying little weeds around the plants that would otherwise be competing with them. If you can mix in some compost with the dirt that you are filling in, all the better, of course. In the second year, a new and thicker plant will replace the spindly first year's one, and if the soil is rich and the weather good, maybe two or three shoots will grow. Leave them. You want the plant to build up a big root system fast so that next year you can begin to harvest a few spears. If you planted roots, you might take a few spears in the second year, but I wouldn't really advise it.

In the third year, you can begin to harvest, but take only a few early shoots from each original plant and let the rest grow. By the fourth year, you can start picking in earnest, but the trick here is to leave one of the earliest shoots to grow at each original plant so that from the very beginning of the season, root invigoration is taking place. Then, quit harvesting a month after you begin so that more shoots can come up and grow all summer. By the fifth year, you should not have to worry about taking too many shoots except to quit harvesting about a month after you begin. In the sixth year and thereafter, you can continue picking a few late spears even later than that, because enough spears will have grown up and be past harvestable size by then to ensure a healthy crop the next year. The more top growth over your bed, the better insurance of a good crop the following year, and the shade of that growth helps keep weeds from growing underneath from July until frost. After frost, run your mower over the bed, grinding up the old residue into mulch. You can wait and do that in early spring instead if you wish.

The worst weed in the asparagus bed is volunteer asparagus that grows from the seeds of your crop plants. If allowed to grow, these seedlings overcrowd the bed and give you a bunch of pencil-thin shoots, not the thick succulent ones you want. Therefore, the real Cadillac of asparagus beds is composed of only male plants. Both male and female plants bloom, but only the female bears seed inside red berries. As far as I know, you can't buy just male roots, and knowledgeable gardeners eventually start a permanent bed with roots from a mixed row, taking the male plants for transplanting.

Planting roots or seeds in the trench is done mostly because as the years pass, the root crowns gradually rise higher in the soil until they eventually emerge. The plants then need to be lifted and reset. It also appears that the more shallow the crowns are, the more spindly the shoots. Mulching yearly tends to raise the bed a little as the crowns rise and so adds years of good production to a bed. Mulching with manure and compost also gives the asparagus the nutrients it needs for good growth. As the mulch rots, it does something else for low maintenance that more than repays the time applying it: The soil becomes so soft and loose that you can work it with your fingers. Once the shoots start springing up, I have found no other way to weed the asparagus bed properly than with my fingers, working gently around the stalks to loosen and bury small weeds as they come up. One weeding like this in May and another in June, and you are finished for the year. The shade of the stalks, plus the addition of new mulch (which should only be applied after harvesting is completed, especially if you use chicken manure like I do), controls weeds the rest of the year.

In harvesting spears, it is better to break them off than cut them with a knife below soil level as some books mistakenly instruct. Break the spear *where it wants to break easily,* and you will be certain that the spear you take to the house is all tender. If you cut low, a portion at the lower end may be too tough. Experience soon teaches you the gentle art of breaking. Also, the biggest, fattest stalks are generally the tenderest if harvested at the proper time. Friends of ours confessed that when they first prepared a batch of our asparagus, they trimmed off the butt ends. When they tasted how good and tender the fat stalks were, they retrieved the trimmings and cooked them, too!

Rhubarb Never Fails

Rhubarb is good for low-maintenance gardeners because it is so forgiving; it never *demands* to be harvested. In fact, you can grow a plant or two as a sort of ornamental, right out on the lawn if you wish, and never harvest it. It's easy to mow or cultivate around, too. Those huge leaves keep weeds from growing up through the plant, and if you mow and till off some of the lower leaves, no real harm is done.

Rhubarb is indestructible throughout the Midwest and I assume elsewhere. Ultrahardy, adaptable to any reasonably well-drained soil, and impervious to most insect attacks (the leaves are slightly toxic with oxalic acid), you simply stick a root in the ground and fertilize it a little until it gets established. You can buy seed; the Victoria variety is a good one, and Burpee is one source for it. Other varieties are MacDonald and Valentine. But you need not necessarily buy rhubarb seed; you should be able to get a start from a plant in your neighborhood. Most old plants need to be dug up and the roots divided anyway. Quite a bit of variety exists in the ubiquitous rhubarb plants of any neighborhood, and some are better than others, at least in terms of vigor. "Improved" varieties tend to have redder stalks, and although they do not necessarily taste any better than the greenish red stalks of other older strains, many gardeners find them more desirable. But in our garden, the reddest stalked plants are the least vigorous. Getting a start from an old plant in your neighborhood guarantees you a strain acclimated to your soil.

Winter Onions Grow Like Weeds

What we call winter onions are perennials that produce bulbs at the tops of the stalks and bulblets on the roots each year. You may know them as nest onions or as Egyptian tree onions. Whatever they are called, your greatest challenge in growing them is keeping them from taking over your landscape, and I speak only a little facetiously. I have never seen anything so tough. Mine grow even in partial shade, which they should not. I run the tiller down both sides of the row occasionally to kill the new plants that form when the bulblets on the stalk fall over to the ground. I've even mowed the plants off in midsummer to curtail their growth. And when the onions get too rambunctious, I run the tiller right over them. But nothing daunts them. Whoever first called them "multiplier onions" should get a Pulitzer prize for accurate reporting.

I keep these weed onions, or they keep me, for a good reason: Not only are they low maintenance, but they can (in fact, must) be harvested in the very earliest spring or late winter when there is nothing else fresh from the garden. They begin to grow in the fall, and as soon as the snow recedes in February or March, they perk right up and start growing again. I have harvested them when snowdrifts were still melting 3 feet away. As soon as the weather warms enough to awaken other plants, these onions become too bitter, but how delicate they taste in February! You can pull up a cluster, gently separate the bulbs in the bunch, and then peel the skin away and the outer covering of stalk to reveal scallions of unexcelled delicacy.

Winter (or nest or multiplier or Egyptian tree) onions.

These onions are similar, but not the same, as the evergreen long white bunching onions available from most catalogs. Bunching onions do not form bulbs and won't survive hard winters, or if they do, will not survive forever the way winter or Egyptian tree onions will. Onion maggots do not bother Egyptian tree onions, nor does any other bug or disease that I know of. They are available from Thompson & Morgan, Inc., P.O. Box 100, Farmingdale, NJ 07727. Remember, these onions will not take the place of regular spring onions in May, but there is no other onion in the North for late winter and early spring eating.

The Annual Vegetables with the Least Problems

The hardest job you'll probably have with the vegetables below is preparing the planting bed for them every year—an inevitable chore for anyone who grows annuals.

SWEET POTATOES

The sweet potato ranks at the top of this list in my northern garden and I'm sure it ranks high in the South, too. Centennial is the variety I like—the deep orange, moist-textured kind often referred to as yams in the South. The white and the lighter yellow sweet potatoes are too mealy in texture to suit my taste. Buy plants and set them out after all danger of frost and chilly weather has passed. If the ground is dry, water the new plants once or twice. They take right off and vine so thickly that after a weeding or two, they will shade out most weeds in their territory. In 30 years I have never seen anything attack the plants. Sometimes mice or bugs eat at the tubers a little, but they never do any serious harm. Be sure to harvest before a heavy frost kills the vines, as the green vines wilting suddenly from frost can impart an off-taste to the potatoes.

RADISHES

Radishes are the other no-care vegetable in our garden. They grow so fast, pests are rarely serious problems. There are many kinds of radishes, including fall and winter ones. Weird kinds like Munchen Bier has podlike fruit aboveground that's good for salads, and April Cross or Mooli from Japan is a white radish that won't bolt so badly when hot weather comes. (Both these varieties are available from Thompson & Morgan mentioned above and listed in Appendix B.) Radishes are not a major part of anyone's diet, but they are one of those foods that add some welcome variety to many fresh dishes. Of course, they make fine eating all by themselves, too. If you want to impress the veteran gardener next door, you can easily do it by planting some of the more unusual varieties—ones she's probably never even heard of. And doing so won't take any more time or effort than planting the common little red radish everybody else grows.

ZUCCHINI

Zucchini is, of course, on everyone's low-maintenance list of vegetables. It is much easier to grow 1,000 zucchini than to grow 20, so plant only four seeds and stand back. Zucchini actually do have pest problems enough to stop less aggressive species—from striped cucumber beetle when young, to borers when old, but even so, you will get more squash than you bargained for.

TOMATOES

Where soilborne wilts are not a problem, the tomato is a surprisingly carefree vegetable to grow, which is why everyone does grow it. The trick to growing tomatoes without working hard at it is to ignore all the stakes, wire cages, and various other trellis arrangements that fussy gardeners tell you are necessary for success. And ignore all that malarkey about pinching off suckers. These so-called suckers are fruit-producing stems, and they are pinched off only when you are training tomatoes to stakes and have to limit the number of fruit, or when you are trying to grow a bigger tomato than your neighbor. When your tomato plants have started growing well and are beginning to blossom, spread straw mulch around them and let the poor things grow like they want to, over the straw. The tomatoes will be clean, they will suffer less from blossom end rot because the mulch will keep the soil cool and moist, and even if you don't get the biggest tomato on the block, you will get a whole lot more than your neighbors who boast about their fancy staking systems.

LETTUCE

Lettuce presents very few problems—none at all for me and my family. A bed of it, grown in a 5-by-5-foot cold frame, will provide, before it bolts, all a family needs. The only weed of note in our cold frame is sour grass, a type of oxalis that can be added in small amounts right to the salad with the lettuce. Its lemony flavor adds a nice touch. Rabbits are the worst pest in our garden, but contrary to tradition, they don't eat lettuce.

OTHER SALAD GREENS

For another salad ingredient with no maintenance at all, plant a linden (basswood) tree. The young leaves are quite tasty in salads. And the flowers and young leaves of the common violet plant found in many lawns in spring are a delight in salads, too. And of course dandelions before they blossom are good wilted with vinegar and garnished with chopped boiled eggs and bacon bits. If you are drenching your landscape with toxic sprays, you'll have to forgo such delights.

CORN AND SNAP BEANS, SOMETIMES

I would like to add sweet corn and snap beans to the list of easy-grow vegetables, but in some regions there are problems with these vegetables. Corn earworms can infest the ears, although the worms destroy only a small part of the ear and can be cut out before boiling without much trouble. If you roast your corn in the shuck, however, it is not very appetizing to open the shuck and find a couple of roasted worms inside as well. In our area, we seldom are troubled with earworms, but the raccoons make growing sweet corn useless if you don't put an electric fence around the corn. And that's high maintenance.

Where snap beans don't become infested with Mexican bean beetles, they are very low maintenance. Usually the beetles don't get bad until the supply of beans is diminishing. The trick then is to mow off the plants about 4 inches high—or as high as you can set your mower. Your mower should have killed many of the beetle larvae on the old leaves, and you can gather up the shreddings and burn them to eliminate the rest. If the weather is not too dry, the plants will grow back and set another smaller crop. This second crop will usually be much less infected, maturing in the later, drier part of the summer, which is usually too hot and dry for bean beetles.

Low-Maintenance Cultivation

We are going through another wave of popularity for intensive raised-bed gardening right now. This happens about every 30 years. Gardening on raised beds is fine, but it's not low maintenance. And though all garden writers will rise up to smite me in a high dudgeon with their spades, raised beds are not practical wherever summers tend to be hot and dry, which is most places. If you pile up soil higher than the natural grade, you must be prepared to water frequently, maybe incessantly, because those beds will dry out faster than conventional soil surfaces. The natural capillary action of the soil drawing up moisture from below is disrupted by raised beds. Subsequent necessary watering takes time, is wasteful, and costs money not necessarily recovered by intensive double and triple cropping. Moreover, much more hand weeding is required. Intensive raised-bed gardening is practical only where space is very limited.

The typical backyard is ample enough for a garden without raised beds—with room enough between rows to cultivate weeds with a hand-pushed cultivator or a motor-driven tiller. *After* the soil has warmed up well (about July 4 is the best time to do this in the North) and the weeds have been cultivated several times and the soil subsequently aerated, apply leaves and grass clippings you have saved as mulch. You'll find that most of your garden maintenance work is finished for the year.

The main reason for putting your garden in rows wide enough for some kind of mechanical weed control is that at the same time you can greatly reduce hand weeding in the row by rolling dirt from the passing cultivator blade against the crop plants and covering small weeds there. The art of covering weeds is ancient, but in these days of herbicides, it seems to have been forgotten. When you plant a crop or row of vegetables, you cultivate weeds several times before planting, and if the ground is warm enough for prompt germination, the crop plants usually get a head start on the next wave of weeds. If not, as in the case of slow-germinating carrots, you will have to weed by hand in the row once or perhaps twice. But whatever, once the crop plants are about 2 inches tall and the weeds only an inch tall or less, rolling dirt into the row with the cultivator will bury weeds and not harm crop plants. The depth and speed of the cultivator determine how much dirt is rolled. In loose dirt, you can experiment with the art by using a simple hoe, pulling it along the side of the row, and letting dirt flow in around the plants as the blade plows along. Even with just a hoe, you can weed a row quite swiftly this way. A few weeds will still come up around the crop plants, but not many.

Cultivators

Rows need not be wide to accommodate hand-pushed mechanical cultivators or the newer small motorized tiller-weeders. A hand-pushed wheel hoe of the Planet Jr. type needs only 8 inches of space between plants (although it is better to make the rows wider—at least a foot to allow for the expansion of the plants). The centuries-old Planet Jr. wheel

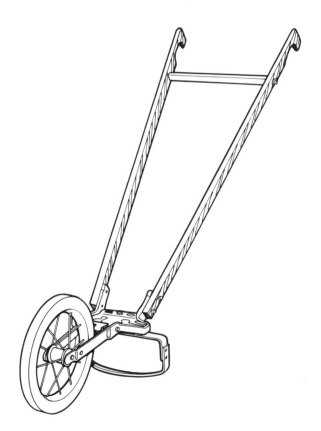

The Jupiter Wheel Hoe.

hoe is now called the Jupiter Wheel Hoe and can be found in many gardening catalogs. The handles come back at a lower angle to the wheels than most push hoes, making the hoe easier to push than other large wheel hoes, but both kinds are quite suitable to the task. Hilling attachments are available for all, and most of the shovel or tine types of cultivators will roll dirt into the row.

The small motorized tiller-weeders require hardly more than a foot of row space for passage. Mantis (Mantis Manufacturing Company, 1458 County Line Road, Huntingdon Valley, PA 19006) and Sunbird (Sunbird Products, R.D. #4, Box 462, Middlebury, VT 05753) are two well-known ones, and because of their current popularity, by the time you read this most of the tiller manufacturers will no doubt be out with their own versions.

If you have a conventional tiller for primary cultivation, you can also use it for weeding as crops grow. By removing the outer tines, you can use it to weed between narrower rows. Most conventional tillers have optional hiller blades that not only roll dirt to cover weeds effectively, but also to do more pronounced hilling, as for potatoes.

CHAPTER 10

LANDSCAPE WALLS AND WALKS

An old jingle tells the low-maintenance story effectively when it comes to garden, terrace, or other freestanding walls you might wish to accent your landscape with:

Wood or metal, cheap and fast;
But only masonry will last.

Masonry and Stone versus Everything Else for Walls

We Americans have never taken to stone walls too readily, Robert Frost and New England to the contrary. We associate them with wealth and/or lots of labor. When we want a wall for privacy around our homes, we naturally lean toward wood or sometimes give in to the ugliest temptation of all—a nice chain link fence filled in with those god-awful plastic or aluminum strips.

Wood and metal may be faster, but are they really cheaper? It is hard to quote a price for chain link fencing with aluminum fillers because the fence is available in a number of gauges—at least 9, 10, 11, and 12—and the thicker the gauge, the higher the price. Then one must count in the innumerable posts, top rails, end rails, post caps, end rail caps, tension bars, tension bands, etc., which significantly add to the cost. But with the aluminum fillers for privacy woven into the chain link fencing, and using the heavier, longer-lasting gauges, the price is over $8 a running foot easily, and that's not counting installation charge—nor your labor if you do the work, nor the concrete you ought to put around the end and corner posts in the ground.

Solid wood privacy fencing—stockade fences as they are called, or solid picket fences—is not really cheap either, and the quality of the wood is questionable. For example, I'm looking at a mail-order catalog that offers a stockade fence of "western white wood stained to look like red cedar." There happens to be no such species of wood called white wood. So what is it? Mostly white cedar, I would hope, but white cedar is not specified as it is in the posts, so you don't know. Also offered, a little cheaper, is a fencing called "mixed northern white woods." Obviously the wood could be anything and therefore not likely to last very long unless you continually paint it or stain it. And even then I wouldn't bet that the $5 to $6 a foot these privacy walls are going to cost you, installation and painting not included, is worth it. If you can find good red cedar fencing, split out of enduring heartwood, you are going to pay quite a bit more.

The point is that even if we disallow the greater beauty of stone or masonry, does it cost that much more to build something that can last forever? I can't say what a masonry wall will cost per running foot since materials vary in price so much, and much depends on whether you do the work yourself, but believe me, there are used bricks available that will cost you much less than wood or chain link fencing, and laying up bricks is not necessarily as hard a job as installing a chain link fence. Just slower. And even if the wood fence is faster and easier, you will do it three times in your lifetime, not once as with brick.

Of course there are practical objections to masonry. As a garden wall, it is awfully permanent, and you may want to move your garden. Some people move gardens around like they do furniture. To each his own. A masonry wall around a terrace or patio may be more practical. In either case, the rewards are worth it: You achieve protection from prying eyes, rambling dogs, raucous noise, and cold and damaging winds, to a degree no other kind of wall can provide. Indeed, centuries ago gardeners learned that stone or brick walls actually soaked up heat during the day and gave it off on chilly nights to protect tender plants espaliered against them.

Since building a masonry wall is considered such a laborious proposition, allow me an offbeat but contradictory example. Twelve years ago I dry-stacked bricks into a circular little wall for a wishing well in our yard. I did not install any kind of foundation under it. The first two or three courses of brick are belowground. That's all. On the inside of the circular wall, the bricks touch the ones contiguous to them. On the outside, they are about 2 inches or more apart, straddling the two bricks immediately below. In twelve years of extreme freezing and thawing, that circular wall has hardly budged. I have had to adjust a brick that shifted slightly out of place only three or four times. Some of the stability of the wishing well wall has to do with the circular shape. Shifting, if any, tends to work the bricks tighter together in a circle rather than farther apart. I know this is true because, unlike the wishing well, the square fireplace I built of dry-stacked bricks nearby (also without a foundation) requires some yearly realignment of the bricks.

But the point is that in a freestanding wall, much can be forgiven the amateur builder, and his wall will still stand. You certainly want some kind of foundation under a wall that is going to be at least 6 feet tall for privacy. But you do not need a formidable house footer. If it extends below the frost line (and that is the main point), the foundation need not be solid concrete or mortared masonry units. You can pile in rocks solidly, or dry-stack bricks or concrete blocks level and straight and that will do. (Frank Lloyd Wright once argued that in some situations, gravel would be a better footer than solid concrete because if thawing and heaving did occur, the movement would be absorbed by the gravel, not transferred to the house frame. Some of the older information on building field walls of stone appears to support that conclusion.) Once above ground level, if the wall is kept plumb, you can dry-stack bricks, crisscrossing alternate double courses, or dry-stack a single course of decorative cement blocks, and you will be

The regular curves make these serpentine brick walls surprisingly strong, despite the fact they are only one wythe thick.

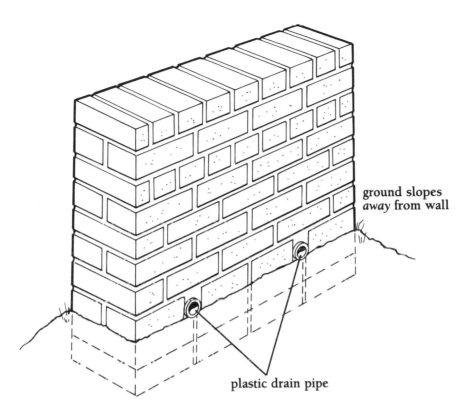

ground slopes *away* from wall

plastic drain pipe

Freestanding brick wall.

amazed how long they will remain stable. You might say that mortar's most advantageous purpose is to keep passersby from walking off with your bricks or blocks! I'm not necessarily suggesting you actually build the wall this way, but just want to impress upon you that if that foundation is solid and the wall plumb, you will be forgiven minor mistakes in your mortaring job.

Mortar does not add as much strength in a freestanding wall as you think. A family near Findlay, Ohio, has a serpentine brick wall of just one course of brick along one side of their property—modeled after the serpentine wall on the University of Virginia campus that Thomas Jefferson supposedly designed. It is not so much the mortar that holds that seemingly fragile wall so strongly, but the shape—the curvature, as in my wishing well wall—that exerts integral strength. It works in much the same way the key in an arch is held in place by the arch and in turn gives great stability to the arch.

After making sure that the foundation reaches below frost line and plumb, you need to make sure water does not linger in the wall or against it. The ground should slope slightly away from the wall. If the wall is on a slope, provide small openings through the wall at ground level every 10 feet or so to allow runoff water to run on through. Short lengths of plastic pipe will do. Mortared retaining walls should have the same kind of base drainage. It is also important that the top of the wall is sealed (mortared), tilted to the side slightly, or otherwise shielded from rain so water runs off, not down into the wall where it might freeze and cause cracking.

Fencing

Several years ago I did a little private survey into what I call The Things That Really Matter in the Local Community. Once past the usual subjects of family gossip, the number one cause of anxiety and crisis among neighbors, whether I surveyed in Iowa or Ohio or anywhere else, was their neighbors' dogs. Dog owners, despite all kinds of ordinances, will not confine their dogs to their own property and when they do, the damn things howl all night. There is no easy solution to this problem. But you can build a dog-proof fence around your property if there's not an ordinance against that, too. Fencing is not low-maintenance landscaping, but it can contribute to low-maintenance sanity.

A second observation about fences: If you do not have anything to pen in or pen out, why do you want a fence? Decorative fencing, for example those split rail fences, have a life of about 12 years before repairs become necessary and are just one more thing you have to dodge with the mower.

Wrought-iron fencing is both decorative and practical, but very expensive even if it does last forever. But because old wrought-iron fence appears to be about as expensive or more so than new, you probably can get your money back should you ever decide to sell any that you buy now. If you have the money to spend, it is probably a good investment.

Next best in terms of low maintenance and price is a good chain link fence. A free instruction booklet on how to install chain link comes with your purchase so be sure to ask for it. You'll need it. If you can afford it, professional installation is a wise investment. Haggle for a good price.

A regular livestock fence in suburb or city will cause more palpitations among the neighbors than howling, loose-running dogs. But in the country it is a good buy if you know how to use a woven wire fence stretcher and buy top-of-the-line fencing. Top-of-the-line fencing should have 9-gauge top and bottom wires and no smaller than 11-gauge for the other wires. For keeping dogs in or out, 6-inch rather than 12-inch mesh is stronger. The wire should be heavily galvanized and contain copper to fight rust. A 330-foot roll of this wire (20 rods) will cost around $120 to $130, and the next heaviest about $80 to $90. From long experience, I can tell you the extra $40 is worth it in terms of long life. For directions on proper installation of livestock fence, see my book *Gene Logsdon's Practical Skills* (Rodale Press, 1985).

Sidewalks and Driveways

Concrete is better than blacktop for low maintenance since blacktop should be recoated with a sealer every few years. Mortared stone and masonry walks equal concrete in low maintenance but are slightly more laborious to build. Gravel and unmortared masonry or stone make rather high-maintenance walks and drives because weeds and grass coming up through them must be constantly controlled. Gravel drives need periodic, even yearly, applications of new gravel, unless at least a foot of large (fist-size) stone is laid down first. Even then, in areas of freezing and thawing and heavy rains, the gravel will continue to sink slowly into the ground. There is a general feeling among quarrymen that crushed stone, the individual fragments of which are more squarish than round, holds up better than round, pebbly gravel. Another maintenance problem with gravel or crushed stone is that car tires dig ruts and throw stones out to the perimeter of the drive. Also, when clearing snow, we inevitably throw some of the gravel on the lawn. In any case, gravel or loose stone drives have to be leveled occasionally.

Despite their drawbacks, gravel is about the only choice for a long drive unless money is no object. Excavate about a foot and lay down a bed of fist-sized stone, then surface with about 3 inches of gravel or No. 7 crushed stone. The driveway surface must be higher than the surrounding terrain, and if it blocks the natural flow of runoff rain, some sort of drainage pipe should be installed through the drive to carry away water.

In most urban and suburban situations, your driveway comes with the house and invariably is concrete or blacktop. If it is an old concrete drive, with enough cracks in it to merit repair, the best choice is to resurface it with blacktop, just as engineers are doing on highways. Part of the cost of blacktop is in preparing a foundation under it, and in this case, the old concrete drive serves the purpose.

Concrete Sidewalks

Blacktop, or hot mix as it is sometimes called, is almost always installed by professionals. But invariably, sidewalks are built by homeowners since the skill and time involved are perceived to be minor. Sidewalks involving concrete are not really all that "minor," and a local contractor who specializes in that kind of work at a reasonable price might be a wise investment. If you proceed on your own, here are some general guidelines—which also apply to pouring a concrete driveway:

• A 4-inch slab is thick enough. For forms, use regular 2 × 4s raised just slightly above the soil surface.

• Concrete can be poured right on a good, solid earthen surface. There is no need to put down a gravel bed first, although many people do. If you do, wet and tamp the gravel down well so it settles and doesn't draw water out of the concrete.

• To minimize cracking, lay down standard reinforcing wire mesh before pouring the concrete. For a driveway, you can use the full width of a standard roll, but for a walk, the roll will have to be cut to fit. You will pay more per foot for nonstandard pieces, but if the hardware store does the cutting for you, the trade-off is not bad. It takes good wire cutters to cut the stuff—a tool most homeowners don't own. Ideally, the reinforcing mesh should be positioned so there are 2 inches of concrete under it and 2 above, but don't worry if you don't get it just right—it's very difficult to do exactly.

Unroll the wire, hold it down flat with bricks or stones if necessary. The natural rumple of the mesh will cause it to run unevenly through the slab, from perhaps a little too low to a little too high, which is fine. The only problem you must guard against is the tendency for the mesh to rumple up above the concrete surface. If it sticks up when you are troweling, you can generally push it down and it will stay. If the ends of the mesh wires stick up, you can bend them and then push them back into the concrete.

• You need a steel trowel, an edger, and a groover to finish a concrete sidewalk attractively. A wood floater is nice to have to go over the wet concrete first; it will settle the large aggregates. But you can accomplish that task with the steel trowel in a pinch.

• Rather than trowel the surface smooth, which results in a "slippery when wet" walk, you can texture it with an old broom after the surface is semisolid.

• Use the groover to put a contraction joint in the walk about every 6 feet. Use a board for a straightedge and run the groove at right angles to the sidewalk's edges. These grooves give the concrete space to move instead of cracking, or as most concrete workers say wryly: "If the slab does crack, it cracks in the groove and you don't notice it."

• Expansion joints instead of grooves (⅜-inch-thick strips of wood) aren't usually necessary in normal-size sidewalks but are advisable in drives or terraces. A really neat way to provide expansion joints in terraces is to use 2 × 4 redwood planks as dividers between various square or rectilinear sections of concrete. If from heartwood, the dividers will last a very long time and make a very attractive design as they age to a silvery gray.

• After the concrete sets up but is still moist and workable, run the edger down both sides of the walk to round the edge and smooth it. The edger leaves a margin of about 2½ inches, which adds a decorative touch.

• As mentioned earlier, be sure the sidewalk does not rise much more than an inch above the surrounding yard so that you don't have to worry about hitting it with the lawn mower blade.

Variations on Concrete Walks and Drives

There are many, many ways you can combine concrete and stone or masonry units to make attractive sidewalks. Embedding bricks or slate or whatever into wet concrete is not, however, as easy to do as it would appear. It is difficult to scrunch bricks, for example, into a bed of wet concrete and get them even and evenly mortared. The proper way to do the job is to pour about 2 inches of concrete down and then set the stones or bricks in it. Then fill the joints with mortar. You can, as some professionals do, squeeze mortar out into the cracks through a bag that has a funnel opening at one end. Or you can simply use a large tin can you have flattened slightly at the top to make a pour spout. You'd better have a steady hand for these last two. Another method is to sprinkle a mixture of dry sand and mortar (two parts sand, one part mortar) over the stone or masonry surface, sweep the dry mortar into the cracks, then soak it with a *gentle* spray of water.

Another alternative is to make the concrete surface look like flagstone or brick. You can use the pattern forms described in chapter 2 to imprint a brick or tilelike surface into the wet concrete. Or you can lay out your own design of irregularly shaped flagstones. Make a jointer out of a piece of ¾-inch copper pipe that is about 18 inches long to fake the joints in your irregularly shaped "flagstones." Bend about 4 inches of the piece of pipe out to a 60-degree angle at one end, and a 60-degree angle in the opposite direction at the other end (see the illustration). One end is your handle, the other your marker. Of course, you can use a regular jointer if you have one, but it will make a joint a little too narrow for the space usually left between flagstones. Mark your "joints" in the wet concrete surface after the concrete has begun to solidify. Then at the proper time, trowel the

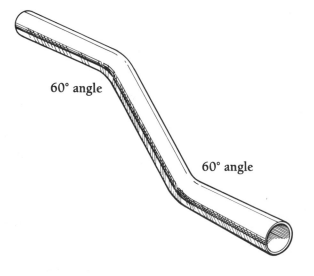

60° angle

60° angle

My homemade jointer.

whole surface, going lightly over your joint marks. When the troweling is complete, smooth over your joints again and sweep out any loose concrete with a whisk broom. The walk will look remarkably like flagstones.

For driveways, sidewalks, and terraces, there are on the market some very beautiful concrete surfaces (mentioned briefly in chapter 6) that mimic closely the beauty of stone, brick, or tile at a lower price. Concrete block "pavers" in many colors, textures, and shapes are now being produced by larger concrete block manufacturers throughout the country. Although pavers have found a ready market from institutions and businesses willing to spend the money for a very distinctive look, they're not that terribly expensive for a home installation, so long as you don't have an unusually long or wide drive to pave. Check with the nearest concrete block factory or write National Concrete Masonry Association (2302 Horse Pen Road, Herndon, VA 22070).

Even more radically beautiful are special patented concrete products that mimic stone and masonry for walls, floors, walkways, and driveways. One company that makes these is a firm that I mentioned earlier: the Bowmanite Corporation (see Appendix A). Another is Coronado Products,

Concrete pavers mimic stone and flagstone in this outdoor path.

Even indoors, concrete pavers look surprisingly good and much like real tile.

Inc. (1325 6th Avenue North, Nashville, TN 37208-0568), although most of Coronado's facsimiles are for interior walls and floors.

These surfaces are installed only by specially trained and equipped crews, and with an almost unlimited choice of color, texture, and design. It is hard to believe concrete could be so beautiful. Bowmanite even has for sale a concrete paving it calls Solarpave, through which water from a swimming pool or whatever can be circulated and heated by the sun, for a price the company says is competitive with rooftop panels. Another new idea from Bowmanite is Grasscrete, a "porous, structural concrete pavement, cast in place, that drains stormwater runoff and produces oxygen like a lawn." Grass can grow in strips right up through this pavement!

Unmortared Walks

The mention of grass brings us back to the typical unmortared sidewalk and garden path most of us settle for because of low cost—and through which we try in vain to keep grass from growing. But if the following guidelines are kept in mind, a homemade unmortared stone or masonry walk will prove to be quite low maintenance.

1. Instead of a conventional walk, use the "stepping stone" idea. Larger flattish stones or precast concrete units are embedded in the lawn more or less irregularly and individually. Since there are no cracks between the stepping stones but perhaps as much as a foot of space, there is no upkeep, no precision to be enforced on nature. You just mow over the stepping stones and don't worry about them. If one or the other heaves up a bit in time, just dig out a little dirt from under it and resettle.

2. For a standard, continuous walk, it is important to first lay down a foundation. Excavate about a foot of dirt, then fill with about 6 inches of cinders or gravel, then 3 inches of sand, more or less as needed to bring the brick or stones you are setting in up to grade. Then with bricks or stones in place, sweep in sand to fill the cracks between them.

3. Crucial to the low-maintenance success of the walk, especially if it is brick, is edging. Unmortared stone or masonry walks tend to creep apart

Stepping stones make an almost instant maintenance-free walkway. With a heavy mulch like this surrounding them, mowing and trimming around them is unnecessary.

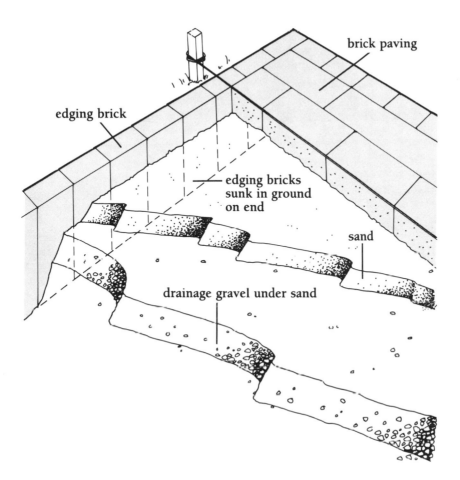

An unmortared brick path.

brick paving

edging brick

edging bricks
sunk in ground
on end

sand

drainage gravel under sand

with freezing and thawing, and to prevent that, you need to sink a border along both sides 6 to 8 inches deep. Bricks set on end in the ground make a good edging. Flat, longish stones will work as well. Landscape ties that are embedded a few inches in the ground and held in place with spikes driven through holes first drilled in the ties make tight and neat borders.

4. Really long-lasting unmortared walks owe their endurance against heaving to good drainage. The classic walk or garden path has a tile drain underneath the gravel bed, but in a typical suburban or urban situation today, there may be no way to outlet such a tile. The gravel itself improves drainage. The walk should in addition have a grade or slope to it so water flows away and never stands on or next to it.

Part 3
The Low-Maintenance Interior

CHAPTER 11

FLOORS AND

FLOORCOVERINGS

Since floors take the most wear and tear in the house interior, the choice of flooring materials is of high priority for the low-maintenance house. The first consideration in making that choice is the one usually considered last, if at all, and it applies not only to floors, but to the rest of the house interior as well: One must have clearly in mind the difference between quality as expressed by durability and low maintenance, and value as expressed by fashion and taste. Especially when remodeling a house, these two aspects can become confused and money can be wasted or at least misspent.

A true story most recently reported in *Remodeling World* (November 1985), a most helpful magazine for owner-builders and remodelers by the way, illustrates the point. When the Pennsylvania Academy of Fine Arts was remodeled recently, architect Hyman Myers discovered that the white plaster columns in the interior galleries covered ornate Victorian cast-iron columns. The plaster was laboriously and painstakingly removed and the original pillars repainted to their original colors, the result hailed as a triumph of authenticity over sham.

No doubt. But the original columns were covered because they came to be considered if not downright ugly, at least unfashionable. I can just hear an interior decorator at the turn of the century justifying the plastering of the ornate columns by saying that all that blue, gold, and rust red "metal gingerbread" detracted attention from the paintings and that simple clean white columns would be better. Actually the change came only gradually. The columns were originally installed in 1876 when ornate cast iron was fashionable. By 1890, human nature being what it is, society tired of the columns' playful colors, and they were overpainted with a dull, uniform brown. By 1910, dull brown had had its day, and the lower half of each pillar was encased in plaster. Twenty years later the top halves of the pillars were also plastered over, no doubt to the applause of Moderne and Art Deco stylists then ruling the world of interior design.

Interestingly, the cast-iron pillars might not have been discovered were it not for Hyman's hunches. Only *after* the columns were restored were records found indicating their existence. Although their entombment was certainly a public event, people who were alive at the time it happened didn't record the event in newspapers or magazines, or in any way that would have passed the information on to the next generation. Memory of the event was buried in plaster with them—a harsh commentary on the instability of the community that runs our public institutions. You can be sure—as sure as night follows day—that the interior galleries of that museum will not stay as they are now, restored authentically. If the building endures, changing fashion will again dictate something different. Ornate cast iron fascinates us today because it has become uncommon. In 1890, traditionalists were making the same kind of snide remarks about it as traditionalists do today about plastic and fiberglass.

Remember this when you remodel or build your home. Books and magazines will exhort you to hire interior designers and architects to advise you. Some of them know structural principles you need to follow (carpenters and builders know them better), but mostly they will tell you what is in "good taste" today. They will reflect the bias and opinion that pumps vitality into today's trends. Some 20 years from now, the next generation of trendies will champion other fashions.

For example, there is now a sort of minitrend back to real linoleums to authenticate houses built when linoleum was king of the practical floor coverings. You could argue the pros and cons of linoleum forever. For sure, the kind of mastic they often used in the '40s was the eighth wonder of the world, as you know if you have ever tried to take up off the floor old linoleum from that period. It is easier to remove the whole underlayment! The point is, regardless of style or taste, sheet vinyl is lower maintenance than linoleum, if for no other reason than that you don't have to clean and wax it as often.

Listen to your own heart. What *you* think is beautiful is as worthy of respect as what Frank Lloyd Wright thought was beautiful—especially if you don't have to spend your spare time cleaning, painting, waxing, polishing, or repairing it.

The second consideration about floors and flooring (that also applies to walls, ceilings, etc.) is whether to do the work yourself. Interior work on a house often falls to the homeowner because once in the house, he or she can undertake projects in spare time, substituting "free" labor for cash. As a general rule, amateurs should be able to lay floorcoverings that come in small pieces—tiles—following directions that accompany the tiles and possibly renting equipment from the floorcovering dealer. Sheet coverings—6-, 9-, 12-, and 15-foot rolls of vinyl for example—require a little more savvy (although maybe less equipment). Basically, however, if you can measure accurately you can handle either job.

Compare the price of the flooring if you do it and if the dealer's crew or an independent professional does it. Then consider the fact that the professional's seams most likely won't lift or curl as soon as yours will, if at all. Also consider that the professional flooring contractor will make sure the subfloor is smooth and solid as need be so that hammer dimples and other bumps and gouges in the underlayment won't start showing through the vinyl floorcovering in a year or so, or that ceramic tiles won't start cracking on the grout lines and popping up. Put a value as you see it on those avoidances of maintenance and subtract that from the price you pay to hire out the installation work. The difference, a subjective one to be sure, might just show you that hiring out the work makes more sense in the long run.

Subfloors and Underlayments

For low maintenance, the subfloor is as important as the floor-covering. If you are laying a floor on a basement concrete slab, moisture from below may be a problem—especially if a vapor barrier was not installed under the slab. One way to solve that problem is to apply mastic to the cleaned concrete and then lay down a sheet of plastic vapor barrier. Then nail furring strips through the vapor barrier to the concrete, using hardened concrete nails. At this point, if you want to insulate the floor, which is an excellent idea, cut pieces of ¾-inch or less rigid foam insulation to fit between the furring strips (which are ¾ inch). Overlay strips and foam with another layer of ½-inch rigid foam. Then screw the plywood underlayment through the insulation to the furring and you are ready to lay the floorcovering, having in the meantime raised the floor's insulative value from an R-value of about 1 to one of about 12.

On aboveground wood floors, preparation of the subfloor is even more important to the durability of the floorcovering. For ceramic tile and other grouted tiles, the subfloor must be solid—no give in it—or the grout lines might crack and individual tiles work loose. Normally, the joists under the floor will be sound, but of course if they are not, they must replaced. The plywood subfloor, hopefully ⅝ inch thick, should be renailed with ring shank nails wherever any give is apparent. If you are laying heavy slate, consult with a carpenter to make sure the joists are hefty enough to bear the weight.

If you are laying new floor over old linoleum or vinyl, the old floorcovering must be throughly cleaned of old wax and dirt so the mastic will adhere to it. All loose seams need to be cut back. All bumps need to be sanded smooth, holes or gouges filled with patching compound, and loose nails removed. All these flaws on the floor surface will show through new resilient floorcovering after awhile if not smoothed away. In some instances, it is wise to add another underlayment of ⅜-inch plywood over the old floor if this does not raise the floor too high.

Wherever there's a likelihood that water will be spilled on the floor, like bathroom and entranceway floors, use exterior-grade plywood, good side up. Particleboard, flakeboard, and waferboard might swell too much in such circumstances and crack the grout. Really quality subfloors under grouted tiles are at least 1¼ inch thick including underlayment, and they are fastened down with ring shank nails every 6 inches on the joists. Allow a narrow crack between plywood panels (1/32 to 1/16 inch) for expansion, especially next to walls.

There is a new brick flooring—actually a brick veneer—that needs no special subflooring. This Pee Dee brick veneer (Deiner Brick, P.O. Box 130, Park Avenue and Cuthbert Road, Collingswood, NJ 08108) is installed with "crystals"—sharp ceramic sand—instead of mastic. The crystals and the ½-inch brick veneer can be installed without a special subflooring because the crystals allow the brick to float without cracking. A two-ply layer of felt is installed first, then the brick veneer, then the crystals. A final coat of silicone sealer is put over all. The installation is supposed to be easy for homeowners because the bricks can be cut and arranged before being set permanently in place.

Ceramic-Tile Floors

For low maintenance, ceramic tile is hard to beat both for durability and low maintenance, and today, for the variety of colors, textures, and designs you can choose from. Because of their relatively higher costs, ceramic tiles today are usually limited to bathroom walls and countertops, if used at all. But if you're willing to spend some more money, install them in floors, too; you'll get your money's worth out of them. Ceramic tile may break, or come loose, it never wears out. New techniques in decorating with ceramic tile now give you choices for almost any part of the house, including beautiful pattern tiles for decorator accents.

For floors, ceramic tiles carry various "abrasive-resistance ratings," which guide you as to choice. A moderate traffic area can get by with a rating of 2, for example, but a heavily traveled hall or foyer needs a 3 or better. For bathroom floors, slip-resistant and moisture-proof tiles are needed. Ceramic tiles are baked clay and when baked hot enough, they absorb practically no moisture at all, especially those made from the highest refined clays and fired at temperatures over 2,000°F. These are referred to as impervious tile. Fully vitrified tile, the next classification downward, will not absorb more than 3 percent water, which is acceptable for even wet locations. Semivitreous tile absorbs from about 5 to 7 percent water, and nonvitreous tile something more than that. But even nonvitreous can be laid in wet locations *if no freezing will occur there,* and it should be laid in mortar over a moisture barrier.

Ceramic tile may be glazed or unglazed. Unglazed tile is usually of earth tones—the colors of the clay itself—that run all the way through the tile. Glazed tile has a baked-on surface—a glass surface that is smooth and easy to clean. Glazing allows an almost unlimited number of colors and designs in ceramic tile.

There are three general kinds of ceramic tile, as discussed below.

QUARRY TILES

These are unglazed. Their earthy tones, mostly reddish, go all through the tiles. They are formed by extrusion of natural clay or shale through a die and are wire-cut at proper intervals. In size they range from about 3 inches square up to 12 inches square and cost from $2 to $3 a square foot. Other geometric shapes are available. Quarry tiles are stain resistant, but not considered stain-proof. They are very strong, hard, and semivitreous, with a water absorption rate of 5 percent or less.

CERAMIC MOSAIC TILES

These are what everyone thinks of when ceramic tile is mentioned. Mosaic tiles are rather expensive and so their floor use is limited for most of us. They may be porcelain or natural clay and come in small sizes—as small as ¾ inch square up to 4 inches square. They are almost always arranged on larger pieces of fabric or paper for easy handling. Some are glazed, some unglazed, and the styles designed for floors contain an abrasive additive to make them less slippery. To appreciate the beauty as well as the low maintenance possible with mosaic tile, write for American Olean's catalog (1000 Cannon Avenue, P.O. Box 271, Lansdale, PA 19446-0271) or *The Ceramic Tile Manual* available for $21 plus shipping from the Ceramic Tile Institute (700 North Virgil Avenue, Los Angeles, CA 90029).

PAVER TILES

Paver tiles can be glazed or unglazed, porcelain or natural clay. For the unglazed, the price starts at about $2 a square foot and goes up, considerably, in the porcelain pavers. Ceramic pavers are formed in molds and generally have more precise edges and dimensions than quarry tile.

A Word or Two in Support of Concrete Floors

Like concrete walls, the tendency is to cover concrete floors with something whether it is necessary or not, especially when the house is a split-level and the lower level with its concrete floor is used for everyday living space. Concrete is not necessarily uglier than the vinyl tile put over it and can serve as a cheap, permanent, zero-maintenance floor itself. As Alex Wade says in his book *30 Energy-Efficient Houses . . . You Can Build* (Rodale Press, 1977), "A nicely troweled concrete slab makes a perfectly serviceable finished floor. A coat of clear polyurethane varnish will make it easier to clean and a few colorful area rugs add the final touch." The slab will also radiate heat well if you don't cover it all with a rug.

A professional can put a finish on concrete as smooth as glass. Polishing and waxing can give it a deep blue-gray sheen, or you could add tints to give it a brownish or blackish shine. After all, terrazzo is just a concrete floor with marble or special stone chips in it instead of gravel, the surface then ground and polished. It is possible to imprint designs into a concrete floor to make it look like slate or stone, too. (See chapter 6 on patios and chapter 10 on walks, driveways, and other landscaping features for further discussions on the decorative uses of concrete.)

Mexican paver tiles, as they are called, are not precisely sized, but are more or less handmade and quite popular now due to the yen for the "country" look. Often the wet clay is rolled out with a rolling pin right onto a hard clay surface and cut into 12-inch-square pieces with big "cookie cutters." Left to dry outside in the sun, some actually show tracks of chickens in the finished surface, though I suspect enterprising Mexican artisans encourage their barnyard fowl in this droll caper because it makes the tiles sell better. The tiles are often fired in homemade kilns, some of which ought to receive grand prizes for originality. For example, one "kiln" I've heard about was actually an old car body. The inside of the car was loaded with tile and then the car was covered with old tires. The tires were set on fire and the heat of the fire baked the tiles. (I wonder what the EPA would have to say about that.) Mexican pavers absorb water readily and should be given a silicone sealer coating. Somewhat cheaper than other ceramic tiles, they are excellent for patios and foyers, but not recommended for bathrooms.

Laying Ceramic Tiles Yourself

Instructions come with boxes of tile that tell you exactly how to install them—better information than I can give here because it will bear specifically on the particular kind of tile you have selected. But I can add a few words in general.

In laying out lines on the floor to guide you in setting the tile straight and square, remember that no floor is perfectly square. Generally, a center line is drawn from the middle of the doorway perpendicular to it across the floor. All square measurements are then taken from this line. You can mark off a line square to it along adjacent walls. After that, nail a straight batten along two adjacent walls, forming a true right angle just out from the wall. If the battens can be arranged so that the tiles installed inside them come out even, in other words, without cutting, so much the better. The tiles are then laid, the battens removed, and the uneven portions along the walls filled in with the cut tiles.

Another way to lay out a floor, especially on a small irregular floor like a bathroom, is simply to make a trial layout of the tiles on the dry floor, making appropriate guide marks on the floor when the tiles are in place. For looks, all square measurements should be taken from the center line down the middle of the doorway, as in the previous method. This is a foolproof way for a beginner, especially if he or she divides the small room into smaller portions, like the space around the toilet, the entryway, the space between vanity and shower, etc. A good square is about the only tool needed for this placement and measurement.

The cut tile should always be up next to the wall where the trim will hide the uneven line. Any "cheating" you need to do to adjust your square lines to the unsquare walls should also be done at the wall where the trim will hide it. Where the tiles form a definite pattern and it takes, say, 17½ inches from one wall to the other, it is a good idea for a balanced look to

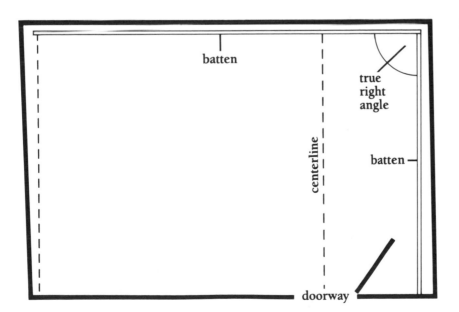

Squaring up a floor for tiling.

cut ¼ inch off the tiles along both opposite walls rather than ½ inch off the tiles along just one side.

To cut tiles, you need a snap cutter and a nibbler for taking off small bites or especially for cutting curves in a tile. You can rent both from the person who sells you the tiles. An ordinary glass cutter can be used to cut straight lines in place of a snap cutter; score and break the tile as you would a piece of glass. You also need an abrasive stone to smooth off rough cut edges, plus trowels, a straightedge, perhaps a chalk line (in lieu of battens), and a sponge or two.

I've already mentioned the importance of the mastic and grout, since generally speaking it is these materials that fail, never the ceramic tiles themselves. The really classic way to install ceramic tile is in a bed of mortar 1 inch thick, and it is still the best way for a wet location. Most tiles, however, are being laid in epoxy mastic today, since the new mastics (like Latapoxy 210) are suitable even for bathroom floors and are very easy to apply. They usually come in three containers: an epoxy resin, a hardener, and a blend of cement and sand. These are all mixed together according to the instructions given and applied evenly to the subfloor with a trowel that has notched edges. The notches leave the mastic in little ridges that makes seating the tiles securely an easy task.

Once the mastic is spread, the tiles are pressed into it, allowing 1/16- to ⅛-inch space between for grout joints. (Some brands of tile come with separate spacers to insert between the tiles; other types come with built-in spacers—tabs on the edges of the tiles that are pushed together tightly during installation and then covered with grouting. American Olean [see Appendix A for address] is one company that makes tiles with built-in spacers.) If the mastic keeps bulging up in the joints, you have applied too much of it to the floor. Excess mastic must be rooted out of the cracks with a nail or similar tool before it dries.

After the mastic dries, apply grout over the tiles, squishing and packing it into the cracks. Many floor contractors add latex to their grout to make it spread easier. They also dampen the tiles first with a sponge for the same reason. Use a rubber trowel or window squeegee to apply the grout. Remove the excess with a wet sponge. Make the grout joints even and slightly indented with an old toothbrush handle or similar tool. Dig out any grout that has gotten down into the expansion joint between subfloor and wall (see "Subfloors and Underlayments" above). Caulk that crack after the floor is finished and dry.

Unless directions say otherwise, you should apply a silicone sealer to the grout joints. Your ceramic-tile floor is only as good as its grout.

Sources of ceramic tile include American Olean Tile Company (1000 Cannon Avenue, P.O. Box 271, Lansdale, PA 19446-0271); Olympia Floor and Wall Tile (1000 Lawrence Avenue, Toronto, ON M6B 4A8, Canada); and Elon, Inc., which is an especially good source for imported tiles, including Mexican ones (150 East 58th Street, New York, NY 10155).

Ceramic Tile for Thermal Mass

If you are building a passive solar house or addition to your house, you have another reason for taking a close look at ceramic tile even though it may cost more than other floor coverings. Ceramic tile is much better than carpet, vinyl, or wood in terms of heat storage. Tile both absorbs and conducts. Therefore, it soaks up sunlight streaming onto the floor and conducts it on into the concrete subfloor. At night, as the room cools down, the heat in the concrete easily radiates from the tile into the room. This is true of other masonry floors as well, but none of them have quite the conductivity that fine ceramic tile has.

Resilient Floorcoverings

Innovations in resilient floorcoverings increase almost monthly, with vinyl leading the way. True linoleum, despite its higher maintenance, is enjoying something of a comeback. It is still made by the Krommenie Company in Holland and distributed by the L. D. Brinkman Company (1251 South Rockefeller Avenue, Ontario, CA 91745). Cork flooring is comfortable to stand on, absorbs sound well, and if you drop a dish on it, you might be lucky and the dish will bounce rather than break. But cork by all standards scores poorly for low maintenance. Rubber and synthetic rubber floorcoverings have their devotees, also. Both are excellent where a nonslip surface is desirable, absorb noises well, and are naturally cushioned. Rubber is resistant to most chemical spills. Synthetic rubbers like Noraplan Duo (Nora Flooring, 4201 Wilson Avenue, Madison, IN 47250) never need waxing.

But it is vinyl that makes most of the headlines these days in the resilient floorcovering world. New methods allow not only a seemingly limitless number of colors and patterns, but also almost perfect mimicry of wood, stone, marble, and other natural materials—you name it.

There are two main categories of vinyl sheet flooring and vinyl tiles: inlaid and printed or photogravure. Inlaid flooring is made up of many tiny bits of vinyl compressed together at high temperature. The color goes deeply into the material and can't wear off. Inlaid vinyls are rather stiff and hard—which is good for low maintenance—but makes them more difficult to install.

Photogravure vinyls, as the name indicates, have the patterns printed on them and are then overlaid with a clear layer of vinyl for protection. Most floorcoverings in this category have a layer of cushioning in them. They must be sealed at their seams with a special solvent that glues the two seams together to keep out moisture. Cushioned vinyl will show up deformities in the underlayment quicker than inlaid vinyls will, and although great improvements have been made, many householders still contend that they do not hold up as well as inlaids.

Both kinds can be purchased in so-called no-wax finishes. This does not mean no-work, however. After installation, the floor should be washed with hot water and a mild detergent, unless the vinyl carries instructions to the contrary. After that it needs regular mopping. After a few years, the flooring will lose some of its gloss and needs to be buffed occasionally. On some urethane-covered flooring you can restore the gloss with an acrylic floor dressing recommended by the manufacturer—wax won't set properly on urethane. Dirt will build up on no-wax floors despite mopping, especially if the surface pattern is textured. People who really hate to clean floors should buy flat matte surfaced vinyl.

Laying Resilient Tile Floorcoverings

Measuring for vinyl, rubber, cork, and other similar tile is done about the same way it is for ceramic tile. Tiles are easier to install than sheet floorcoverings for the amateur. However, from the standpoint of low maintenance, any resilient floorcovering is better in sheet form than in smaller tile pieces. Why? The more seams, the more maintenance. A floor that can be covered with a single piece from a 15-foot roll has no seams to curl up or to catch dirt and moisture.

But if an occasional tile does curl or buckle, it is at least easier to repair than sheet floorcovering. Vinyl will soften if heated (don't heat too much!). Direct a hair dryer, or heat lamp if you have one, on the curled up edge until the tile softens a bit. Then pry up the edge or corner with a knife or old screwdriver and direct the heat under the tile. Moisture is almost always the culprit and you want to dry the area under the tile completely. Then scrape and vacuum out all the dirt and old adhesive you can. When the underside is clean and dry, apply new adhesive and push the tile back in place. Weight it with something heavy until the adhesive sets.

If you have to replace the whole tile, begin by lifting a corner as described. Cut off the corner so you can work a stiff putty knife under the main part of the tile. Get it warm and soft with your hair dryer first. After removal, clean and dry the space under it, spread adhesive, and lay down the new tile. Butt the new tile at one edge up against the adjacent tile and push the tile straight down into place. Don't try to slide it in place. Spread the adhesive with a notched trowel—or an old saw blade. Use anything with a notched edge that will leave the surface of the adhesive slightly rippled.

A bubble or buckle in the tile—and this holds for sheet floorcovering too—either from moisture or a popped nail, should be softened with heat as above. Then cut a slit in it, removing the nail and/or dirt. Dry the area under the slit thoroughly, and push in adhesive. Weight down.

Getting a new tile to match your floor is difficult. Even the same design may not match in a new batch of tile. The wildest, but maybe best solution is to get some tiles totally different than those on the floor, replace the bad one and several good ones scattered appropriately around the room and call them, with a very straight face, accent tiles.

Laying Resilient Sheet Floorcoverings

Putting down sheet floorcoverings, like laying carpets, is slightly more difficult than laying individual tiles. But if you can measure accurately, you can do it. Armstrong (150 North Queen Street, Lancaster, PA 17604), a leading manufacturer of sheet vinyl and other floorcoverings, is so sure the do-it-yourselfer can lay sheet vinyl that if you use its "Trim and Fit" kit and make a goof while cutting or fitting, retail stores you deal with will replace both the flooring and the kit. While Armstrong was the first to make such an offer, now other flooring manufacturers sell similar kits with the same guarantee.

Essentially what you do with any sheet floorcovering is to make a pattern of the floor on felt paper that comes in 3-foot rolls, taping strips together to pattern the whole floor. You cut the felt roughly an inch away from the walls, cabinets, etc. This edge is not the pattern line. The actual pattern line is traced on the pattern using a square. The blade of the square has to be wide enough to extend from the wall over onto the pattern, and since the conventional square is 1½ inches wide, it will do that. With one side of the square's blade against the wall, you trace the wall's outline on the pattern on the other side of the blade, going all around the walls and cabinets and door frames. Every angle, however slight, needs to be recorded on the pattern.

Then the pattern is laid over the floorcovering, centered correctly, and the pattern line transferred back onto the floorcovering with the

Cutting and laying vinyl sheet flooring.

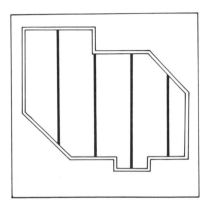
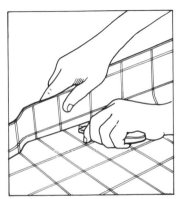

adhesive at seam

square, reversing the procedure by which you traced it on the pattern. If there must be a seam, cut the flooring so that the design matches on both sides of it.

Latex mastic is used to glue down the floorcovering, but epoxy must be used to glue down 3 inches of the flooring on either side of the seams, as per the instructions that come with most resilient vinyls today. After the first piece of flooring is glued in place with mastic, lift the seam edge and spread the epoxy underneath. Then spread another 3 inches of epoxy on the floor where the second strip will butt against the first. Apply the mastic for the rest of the second strip and then lay it down in place. If the second strip does not want to lie down flat at the seam, put a weight on it or tap the two seam edges together until the epoxy sets up. Instructions with your vinyl will cover all this in detail.

I am loath to give more detailed directions anyway, because likely as not they will be outdated very soon. A case in point is Armstrong's new type of vinyl flooring it refers to as "tension flooring." It is glued only around the edges and then it shrinks tightly onto the floor surface. Some kinds may even be stapled around the edge rather than glued, so that laying vinyl becomes quite similar to laying carpet.

Stone and Masonry Floors

Stone, especially slate, and masonry are so enduring, fireproof, and beautiful that many homeowners overlook minor disadvantages and are using them not only for foyers but living areas and even kitchens, where a dropped glass is a goner for sure. Some masonry floors do stain easily, but an acrylic or silicone sealer can prevent that problem fairly effectively. Modern scientific testing does not support the common belief that masonry floors don't "give" and therefore tire feet and legs more quickly, especially in the kitchen where one does so much standing. The National Bureau of Standards maintains after testing that the human body does not weigh enough to cause "give" in any of the so-called resilient floor-coverings: you'll get just as tired standing on a vinyl or wood floor as on a stone one. In any event, we should, without doubt, give more consideration to stone and masonry for the more traveled floors in our houses. For example, we persist in carpeting stairs where hard-wearing and beautiful marble would soon pay for itself.

Marble Floors

Marble floors are probably not practical in kitchens or anywhere else where spills are probable. Marble stains a little easier than many other

Removing Stains from Marble

The Marble Institute suggests using a poultice to remove stains from marble. Here's their proven method: Soak common chlorine laundry bleach or a 6 percent hydrogen peroxide solution (depending on the stain, see next paragraph) into a white absorbent material like paper towels, powdered chalk, talc, or molding plaster to form a paste. Apply the paste with a wood or plastic spatula or stick (anything that won't scratch marble) over the stain about ½-inch thick. Tape some plastic film (a plastic bag will do) over the area and allow your "bandage" to set for 48 hours. Moisten the poultice at the end of that period to control dust and remove it with your spatula, wiping the area clean with cool water and a clean cloth afterward. Repeat treatment if necessary.

In order to remove oil stains from dairy products, cosmetics, mustard, and the like, you must add acetone to the poultice. Use it only with good ventilation and keep it away from fire. Vegetable stains from leaves, tea, coffee, flowers, bird droppings, etc., require the hydrogen peroxide poultice treatment. Urine stains, if not wiped up right away, respond to the chlorine bleach treatment. Rust spots can be removed with a rust-removing product and scouring pad. If this fails, get in touch with a marble dealer for the appropriate chemical cleaner. In fact, commercial products are available for all the conditions discussed above, although they will cost more than if you make them up yourself. American Olean (see Appendix A for address) carries a full line of ceramic and marble cleaners.

good floorcoverings, if the spill is not wiped up immediately. Marble does wear a little over the years, but because the color goes all the way through, the wear is hardly noticeable until the second century of use. Marble can be slippery, but marble that's to be used for floors, stair treads and thresholds is given a honed surface rather than a polished one because it is not as slippery.

Slate Floors

Slate is the stone floorcovering of choice today. Individual slates are laid in thin-set mastic and the grout is applied later just as for ceramic tile. It is imperative to put a coat of silicone or acrylic sealer on the slates to keep them bright and easy to clean. In fact, a smart thing to do is to put sealer on before grouting, being careful not to spread the sealer into the joints. You'll find that any grout that you accidentally get on the slate will clean up a lot easier if the slate already has sealer on it. Then after the grout had dried, put on a second coat of sealer, being sure to seal the grout as well. After that, a yearly cleaning will do. At home we use Murphy's oil soap to clean our slate, and we don't get it done every year, either. After a scrubbing with that soap we apply a slate wax. Then any water or mud that dribbles off winter boots and shoes is easy to wipe up with a mop.

Concrete Floors

Not quite so well known as real slate, brick, tile, or granite are the new concrete floorcoverings made to look like them. They are laid like slate and though not as durable, they will last a long, long time. Jim Pardue, vice president of sales at Coronado Stone (Coronado Products, Inc., 1325 6th Avenue North, Nashville, TN 37208-0568), which makes concrete products of this nature, says that installed, the price of pavers that simulate brick, stone, or whatever runs about $4.50 a square foot. He recommends about a ½-inch joint between pavers. Each tile is handcrafted at Coronado, and one is hard put to believe they are really concrete when laid into beautiful floors. The tiles come with one coat of acrylic sealer on them and Pardue recommends that the homeowner apply a second coat before or after installation. After that, a periodic mopping with a common kitchen floor wax is all the care necessary. There are designs for every kind of decor and every room.

Brick Floors

Brick, like other masonry floors, works well in passive solar systems since it will soak up solar heat and give it back as heat throughout the night. At a cost that starts at about $1 a square foot, it is also among the cheapest of the durable, low-maintenance floors. Brick floors should be coated with a sealer, otherwise sulfates from the mortar might form a white powder on the surface. This is true of all masonry floors laid on concrete. A synthetic floor wax serves as a suitable sealer for this purpose.

Terrazzo Floors

Terrazzo, which is concrete with marble or granite pebbles in it that has been sanded down to a smooth finish, is probably the ultimate floor for low maintenance. It needs to be sealed or waxed, but there should never be any repair work required, barring an earthquake.

Wood Floors

We, of a woodland culture, speak lovingly of the "warmth" that a wood floor (or a wood anything) casts onto a house interior. This is mostly sales hype. We now have vinyl floors that so faithfully imitate wood grain and even come in narrow strips the same shape as wood floorboards, that any difference in "warmth" is entirely imaginary. Wood floors are basically high maintenance and only because of the new finishes that add a protective coating to them do they merit inclusion in this book.

Moisture is the bugaboo of wood, and I do not mean the occasional spills of water all floors are subjected to—or at least I mean those spills least of all. Rather, it is the swing from high humidity in summer to low humidity in winter (which will be discussed in more detail in chapter 13) that can be the biggest problem. White oak, hard maple, mesquite, and ironwood are floor woods so hard they will wear forever and then you can sand them down and they will wear forever again. But alternate moisture and dryness will swell and shrink them as easily as any other wood, and cupping and crowning (bulging upward) can occur. Thus, the wood should be treated with a varnish or sealant that makes it more or less impervious to the entrance of moisture. Often hardwood floors are sealed on the upper surface, but that doesn't do much for moisture coming from below.

Especially in new housing, it is unwise to lay raw wood floors down where concrete or plaster has not thoroughly dried, or after the wood has been exposed to humid weather. The fact that the hardwood floorboards have been kiln-dried makes no difference. Raw kiln-dried wood readily absorbs moisture on humid days and swells. If nailed down on a concrete or plaster subflooring that is not completely dry, the boards may cup. Then you need to sand them down flat. Then, after the house dries out and is heated up its first winter, the floorboards shrink and pull down at the joints, causing the boards to crown, necessitating another sanding and refinishing.

The safest and generally more expensive route (up to about $5 per square foot) is to buy prefinished hardwood floorboards, or have the bundles of boards stored at normal house heat and humidity for a month or so before installation. The latter course is much more easily accomplished in remodeling than when building new. For both unfinished and prefinished hardwood flooring, one good source of many is Harris-Tarkett, Inc. (P.O. Box 300, Johnson City, TN 37605).

The great thing about wood is its versatility. You *can* sand it to renew it or to give it a different finish. New methods allow white oak to be bleached to an almost white floor, stunning even if it does show dirt more. Red oak is used a lot today for floors, although it is not nearly as hard and long lasting as white oak, and don't let anyone tell you it is. But red oak still will last a long time and can be stained to look much like cherry or mahogany. If you have money to spend, you can invest in exotic wood floors—rosewood or ebony even. Or use these woods sparingly in mosaic designs with cheaper maple or with ceramic tile.

If you really love wood, you can install wood that makes for a practical kitchen or even bathroom floor because the boards have been treated, impregnated actually, with polyurethane plastics, and are just as "no-wax" and impervious to moisture as the vinyls. Or so the advertisers say. I tend to agree with Paul Hanke, writing in *New England Architect and Builder Illustrated* (September 1985): "Wood flooring...is subject to wear and tear particularly since the finish (urethane or oil and wax) is surface-applied and must be regularly renewed....Water is taboo for wood floors and they are a poor choice for areas where sinks, tubs, or washers may overflow."

Wood floors come in planks, generally 4, 6, or 8 inches wide or in narrower strips or in various block designs generally referred to as parquet. Planks are usually nailed down, the nail holes filled with wood plugs that become part of the floor's design. Or the nails are driven in at the leading edge of the boards, below the surface where they don't show. The narrow strips, perhaps the most popular hardwood flooring, are narrow to reduce the possibility of warpage, which increases with the width of the board. Both plank and strip are usually tongue and groove today. Parquet floors may be nailed to the underlayment, but they are usually glued.

There is now a new way to install wood flooring developed in Europe. Whether strip, plank, or parquet, the flooring is laid down on several crossed layers of subfloor and is not glued or nailed. This "floating" system is easier for do-it-yourselfers than conventional methods and allows you to take the floor with you when you move. Harris-Tarkett (address above and in Appendix A) sells special underlayments for this kind of floating floor installation, plus other installation tools and materials. Local lumberyards that carry wood flooring should also be prepared by now to advise you about this method of installation. You can use it right over old vinyl or carpeting if you wish. It's more expensive in terms of materials, but less expensive in terms of labor.

Sanding an old wood floor back to the look of a new one is a mess of a job, but because we treasure our wood, it will add value to your home more than carpeting or the best vinyl would. Rent both a big floor sander and an edger. Don't try to do the job with a little carpenter's belt sander. Sand with the grain mostly, but if the floor is badly cupped or rough, sand first at an angle slightly biased to the grain and then sand with the grain. Use a rough sandpaper first, then a medium to fine grit. Wear a respirator. When

Cross section of a Tarkett floating wood floor system. The layered wood strips are glued to one another, but not to the floor itself. The entire floor can be removed by pulling apart the strips and breaking the glue bond.

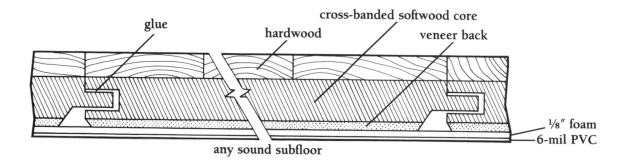

glue   hardwood   cross-banded softwood core   veneer back   ⅛" foam   6-mil PVC

any sound subfloor

Once installed, the Tarkett floating wood floor system looks like any other wood floor. Only a cross-sectional view (see illustration on page 198) gives away its secret.

you are finished, wait a few days for the dust to settle and then clean up. The main trick to sanding with a power floor sander is not to let the thing stand in one spot while it's running or it will quickly gouge a rut in the floor.

The best finishes or sealers for low-maintenance wood floors may not be the best for the wood. Shellac and wax give a soft, mellow, beautiful finish that allows the wood to "breathe," but you will have to wax often to keep it looking good. Urethane varnishes provide the toughest surface, so tough in fact that they may chip rather than flex like a phenolic varnish. The latter is usually recommended where foot traffic is heavy as in the kitchen or foyer. Gymseal (The McCloskey Corporation, 7000 State Road, Philadelphia, PA 19136) is one of many phenolics recommended for floors.) So-called alkyd varnishes like Fabulon's Acrylic Wood Finish, available at most hardware stores, are also recommended in this situation. But the hard polyurethanes are difficult to beat for low maintenance. Any good paint and varnish dealer would love to educate you in detail on this subject. Even more low maintenance can be obtained with penetrating sealers, often incorporating polymerized tung oil. There are many brands.

Before you sand and refinish, consider simply cleaning the old wood floor with a mild paint remover—deglossers as they are called. This can be especially effective in an old country house where you wish to preserve a feeling of yesterday. The patina of the old cleaned wood might be more appropriate than a newly sanded, glossy surface. If a few spots don't come very clean or still show old stains, plop area throw rugs over them. Now that's low maintenance.

Carpeting and Rugs

Homeowners shopping for a new carpet think mostly about color. Like the kings of ancient Assyria in the Fertile Crescent of Mesopotamia who treasured new and rare blue and purple dyes in wool as much as they did gold and silver, so we all, being human, are moved by new and/or unusual colors. Also the rug must, by heaven, *match* the room's decor.

Unfortunately, this attention to color does not always serve durability and low maintenance. For example, technology has now found ways to treat nylon fibers so they resist soiling and staining to an amazing degree, opening the way to an almost unlimited range of new light rug colors. Pastels, once unheard of for a rug, are now fashionable and stunning, to say the least, after years of dark-colored carpets. The fashion, from a low-maintenance point of view is somewhat self-defeating, however. Because of their lighter hues, the new rugs show dirt more even if they do clean up easily. So to keep them looking their best they have to be cleaned more often. Smart is the homeowner who takes advantage of the best of both worlds: buys the dirt-resisting nylons to be sure, but in richer hues like wine burgundy, pine green, or cordovan brown. These colors will show light-colored hair, threads, and bits of paper and dirt more readily—all of which can be vacuumed easily—but won't show the more persistant dirt and stains so fast.

Of the four major kinds of interior rugs—wool, nylon, polyester, and acrylic—wool remains the most durable and, all things considered, the best choice for low maintenance. Yet wool is the most expensive. A good one will cost around $45 a square yard and up, mostly up, so people turn to synthetics that provide a fairly good rug for half the cost of wool. Wool is naturally nonabsorbent and so somewhat stain and dirt resistant; it is very slow to burn and is quite fire resistant. It also resists crushing of the pile better than any other rug material. Wool will fade or deteriorate in direct sunlight, but so will nylon and polyester. Wool is subject to insect attack—clothing moths—but all good wool carpeting comes factory-treated against this danger.

Wool rugs are so durable in fact that handwoven types have become collector's items. Oriental rugs actually increase in value with use—"the surface patinates and the colors mellow" is the phrase to use if you want to impress your friends. I'm told that the airport terminal at Cairo is carpeted with Oriental rugs over which millions of feet have trod, just to show the world how well a really good wool rug will wear.

Collecting Oriental rugs became a fad in the '70s until the price rose and there was little money to be made by new investors. Prices peaked, at least for the time, about 1980. But you can use the rugs maybe until the next round of price increases and they will still be in very good shape and still valuable. Value of course varies. The really priceless Oriental rugs in museums have as many as 2,000 knots per inch, which is almost unbelievable. Even 500 knots per inch makes an extremely valuable rug, and 150 to 200 quite acceptable in some designs and shapes. (See Appendix A for a list of sources for Oriental and handmade rugs.)

The Navajo rug is an extremely durable type that has become so sought after by collectors that it is too expensive for practical floorcoverings. Normal sizes today are too small for floors except for throw rugs and are used principally as wall hangings. But you can use them on the floor and be assured that normal use won't harm them much in a lifetime. *The Wall Street Journal* recently said that next to real estate, Navajo rugs are the best investment you can make. Rugs measuring 3 by 4 feet were selling from $150 to $500 in early 1986, and one about 4-by-8 feet went for $1,400, all of which would resell in Santa Fe for probably twice that. Average prices have tripled since the early '60s. The irony of this situation is that farmers get very little for their wool, and Navajo weavers, except in some cases, hardly make minimum wages.

Of the three principal synthetics, nylon is the best for low maintenance and generally costs more than polyester or acrylic. All three are fire resistant but will melt or scar from a hot cigarette or an ember popping out of the fireplace. Nylon and acrylic resist crushing better than polyester, but polyester is slightly more resistant to abrasion. Acrylic does not fade in direct sunlight as much as nylon or polyester and is a good choice under a picture window that faces a southerly direction. The synthetics are all immune to insect damage. Polyester is usually factory treated against mildew, a problem sometimes. Polyester and acrylic create less static electricity than wool or nylon, although nylon manufacturers are experimenting with metal threads in their carpets that seem to cut down on this annoyance. New rugs, of whatever kind, generate more static than ones that have been around for a while. Static is also worse in winter, when heating the house dries out the air.

Whatever kind of rug you choose, the best key to its real value is its density. The more fibers or strands packed into a given space, the better. Bend a portion of a rug back and if you see lots of backing, the rug is obviously not very dense and should be cheap. A good place for a cheap rug is the spare bedroom, used only when Aunt Hildy comes to visit.

Pile rugs are composed of many loops of fabric woven into a backing usually of jute or polypropylene, the backing coated with a layer of latex and then another backing added. Such rugs are called "tufted" rugs. If the rug consists of warp and woof fibers woven together, it is a woven rug, made on a loom. Tufted rugs are easier and faster to make by machine and so are generally cheaper. You can usually identify them by looking at the backing. The directions of the weave on the back will have no relationship to the directions of the weave on the front. Tufted rugs won't unravel at the edges if you need to cut them. Woven rugs will if the edges aren't bound. The bound edge is called a selvage, and if you see on a carpet edge the telltale zigzag- or diamond-shaped binding, you'll know you are looking at a woven rug.

The looped strands that form the pile can be cut on the surface to make each loop into two separate strands. This is then called a cut-pile carpet. It creates a shearer, smoother, plusher surface than the loops, but it is not as durable or crush resistant. So-called sculptured rugs are composed of uncut loops at different heights. There are other variations in the twist of the fibers or in heat treatments during manufacturing that may increase sturdiness or density. These processes make different textures, but add or detract little in the way of low maintenance.

In weekly vacuuming, carpets will come cleaner and therefore last longer if you use a vacuum that has a beater as well as a sucking action. If you move the vacuum slowly over the rug, it obviously will get more dirt out. Don't be in a hurry. Blot up spills immediately, and if staining occurs, use a spot remover according to directions.

Those people who are always rearranging their furniture may not be as crazy as the rest of us think they are. This is a very good way to get even wear out of your carpet and hence longer life.

A good carpet deserves a good pad under it. Even a cheaper carpet deserves a good pad under it because that more than anything else will contribute to long life. Generally speaking, the thicker the rug the thinner the pad need be, but rely on your dealer for the proper advice.

Three types of woven rugs.

You can install a carpet yourself, but most carpet dealers will include installation with the purchase price. It seldom pays to do it yourself and botch the job.

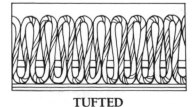

TUFTED

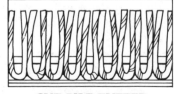

CUT-PILE TUFTED

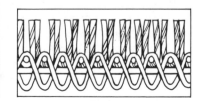

WOVEN

Wet Cleaning Your Rugs

Sooner or later, a carpet will need a "wet cleaning" or what is often called "steam extraction" cleaning. You can rent the commercial machine needed for this job, and instructions on its proper use should come with it. It's relatively simple operation: You begin by first vacuuming throughly. Then you spray a synthetic detergent according to its label directions on the carpet and suck it back up immediately with your rented machine. Don't get the carpet too wet.

An extra sucking stroke for each application stroke is generally a good practice. Allow the carpet to dry overnight before walking on it. If the rug has been cleaned before, you may need to add an antifoam solution to your soap.

To raise flattened-out pile, such as that made by a chair leg, place a damp cloth over the area and hold an iron on it set on high. Press down very lightly on the iron. About 30 to 60 seconds ought to do it.

Indoor-outdoor carpeting is a synthetic called olefin, or sometimes polypropylene olefin. It is very durable and the least expensive of all the carpeting, which proves that price and durability are not always connected. Olefin is the carpeting to use for outside steps or porch, basement, bath or kitchen, *if* you insist on carpeting such areas. Low maintenance would dictate otherwise, however. No matter how inured olefin might be to water and other liquids, cleaning up spills is more difficult than from vinyl or other hard floors. Why do it? I have seen kitchen carpeting that almost reeked with the residue of spills. This may be the fault of the homeowner, not the carpet, but I still ask, why? If you like to stand on something soft at the sink, why not an attractive rag throw rug that you can put in the washing machine when it gets dirty?

As for carpeting on walks, entryways, and porch steps, a year or so of weathering makes it look so shoddy and artificial that I think it detracts from the appearance of the house. Masonry is much, much better.

Braided and rag rugs from scraps are very durable since they usually are made of wool and/or denim. Such throw rugs can be a real bargain at garage sales. Don't try to get dust and dirt out of a woven or braided throw rug by snapping it in the air, because you can easily loosen the weave that way. Hang it on a clothesline and beat it the old-fashioned way. That's not particularly good for the rug, either, but safer than snapping it. Beating does not wear (and certainly does not fade) a rug as much as laundering does.

CHAPTER 12
WALLS AND CEILINGS

The number of choices you have in ornamenting walls and ceilings is staggering. The first low-maintenance concern in walls and ceilings is not weathering or wear, but cleaning, and so some materials, paint for instance, can be more appropriate on walls than when used on floors or outside. But as with floors, taste and fashion in wallcovering can be at odds with low maintenance. Wood paneling is easy to maintain, but because some people find it too common or too dull, they opt for a nice pastel wallcovering even when the primary colors in it soon turn out to be peanut butter and jam from the kids' fingers. Also, sometimes a material good for low maintenance on a floor might have some drawbacks on a wall, as does ceramic tile in the shower wall, as we shall see. In such instances, the difference between low and high maintenance is not so much the materials themselves, but rather how and where they're used.

To Plaster or Drywall, That Is the Question

A basic decision when remodeling a room, adding one or building new, is whether to plaster or to drywall (the latter is referred to by many other names, like Sheetrock and wallboard). It is difficult to get unprejudiced advice on the matter, since everyone has a bias. Builders urge drywall in most cases, mostly because plastering holds up the progress of building the house; it takes more time to plaster. Also union labor has driven the cost of plastering up where it won't compete with drywall. But if

204

you do the plastering yourself you can save appreciable sums of money. Contrary to prevailing wisdom, plastering need not be difficult, if you can be content with a somewhat rough-textured finish. What really takes skill is the smooth white finish the professionals can achieve, especially if it has to be put on a ceiling. But a ceiling is an excellent place for a textured finish, except in a kitchen or other room where dirt is a daily possibility. And I say this as I stare up at my own rough-textured plaster ceiling. The plasterer finished my office ceiling by making light fanlike sweeps with his trowel. The resulting pattern looks very skillful and attractive when in fact it was much easier than making a smooth surface. Heavily textured plaster walls or ceilings should be avoided, however, as they are difficult if not impossible to clean. And rather ugly after you have to look at them for several years.

I would be slower to urge do-it-yourself plastering if I didn't have the support of at least one architect, Alex Wade, who in his *30 Energy-Efficient Houses . . . You Can Build* (Rodale Press, 1977) encourages the idea, too, so long as the goal is "a rough-surfaced, natural gray plaster." You can always paint it. Or if it's reasonably smooth, paper it. And by the time you do a wall or two, you could be ready for the traditional brown coat followed by the supersmooth white coat of the professional plasterer.

The Art of Plastering

No book can tell you how to do it; you just must learn. Start at the edge of a wall. Inside corners are the difficult part. Hold the trowel about 45 degrees to the wall. After you mix the plaster until it's almost soupy, let it stand for half an hour before applying it so that it can set up some. If it gets too dry, add a little water. To learn the proper way to draw the trowel over the wall in order to spread the plaster out evenly requires practice and more practice. A secret is to learn how to release your pressure on the trowel *before* you withdraw it from the wall. Start in a closet where no one will see your early goofs. After the plaster has set up on the wall for half an hour or thereabouts, smooth it better. A supersmooth final surface is applied an hour or more later when the plaster is approaching dryness. It's similar to putting a supersmooth surface on concrete. Only experience can teach you.

Plaster is applied to metal mesh or to a kind of gypsum board usually referred to as rock lath, which has a paper surface to which the plaster bonds. Some rock lath has perforations in it that the plaster squeezes into for a better grip. But both smooth and perforated seem to work equally well. One of the arguments in favor of drywall is that by the time you put the rock lath up in preparation for the plaster, you might as well have put up drywall and be done with it. The point is well taken although rock lath goes up easier and faster since you don't have to worry about the seams, which will be covered with plaster. Rock lath also comes in smaller pieces than the cumbersome 4-by-8-foot drywall panels.

Nearly everyone agrees that plaster is harder, tougher, and stronger than drywall. It will hold pictures, towel racks, shelves, and the like much better than drywall no matter what kind of hanger you use. And drywall has been known to sag away from the wall, pop nails, and open seams.

But plaster cracks, point out champions of drywall, when the house settles. Cracked plaster does not usually come from the house's settling, or should not, if the builder is worth his salt. Cracks from settling are what I call one-way cracks in that they tend to widen farther every year. This kind of damage could show up with drywall, too. More often, cracks in plaster come from expansion and contraction of the house due to temperature and moisture fluctuations.

Our house, plastered throughout, has in 12 years incurred maybe half a dozen of these kinds of cracks. During periods of contraction, they open scarcely more than hairline spaces, hardly enough to fill with the proper Spackle or caulking. In periods of expansion, the cracks come together, forcing out any repair material we may be tempted to use. The cracks have not widened over the years, are barely noticeable, and are best left alone or covered with a double-layer, embossed paper wallcovering (see "Flexible Wallcoverings," below) that has enough elasticity in it to endure such minute expansion and contraction without tearing.

Some builders say they won't use plaster because the moisture in it affects the structural wood as it vaporizes. The wood swells then shrinks as the house dries out, and the expansion and contraction cracks the plaster. This is arguable. So much of the structural wood used in building today is not properly dried to begin with, or if kiln-dried, languishes at the building site in rainy, humid weather and absorbs much more moisture than it could get from drying plaster. If water from the plaster were the culprit, why didn't the plaster in our house crack in the first year?

An advantage of plaster not often mentioned is that when finished by a professional, the smooth white coat is nice enough to stand as the wall finish without *anything* put on it. It is in fact a smart idea to wait at least a year before painting and papering anyway. Hot spots in plaster—accidental concentrations of lime that cause a condition where wallpaper or paint won't adhere well—should be all gone in that length of time. At any rate, new plaster should be allowed to cure at least five weeks before papering. Hot spots can be neutralized with a zinc sulfate solution (available at wallcovering stores).

Drywalling

Nevertheless, drywall is easier than plaster to install if you don't consider the heavy weight of the panels. It is only decidedly inferior to plaster when the ⅜-inch thickness is used instead of the proper ½ inch. Architect Alex Wade says that if two layers of ⅜-inch drywall are installed, with the joints staggered and both adhesive and screws used to hold them instead of nails, they make "a very superior wall finish that rivals plaster in quality." Directions on how to install double-layer drywall are available from drywall manufacturers like U.S. Gypsum and Gold Bond. See your local dealer. Directions for putting up drywall conventionally can be found in many books and supplier brochures. Nail the heavy panels well. Two nails an inch or so apart every foot are better than one every 6 inches. The only real skill involved is in applying joint tape and joint compound so smoothly that the seams don't show. In my experience, it takes a normally handy person about one room to learn the skill. But most amateurs who have put up drywall say they would be better off hiring the work. Most of them do, the second time around.

A favorite ceiling finish these days consists of putting up drywall with screws, then covering the whole ceiling, not just the seams, with about a ¼ inch of joint compound (some people call it glop) or a material almost exactly like regular joint compound that has a bit more elasticity. Then, before it dries, the plasterlike compound is textured with swirls or any other design the homeowner finds appropriate. One plasterer I know who does this work has a texture he calls The Stomp. Using a piece of board nailed to a stick, he pushes the board against the wet plasterlike compound much as you would use a stomper to level a soil surface, only more gently. As the board pulls away from the ceiling at each "stomp," it leaves a dimpled texture. Such designs would not be practical in kitchens or over wood stoves where regular cleaning is necessary. There you want as smooth a surface as possible. But anyone can do The Stomp, and swirls are easy, too. A little imagination could supply an almost unlimited number of designs to imprint in the wet glop, just by carving or gluing patterns on the stomp board.

Another tip about drywall: Champions of wood paneling like to point out that the use of this low-maintenance wallcovering negates all the worry and work of either plaster or drywall. This contention isn't, or shouldn't, be true. Most wood paneling, especially the 4-by-8-foot panels, are so thin and flimsy that alone they do not make a solid or strong wall. Good builders advocate backing them with at least ⅜-inch-thick drywall, which is about the most economical way to make a panel wall solid.

Because of so many variations in individual cases, it is difficult to say whether drywall or plaster will last longer. I've known drywalls to last without needing repair for 15 years, and plasterers are quick to use words like "forever" when referring to plaster walls. But one man who does a lot of work with both materials bared his soul to me. "Well, both are likely to last a long time without much repair, but I'd say that you can expect to find popped nails in drywall in about five years, and a few cracks in your plaster in eight years."

Flexible Wallcoverings

Many years ago, the Typical Homeowner of my age got some unwanted experience steaming and scraping off layers of old wallpaper. And then if he was really lucky, he got to mix up wheat paste glue, smear it on new wallpaper, carry the gloppy stuff to the wall, and hopefully get it stuck up before his arm muscles failed completely. Such an individual reached a point where he wiped the glop of wallpaper glue from his shoes and the sweat caused by the steamer from his brow and swore never to look at another piece of wallpaper in his life.

Such a Typical Homeowner is in for a surprise should he or she venture into a wallpaper store today. First of all, there's no such thing as wallpaper anymore—the proper word is wallcovering. With good reason. Unless some exotic textile is used, almost all the wallpaper today is vinyl, or in the cheaper kinds, paper coated with vinyl or paper bonded to some kind of plastic closely related to vinyl. The choices in vinyl are mindboggling. There is evidently no flexible material that vinyl cannot be made to imitate with amazing fidelity. There are vinyls that look and feel like silks, satins, richly embroidered brocades, metallic foils, grass cloths, burlaps, leathers, anything at all. And even in our little village, I counted nearly 400 sample catalogs. No wonder it takes people so long to choose a wallcovering. Most "ordinary" vinyls start at about $11 per metric roll (28 square feet approximately) and the highest priced I found (leafing madly through 400 volumes) was a richly embroidered flower pattern of 100 percent acrylic that cost $90 per roll!

Wallcoverings of real textile materials, like burlap or linen, are not easy to clean and so are more of a maintenance headache than a help. Such materials, exotic and beautiful as they may be (not to mention expensive), do not double as a vapor barrier as vinyl will. If they should get soiled, they are very difficult to clean. On good scrubbable vinyl, you can bear down with a detergent and get rid of almost any kind of dirt. Do not, however, use any more water than absolutely necessary, especially around seams. Excess water could soak the vinyl enough to weaken the glue.

What the low-maintenance-minded wallcoverer looks for on the back of a wallcovering sample are these words: scrubbable, strippable, and prepasted. "Scrubbable" means just that. You can scrub it. It will hold up in damp conditions. You can use it in the kitchen or even the bathroom. Cheaper plastic-coated papers might be wipeable or gingerly washable, but not scrubbable, and they should not be used in kitchens or other areas where periodic cleaning is necessary, or where moisture is going to be plentiful. Most good vinyls are now fabric-backed, and these are "strippable." When and if you want a new wallcovering, you can peel the old off—no more steaming, scraping, and cussing. Some good wallcoverings are still paper-backed, and these vinyls will sort of peel off, too. The paper backing stays on the wall, but the job is easier than the old-fashioned way.

Finally, especially if you intend to hang the wallcovering yourself, you'll want to see the word "prepasted" on the sample back. Sometimes the word is not there, but a little picture of a tray with a roll of wallcovering issuing from it instead, and the words, "use with a water box" or some such underneath. What both this symbol and words mean is that the wallcovering already has glue on the back, which is activated by soaking it in water. Prepasted coverings should not be confused with papers that have some kind of gumming or peel-back adhesive on them to be stuck directly onto the wall. These latter coverings have not generally proved very satisfactory.

Some of the good fabric-backed vinyls are not prepasted. Rather than hung with the traditional wheat paste glue, new vinyl adhesives are recommended for them. Wheat paste, I'm told, is sometimes affected by mildew.

Hanging Wallcoverings

Wallcovering stores provide all kinds of information on hanging the various materials they sell and even schedule periodic seminars where representatives of the wallcovering manufacturers give lessons on installation. The mistake most often made by do-it-yourselfers, a clerk in the local store told me, is forgetting to put a coat of sizing on the wall first. Special sizing makes the job of hanging vinyls somewhat easier. The vinyl stretches a little when wet and shrinks upon drying, and the sizing allows you to slide the vinyl a bit to position it perfectly against the adjacent sheet and smooth out air bubbles. Also, sizing makes stripping off the wallcovering easier when you want to put on new. Two coats of primer sealer on drywall can take the place of sizing in some cases, but it is advisable to apply sizing, too. Holes in old plaster should be filled and sanded

---

Quilt a Wall

Faced with an empty expanse of wall to cover, some people have found ways to individualize their wallcovering designs beyond the repetitious patterns of the factory. Using wallpaper catalogs or remnants, they cut out squares or other shapes and arrange the pieces in their own quiltlike designs. Each piece is then transferred to the wall one at a time after soaking to activate the glue. The result is some very eye-popping decor. Almost any quilt design can be copied in this way. Of course with all those seams, you are tempting fate—you risk squares peeling off the wall over time. But in a room where moisture and dirt are not problems, the risk is minor.

smooth—otherwise you might soon have a hole or a noticeable indentation in the covering. Surfaces covered with glossy paints won't hold wallcovering adhesive. Wash the surface with paint thinner and when dry, coat with sizing.

Don't try to violate the tried-and-true directions for hanging wallcoverings. For example, don't try to wrap a strip around an inside corner. It might look okay for awhile, but soon it will wrinkle. Check the run numbers on all your rolls to make sure they are the same. Color can vary slightly from run to run. To keep the color uniform on plain textured or solid color coverings, reverse every other strip, top to bottom. Don't use a seam roller on flocked wallcoverings. Instead, tap gently all along the seam with a rounded tool handle or similar object. Where vinyl strips overlap at corners, you will need a vinyl-to-vinyl adhesive to make them stick together.

Old and New Wallcoverings

One type of old-fashioned wall*paper* is enjoying something of a renaissance these days. Among wallpaper aficionados, it is called anaglypta, and it is composed of two pieces of paper laminated together and then stamped with an embossed design to give it texture. Historically, anaglypta was a cheap copy of lincrusta, a deeply embossed linoleumlike wallcovering that was itself a cheap copy of stamped metal. And to carry the history one step further, stamped metal was a cheap imitation of stamped leather, or expensive decorative plaster or carved wood. The historical theorem at work here can be briefly stated: The higher the price of common labor the more unaffordable becomes craftsmanship and quality materials. By raising the "standard of living," we have ironically lowered the "quality of life." The sad lesson, not yet learned, is that money alone cannot level out the differences between wealth and poverty. As we can see from contemporary America, throwing money around freely only widens the chasm between the two.

Anaglypta, made in England, is being sold in America as an ideal covering for cracked plaster walls. Its embossed texture hides cracks and other minor imperfections. You see it advertised in many householder magazines right now. It is sold by Decor International Wallcovering, Inc. (37-39 Crescent Street, Long Island City, NY 11101), and Rejuvenation Houseparts (901 North Skidmore, Portland, OR 94124). Though it hides cracks, it will not keep cracks from widening farther, wallcovering stores assure me. So don't expect miracles.

This type of wallpaper needs to be painted if you wish to clean it. Where cleaning is more or less regular, as in a kitchen, or where moisture is more or less constant, as in a bathroom, oil-base paint is recommended. Otherwise, latex. Directions with the wallpaper spell out priming and

Anaglypta, a real paper wallcovering, is embossed, thus you can use it to hide cracks and other imperfections in the wall behind it.

finish coat details. In terms of low maintenance, this type of wallcovering is debatable. Among the questions asked and "answered" on the manufacturer's brochure is this one: "How long will it last?" Answer: "It can be painted up to eight times." If you paint it every 3 years, that's 24 years. I will let you make your own deduction. As president of the I-Hate-to-Paint Club, I know what mine would be.

If you don't mind painting, there is another beautifully embossed wallcovering on the market that is brand-new. It is made from cotton fibers and is advertised as more durable than paper. Manufactured by Mile Hi Crown, it's available in many stores that sell wallcoverings.

From Flexi-Wall Systems comes a new wallcovering impregnated with gypsum and designed to take the place of real plaster. It will go directly on almost any surface—cement, tile, glass, wood, or plaster. It is also available in many stores that sell wallcoverings. Like all new products, only time will prove or disprove its low-maintenance advantages.

Moldings

Wall trim, moldings, baseboard, and chair rails are now easily available in extruded polystyrene in enough different colors to match almost any wallcovering. You can also get polyurethane cornice molding that looks like fancy plaster or carved wood. All these plastics can be sawed, sanded, nailed, and painted, if necessary. What they lack in vibrancy of the more natural materials they make up for in low maintenance.

Interior Wall Paints

If paint makes low-maintenance sense anywhere (which is debatable), it makes the most sense on interior walls, protected from the weather and from the scuffing that floors get. Paint is a good wallcovering for those people who have a low tolerance for permanence. Cheaper than other wallcoverings, paint allows you to change colors in a room more often than you might do if facing a wallpaper or paneling change. (What is really needed is a paint that changes colors with one's moods, like the mood rings popular several years ago!)

Types of Paints

Oil-base or alkyd-base paints (they are almost synonymous) no longer have any real advantages indoors over latex (water-base) paints although the experts still argue. Being very interested in paint, or rather in trying to escape painting, I have looked deeply into the subject and for awhile believed that oil-base paints could rightly boast that they adhered to wood better than latex. Further reading revealed that at least one expert disagreed, even for outdoor uses, contending that since wood swells and shrinks and since latex is more elastic than oil-base films, it will endure wood movement better and hence adhere longer.

Be that as it may, latex paints have so many advantages that they remain the first choice for interior walls. They mix easily with water and they clean up easily with water. Latex paint odors are not so offensive indoors and go away quicker. Latex dries faster, too, so that you can follow with a second coat almost right after finishing the first. Today, latex paints are almost as washable as oil-base paints, and unless a wallcovering manufacturer specifically recommends oil or alkyd paints (as in the case of embossed wallpapers) latex paints are the right choice. Just remember that no painted surface is going to clean up perfectly after it gets dirty. The only alternative is to clean as best as you can and paint it again. That sounds worse than it really is; it is easier to paint a wall than to try to clean all the dirt off it, especially if you have to do the ceiling, too.

There is one exception to using latex, and that is that it should not be used over an oil- or alkyd-base paint because it will not stick well. If you are covering an old oil-base paint, use oil-base paint to do the job. If you don't know whether the paint is an oil or latex, chip some off and take it to the paint store to see what the experts say.

Latex paints are designated flat, semigloss, and gloss—the flatter it is, the harder (usually) it is to clean. If you do choose to use a high-gloss paint, remember it will have to be deglossed before putting a vinyl wallcovering on it, should you decide to do that someday.

Sealer and/or primer on a new wall or new wood trim almost always should precede topcoats, and two topcoats almost always are better than one. Follow label instructions for the specific paint you choose. And though it be repeated 10 million times, always remember that if the surface isn't clean and dry, even a paint guaranteed for ten years will not last that long. On a wettish surface it won't last six months.

On a masonry wall, as in a basement, the best low-maintenance paint (and the most expensive) is an epoxy concrete enamel. But if the wall

Special Effects with Paints

Besides being relatively cheap and going up relatively easily, there is another advantage of paint that very few people use. You can use it to create your own wall design. One homeowner I know near Canton, Ohio, dared to be different. He really wanted to paint pictures on the walls himself, but doubting his skill, he called in local amateur painters willing to cover whole walls with murals cheaply. What a delightful idea, enjoyed and cherished by everyone who visits. In another house that I saw featured in a magazine, the owners painted modern designs all over the walls to create a cohesive whole running through the walls and ceiling. The design was abstract—nothing was repeated in patterns—yet it was all very pleasing.

Why not, in a child's room, allow the child to paste pictures on the wall or draw crayon cartoons, or paint scenes in whatever droll or haphazard manner the child chooses? A wall to which the kids can do anything they want. And what wonderful low maintenance! At some future time it can be cleaned, repainted, or recovered . . . but I wonder how many parents would. Can you imagine in later years how much such scrawlings would mean to the family?

The closest the more adventurous among us usually come to creating unique wallcovering designs is with stenciling, a kind of "country" decor now popular again. Stenciling allows you to create your own patterns and designs. (Scores of books tell you how to get some dramatic effects from this very simple skill.) Instead of stenciling a row of chickens around your wall, or a row of alternating chickens and cows, why not go all the way, and create a *different* animal in each position. More time-consuming, yes. But you only go around once, as they say.

tends to be moist, you are probably better off with a portland cement paint, especially one with water-sealing capacities, real or advertised.

Roller Brushes and Other Tools

Advances in painting equipment continue to be marketed. The latest is a motor and canister affair that pumps paint through a connecting hose to the roller. When you push a button on the roller handle, paint flows from the hose into the roller. No more bending over to slop your roller into a tray of paint—or what I've done, step into the tray inadvertently while admiring how handy I was with the roller on the wall! One manufacturer is Power-Flo Products Corporation (1661 94th Lane NE, Minneapolis, MN 55434). These power paint rollers appear to be ideal for professional painters. But at a cost of between $50 and $100, homeowners are slow to buy. Once they get over the shock of what good paint costs these days, they settle for a brush or a simple hand roller so that they can keep down costs. Even some of the professionals don't like to use the power rollers because they take so much longer to clean than a simple pan and roller. (A cleanup tip: Line the pan with aluminum foil or plastic wrap, sealing all the edges, before adding your paint. Then at cleanup time, merely pour off any unused paint and carefully lift out the liner. If you were very careful, there'll be no paint in the pan to wash off.)

On walls and ceilings, rollers make better sense than brushes, being considerably faster and, for most of us, easier for applying an even coat. Always buy the spring-loaded kind that allows you to slide old roller brushes off and new ones on easily. The nap on the brushes varies in thickness for different paints—short naps are usually for flat paints, a short stiff nap of mohair for enamel, etc. Your paint dealer can advise you in any specific instance.

Since you can't roll right up to the ceiling or corners, you "cut" these areas with a brush or foam pad, about 3 inches out from the corner. By far the easiest tool to use is a little plastic gadget that you mount a foam pad on and then run along the corner. In fact, they are a great tool for painting flat surfaces anywhere since they apply the paint evenly and leave no brush marks. The foam pads are easier to clean than brushes but because they are so cheap, most people throw them away after use.

There is much ado written about using good brushes and taking care of them after use, but I agree with George Grotz, author of *The Furniture Doctor* (Doubleday, 1983) and other good books. Buy cheap brushes and throw them away after use. Let's face it. What the Typical Homeowner does is buy a brush or two for a certain painting job. Afterward, he cleans them up religiously or thinks he does and wraps them in a cloth for safekeeping. Or he puts them in a can of solvent on a piece of wire just like the books say he should. Then he forgets about them. Two years later

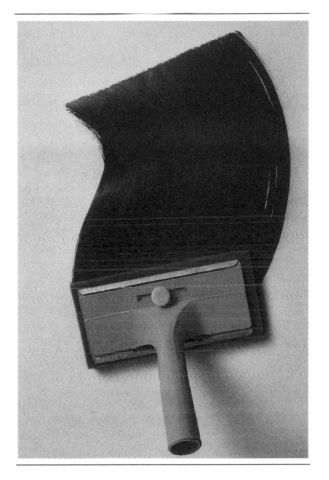

Foam painting pads are very handy for painting a straight edge against moldings and at wall and ceiling joints. And because the pads are cheap, you can just slip them out of their holders and throw them away when the job is done.

when the next paint job comes along, the brush in the cloth is as hard as a rhinoceros hide, and the one forgotten in the can of dissolved solvent is totally petrified. Or more likely he can't find it at all because the kids used it to paint a bicycle and left it in the bottom of the paint can that got thrown away. In actuality, it is seldom that a Typical Homeowner ever uses a paintbrush a second time, and very rarely a third time. Even when I have taken supreme care in cleaning a brush, by the time I haul it out for a third use, the upper half of the brush is stiff and won't hold much paint, and the corner edges are beginning to frazzle. I'm forced to buy a new brush anyway.

According to market statistics, plain old paintbrushes still outsell all other kinds of paint applicators. This is true because the typical homeowner appreciates that a brush is handy and can be taken up immediately to proceed with the job. With rollers, you still have to have some kind of brush for cutting the corners, and with brushes you don't need to spend half the day masking everything in sight as you do with a paint sprayer. Nor do sprayers do as good a job, especially on rough wood. Professional exterior painters I know have developed a technique where they spray and brush simultaneously, the brush working the sprayer paint better into the boards. Only where you have to paint finely turned and carved cornice trim, or newel posts on stairs, or fancy filigreed molding, does a sprayer prove its worth. And low-maintenance homeowners will avoid such ornate decoration anyway because these dust catchers are a real pain to clean and hell to refinish.

Paneling

When we think of paneling, we automatically think wood. But paneling today comes in such a vast array of facings that the only way to differentiate it from vinyl wallcoverings is to say paneling does not come in rolls. Much paneling—more precisely called decorator panels—is actually nothing more than hardboard with vinyl wallcoverings overlaid on it. Panel size is usually the standard 4-by-8-foot dimension, in thicknesses from ⅛ inch up to about ½ inch. Thicker wood strips or boards are often referred to as paneling, but I deal with them under the heading "Planking" (see later).

Plywood panels consist of thin layers of real wood laminated and glued together. Plywood is graded for quality and for exterior or interior use, the wood usually being softwood—fir or pine—with a thickness of ¼ inch up to 1 inch. These are used structurally in framing a house, but not for wallcoverings, except perhaps in a garage or workshop. Some plywood panels have an exterior layer of hardwood, usually birch or oak, and are often used in making cabinets. A good buy in this kind of plywood right now is one with an exterior layer of Philippine mahogany, called luan. Luan panels are comparatively cheap, but the wood is much more attractive than the usual plywood facing. Philippine mahogany is not considered exotic wood like other mahoganies and is, for the time being, plentiful. You can even find pallets made of it.

What distinguishes these plywood panels from the kind of panels used as decorative wallcoverings is that the wood surface is raw—unfinished—and there is little or no provision in the panels' designs for hiding seam lines. The edges just butt against each other, requiring some covering trim to hide the crack. But it is mostly because they are unfinished that they score low as low-maintenance wallcovering.

In recent years, manufacturers have begun facing plywood with fine veneers of choice and exotic hardwoods in beautiful designs. The veneer is then covered with prefinished coatings—usually tough acrylic vinyls. The prefinish means you have nothing to do but put the panels up. No home finishing could equal the factory finish in durability or ease of cleaning. If pizza at little Joey's birthday party mysteriously ends up on the wall, you can wipe it off and use a little mild detergent to clean all residues away. Since most of the veneers are of rather dark-grained wood, dirt doesn't show, and regular dustings can be few and far between. These are usually the most expensive of the 4-by-8-foot panels, but worth it if you like wood walls. A general rule to follow is that if you are putting up these panels in thicknesses less than ¼ inch, from ⅛ up to ⁷⁄₁₆ inch (thicknesses vary), you should back them with drywall to make a solid wall. Even at ¼ inch, that's not a bad idea.

The newest innovations in paneling that allow an almost unlimited choice in facing design are rarely plywood-based at all but are made of some kind of fibrous hardboard (Masonite is one brand everyone knows) overlaid with plastic, vinyl, or a paper-thin covering upon which the design is printed.

The latter is among the cheapest of the panels. Because the designs are printed—actually photographs—they can mimic faithfully the most exotic woods or anything else, but they are rather easily scratched or torn. Often, to keep costs down, these panels come with the cheapest and thinnest hardboard backings. I once lifted one such panel at the corner and it promptly snapped off. You probably know of them—they're the panels usually listed in the red hot sales notices for only $4.99 a sheet. Avoid them.

Somewhat higher-quality panels overlaid with what amounts to vinyl wallcovering in a myriad of designs are worth considering in lieu of drywall and wallcovering, especially if you have confidence in your ability to put up panels but not to put up wallpaper. Remember, however, that panels are more permanent. If you become dissatisfied with the design or color, it is more expensive and difficult to remove panels than wallpaper. With the panels, which are usually called generically "decorator panels," you can buy matching trim and molding, which will give your work a more professional appearance even if you are a beginner. Decorator panels are all washable—good low-maintenance materials.

So as not to be kept out of kitchens, baths, laundry rooms, or other areas of high-moisture or high-dirt possibilities, panel manufacturers have developed ways to bond tough plastic coatings to waterproofed hardboard. Now you can buy panels that look like ceramic tile, onyx, marble—you name it. Some are recommended even for shower stalls if you use the prescribed moldings and trim—a bit risky, I think. These panels are not cheap, but they can be attractive as well as very low maintenance.

When buying panels, check them for damage in shipment or by careless carpenters. Edges tear, chip, and fracture rather easily. If the somewhat flexible plastic-face panels are flexed too much, that tough, hard plastic coat can crack. It is wise to have a helper when installing the cumbersome 4-by-8-foot sizes. Detailed instructions come with all panels as do proper nails and/or adhesive. Be sure to follow the directions, especially those that advise that a particular panel be held at room temperature and humidity for a certain length of time before installation. Observe all provisions for creating a slight crack between panels to allow for expansion. Failure to obey such instructions may result in buckling panels.

Planking

The Cadillacs of wood paneling are the solid-wood boards, or planks as interior decorators prefer to call them. I call them interior wood siding. Good-quality planks tongue and groove into each other with enough room left to allow for expansion. Check the boards and see how they fit. On good plank paneling of the tongue-and-groove kind, the groove will have a notch in it so positioned that the tongue *can't* be seated tightly in the groove. The notch keeps a tiny open place between the abutting edges of the planks. This allows for expansion and contraction, and because this space is consistent, spacing always looks neat and equal across the wall. Prefinished planks are worth the extra money since you would work hard and long to duplicate or even come close to that low-maintenance finish.

Knotty pine is the granddaddy of interior wood siding. Western Wood Products Association (522 Southwest 5th Avenue, Yeon Building, Portland, OR 97204) is pushing western pine, cedar, and redwood interior planking, which are reminiscent of knotty pine, but much more beautiful to a new generation's eyes. This organization has an excellent guide *(Our Real Wood Interiors Design Workbook)* to tempt you with wood planking. For hardwoods like oak, walnut, etc., you should consult local lumberyards by all means. They won't carry these plankings in stock necessarily because they're expensive, but they probably have samples and catalogs of sources. There are even very thin "planks" of real wood (⅛ inch thick) that go on over plaster or drywall with adhesives, almost like wallpaper. Because they are cheaper than thicker planks, they're good for those who love wood but are on a strict budget.

Marlite (Masonite Corporation, 1 South Wacker Drive, Chicago, IL 60607), famous for its man-made panels, makes a hardboard "planking" 16 inches wide, 8 feet long, and ¼ inch thick with very realistic, embossed wood graining. Though thin, the planks actually tongue and groove together. Man-made planking of this kind has an advantage, if it is an advantage, over solid wood in that it won't expand and contract as much. See your local lumberyard; almost all carry or can order Masonite products.

FINISHES

If your wood paneling is not prefinished, the question arises as to what is the best finish. I discuss this subject in detail in chapter 13. Suffice

Wainscoting

If the idea of a whole wall in wood (or the idea of a whole wall of anything) overwhelms you, you might want to give some thought to the Victorian dado wall, which when wood is used in the lower portion, becomes known as wainscoting. Wainscoting was (and still is today) decorative and a good low-maintenance idea, too. The upper part of the wall, above the area likely to be bumped and scraped and smeared with fingerprints, can be kept in plaster or wallpaper fairly easily. The lower portion that gets most of the abuse is covered with boards and topped by a chair rail, a piece of molding running horizontally across the wall. This solid wood takes the punishment as only solid wood can. When it finally is scarred and scratched too much to be repaired cosmetically, you can sand away the wear and tear and refinish it like new. Wainscoting also allows you to have an expensive wood plank wall at only half or less the price, since only half or less of the wall is covered with wood.

Wainscoting boards (usually 1 by 3 inches by whatever height you desire) are available from a number of suppliers. Or you can use any available tongue-and-groove planking. Or make your own board-and-batten wainscoting out of any available lumber. It's easy to install over any wall. Thin wainscoting slats can be glued even to masonry walls. Or you can mount two horizontal boards across the studs and nail the vertical slats to them. Then top the vertical boards with cap molding and rail molding. If the boards you are using are not too thick, you may not even have to take the baseboard off. Cut the slats to fit against the top of the baseboard, then cover the abutting edges with a face trim.

it to say here that nearly everyone who has ever taken the lid off a can of varnish has a firm opinion on the matter. My own feeling is that a good plain wax finish is something to consider. Wax tends to get dirty quicker than a varnish or shellac and wears away where fingers frequently touch it. And if you ever want to put on another finish, removing all the wax might be difficult. But on the other hand, wax is easy to apply, easy to polish or give a new shine to, fairly easy to wash dirt off of, and most important, doesn't show scratches the way other clear finishes do. (Scratches in wax can be often obliterated with a little more wax.) A homemade wax recommended for wood consists of 2 pounds of beeswax dissolved in a gallon of hot turpentine. Be very, very careful heating turpentine because it is highly flammable. Use a double boiler in a well-ventilated place. Just rub the warm wax solution on with a cloth, let dry, and then buff.

Some solid-wood planking is not smooth but retains the texture of rough wood, or in the case of certain popular ''barnboard'' planks, is stressed artificially to resemble old weathered wood. On these planks, a wax finish would not be practical. Barnboard planks are often varnished-stained at the factory and require no other finish. Obviously, textured wood is going to be harder to keep clean and should be installed, in the low-maintenance house, where dirt is a minimal problem. Clean by vacuuming it.

Tile Walls

The ultimate in easy-care walls is ceramic tile, most would agree. Nothing resists dirt and staining as well, or cleans easier. Wear and breakage on walls are almost impossible. Because of its impervious and enduring nature, however, ceramic tile is called upon to cover walls in the most difficult of situations, which is, above all, around the bathtub and shower stall. If bathroom walls were built like in-ground swimming pool walls, there would be no problem. But when we attach a thin water-impervious skin to a stud wall, we are demanding of nature almost the impossible. Someone came up with the solution a decade or so ago—the one-piece molded fiberglass shower and tub assembly. But to keep the price low enough these units are small, very standard, and ugly to many people. One person I know says it's like taking a bath in a plastic bottle. Nevertheless, these one-piece units (that also now come in polyvinyl chloride or PVC, which is cheaper than fiberglass) are good for low maintenance. A large bathroom, totally encased in cast iron covered with good porcelain would be the ultimate, but no one could afford it. Lightweight fiberglass and PVC systems you can install yourself are the practical alternative. One source is Traco Bath Systems (Delta Faucet Company, 55 East 111 Street, Indianapolis, IN 46280).

To clean fiberglass and plastic bathtub and shower assemblies (or even porcelain, for that matter), you should not use abrasive cleansers,

Molded fiberglass and PVC tubs and enclosures are a less expensive alternative to porcelain and ceramic fixtures. They're easier to install, too, but not necessarily easier to keep clean.

which mar the surface. There are now cleansers designed for cleaning just such surfaces, like Dow's Bathroom Cleaner with Scrubbing Bubbles, which TV has made famous. They will not scratch fiberglass. However, in time, fiberglass and plastic will stain in some water, usually picking up a very light brown tinge which cleansers won't remove entirely. This is one reason why investing in porcelain in the first place is lower maintenance in the long run. Over and over again "you gets what you pays for."

Installing Ceramic Tiles

There are different ways to put up ceramic tiles: one right way and several wrong ways. Unfortunately, the way that's most wrong of all is still commonly followed: The ceramic tiles are glued to a plaster or drywall wall and grouted with an organic adhesive or mastic, the kind you should *not* use in high-moisture areas because water will inevitably get through it.

(Organic adhesives originally were made from rubber extracts and now refer to a whole class of mastics that dry and cure by evaporation.) But in this kind of slapdash installation, even using an epoxy grout is not insurance that within a few years the grout will not crack, allowing moisture to seep to the inside. When this happens, the tiles loosen and soon must be removed and reglued. I've seen it happen in too many bathrooms including one of our own. Often the adhesive holding the tiles to the wall remains very intact but the whole outer layer of plaster comes loose! If you merely scrape off the loose plaster, clean the backs of the tiles and reglue, expect the same problem to recur in five years, although you can slow the inevitable leakage through the grout by covering it with a sealer or elastometric caulk, the kind you use to seal the crack between the tub and wall.

As I mentioned, we did one of our bathrooms the wrong way because we were trying to save money over the more expensive right way that we used in our main bathroom. In the latter, we called in a professional ceramic-tile installer. (The other bathroom was tiled by a general carpenter who tried to talk us into cheaper plastic panels, which indeed would have lasted longer without maintenance than the ceramic tile he was installing the wrong way, as he knew fully well.)

The professional, following the *Handbook for Ceramic Tile Installation* (available from the Tile Council of America, P.O. Box 326, Princeton, NJ 08540) nailed galvanized metal lath (mesh) on the stud wall very securely, that is, about every 8 inches. If you don't use galvanized lath, the lath will eventually rust away. Make sure the right side faces outward. The little cups of mesh should slope upward, away from the wall. This is hard to tell by sight, but if you run your fingers upward, the mesh will feel smoother than running them downward. Then he overlaid the metal lath with a scratch coat about ¼ inch thick made of one part portland cement, five parts sand, and ⅕ part lime. When this was dry, he laid on a mortar bed about ½ to ¾ inch thick, leveling the wall. He then bonded the tile to the mortar bed with a latex-portland cement mortar. (There are two other portland cement and dry-set mortars that you can use instead of this mixture. Both work well, but one requires that the tile be soaked before installing—see *The Handbook for Ceramic Tile Installation,* mentioned above.) He then grouted with a portland cement-sand mixture to which latex had been added. This procedure is very similar to laying a ceramic-tile floor, as I describe in chapter 11.

The grout can be further sealed with some silicone sealer (if the grout label calls for it) and by all means, the crack between tub and tile should be so sealed. Incidentally, that crack should not widen with the years. Mediocre building that allows houses to settle and the bathtub to fall away from the wall is something we have all come to expect, but one sign of a really well-built house is that the tub doesn't fall away. Ours hasn't. If it does, resealing with a silicone caulk is important or moisture will get behind the lower tiles.

Pregrouted tiles relieve most of the agony of installation: no more struggling to keep the spaces between tiles straight and even.

Our ceramic tiles were installed 12 years ago and we have had no problems like we've had in the other bathroom. Nor does it seem any are forthcoming.

I realize today that epoxy adhesives combined with portland cement are giving results as good as the old mortar-bed style and are easier and quicker to work with. These new methods are usually referred to generically as "thinset" since the bed of mortar and adhesive is not as thick as it is in the old method. Using these epoxy-cement mixtures with galvanized metal lath for a wall anchor may give good low-maintenance permanence. (Be sure to use one of the new rock lath boards made especially for ceramic tile, like Durock [USG Corporation, 101 South Wacker Drive, Chicago, IL 60606].) But the information I can garner from installers is that the old way is still better, if costlier.

Designer Tiles to Choose From

What makes ceramic wall tile so exciting today is the wonderful array of designer tiles available. Some of the new crystal-glazed and opalescent tiles look like jewels or little works of art. Together with the durability of ceramic and the epoxy adhesives, we may witness a resurgence of ceramic tile to the high level of popularity it enjoyed in the late 1800s when entire rooms were enclosed in it from floor to ceiling—even ceramic baseboards and chair rails! In fact, some of the demand for ceramic tile is coming from the resurgence of interest in Victorian house styles and fashions. (There is an entire magazine published now for people interested in restoring Victorian homes, and it is an excellent source for ideas and products for sale in low-maintenance materials. It's called *Victorian Homes* [Renovator's Supply, Box 61, Renovator's Old Mill, Millers Falls, MA 01349].)

There is, in addition to the fine and numerous kinds of ceramic tile from mass producers, select designer tiles from the same manufacturers and some very unique kinds and designs from sources that are just one leg up from cottage industry. The Moravian Pottery and Tile Works (Swamp Road, Doylestown, PA 18901) is making reproductions of the famed Henry C. Mercer tiles of the early part of this century. Also available are unique styles from Sax Tatterson (Box 15, Taos, NM 87571). The finest stock selections come from Mexico, Portugal, and Italy and are available through American companies like American Olean Tile (1000 Cannon Avenue, P.O. Box 271, Lansdale, PA 19446-0271). The Tile Gallery (300 D Street SW, Washington, DC 20024) is another source of unusual tiles.

Actually, if you have any knowledge of pottery, or are ever tempted to learn, making your own tiles is much easier than throwing a pot on a potter's wheel. Other than a kiln, you really need no special equipment. You can make wood molds and cut designs in the clay with an old knife. Or carve designs on wood blocks and imprint them in wet clay. Many, many books tell you how. Incidentally, the American Olean Tile Company, mentioned above, has over a dozen publications on all aspects of ceramic tile, including the latest simplified methods of installation. Pregrouted tile panels now obviate some of the skills formerly important in tile installation. It may be a good idea to have a professional install tile in a shower, but there's no reason you can't do a kitchen wall or countertop yourself. And what a countertop it will be. Good porcelain ceramic is almost completely impervious to moisture—less than ½ of 1 percent absorption. It is stain-proof and dent-proof (although under hard impact it may crack).

Stone and Masonry Walls

Any stone or masonry used in floors or exterior siding will work as an interior wall, often with dramatic effect. The use of such walls has become more popular in new energy-conserving houses because they provide some heat storage capacity and are ideal in houses with passive solar systems. A good example is the headquarters of Amory Lovins (the high

If laying stone is more than you can handle, these facsimile concrete stones might be for you; they're easier to install than the real thing.

priest of low-energy alternatives) in Colorado—a long sinuous stone wall, which winds around most of the house, provides great beauty and practicality simultaneously. Rough cobblestone walls are not easy to clean, but if they get dirty they don't show it. Construction and labor costs are high whenever a nonconventional material like this is used, and most people, no matter how much they love low- or no-maintenance stone interior walls, are content to limit themselves to fireplace and chimney-facing stone, or at most to one wall in which the fireplace is located.

Real stone walls are heavy and require deep and sturdy foundations. Where the look of stone is desired in a room that can't be bolstered with such a foundation, various kinds of fake stone made of special concretes are available. The word, fake, does not do them justice, however, since they can look remarkably real and are available in all kinds of stone colors and formations, some classier than the real thing. Coronado Products, Inc. (1325 6th Avenue North, Nashville, TN 37208-0568) is one manufacturer with national distribution. Installation requires no special support or wall ties. The stones are usually laid against metal lath with mastic and then grouted in place.

Concrete Block

Concrete masonry blocks, specially scored on the facing and integrally colored, make a low-maintenance wall of great permanence. Most

Concrete blocks, often limited to basement and garage walls, can look pretty good in the living room, too. Use them creatively and you can have a very practical, lovely wall.

often, the structural load-bearing walls are made of these special blocks and their facings serve as the decorative wall finish, too, both inside and out. (They may be given a coat or two of sealer to keep out moisture and make cleaning easier.) Building this way is fairly low cost since once the blocks are laid the walls are finished. No paint, no drywall, no plaster, no paneling, no wallpapering. The concrete mass acts as a thermal mass, too, in passive solar systems, and generally helps to keep a building cooler on a hot day and warmer on a cold night. It also provides great fire safety, which is why condo and apartment builders like it—great savings in fire insurance. In an apartment complex, the blocks cut down on noise better than frame walls. The overall visual effect of the scored blocks is surprisingly attractive, too. Write for the pictorial brochures from the National Concrete Masonry Association (2302 Horse Pen Road, Box 781, Herndon, VA 22070) or better yet, pay a visit to your nearest concrete block manufacturer. As I've mentioned earlier, you'll be surprised at what has happened to the lowly concrete block these days.

Bricks

Conventional bricks can be used in interiors and often are, but available now are thin bricks, more like tile, which you glue to the wall individually or in panels. Your lumberyard carries them. It probably also carries plastic tile "brick" that looks and even feels like real brick but goes up much more easily. Easier still to put up are interior wall panels that have brick facings. The better ones are so well designed that you can hardly tell them from real bricks. Masonite Corporation (1 South Wacker Drive, Chicago, IL 60606) is a leading manufacturer of these panels.

Marble Tiles

Marble tiles for interior walls are now available with a new adhesive that makes installation easy. The makers of Hearthstone Decorator Tiles (Hearthstone Way, Morrisville, VT 05661) believe their "Ultrabond" adhesive is not only easy to use but permanent. Each individual marble tile has an adhesive tab at each corner and one in the middle. All you do is stick them up. No goo of any kind to slop on the wall and then sag and slump while you frantically try to get the tiles on straight and square. Nor do you have to smear grout all over the wall to get it packed into the gaps

Brick wall panels grace the walls and island in this kitchen.

thoroughly. You apply vinyl caulk neatly between the tiles instead. The company recommends a clear lacquer to protect the marble. Detailed instructions on installation are available with your purchase. These tiles go on over any surface, even plastic laminate.

Plastic Laminates and the Like

Plastic laminates are most often used for kitchen and bathroom countertops, and so this section doesn't really belong in a chapter on walls and ceilings. But there is no better place to put it in this book, and I'd hate to leave it out; plastic laminates are to many people the ultimate in low maintenance surfaces. What's more, they *are* sometimes used on walls, in the bathroom and kitchen and other places where there's water splashing around.

A few years ago, Formica and the other laminate manufacturers came out with a new product—what they refer to as their "solid color" laminates. Because the color goes all the way through the laminate, edges do not have the layered veneer look. I doubt this development means a great deal to most people because edges are usually covered up anyway. And I doubt that solid colors necessarily mean these new laminates have more quality. Some, in fact, do not wear as well as the older kinds, but because the color or pattern goes deeper, wear is not as noticeable. Don't expect the durability of ceramic tile, however, and when or if you replace the old countertop with a new one, do expect some hard work getting the old adhesive off. Usually it's nearly impossible, and the new adhesive won't stick well to any old adhesive that's remaining. Most carpenters simply replace the whole countertop. But you can also glue a new layer of laminate over the old. This is sticky work, pun not intended, and before you are through you may wish you had replaced the whole countertop—or covered it originally with longer-lasting ceramic tile instead. (To make laminate last longer, it is not a good idea to use it for a cutting board, as my wife scolds me for doing; a knife can leave permanent marks in it.)

Choices in laminates range from simulated leather to granite, agate, and marble mimics. Choose one of the thicker laminates for a countertop (.05 inch deep) or you are really asking for high maintenance.

Laminates are being used more and more on walls, where they wear better than on countertops. (A thickness of .028 is plenty for a wall.) Here again the choice of designs and colors is almost endless, including leather, stone, and wood-grain mimics and decorative wallpaperlike panels. Manufacturers with good (free) information include: Formica Corporation (1501 Broadway, Room 1519, New York, NY 10036), Nevamar Corporation (8339 Telegraph Road, Odenton, MD 21113), and Wilsonart (Ralph Wilson Plastics Company, 600 General Bruce Drive, Temple, TX 76501).

Corian is an extremely popular choice for new bathroom sink and countertop combinations. It's good looking and wears very well. And because the sink and counter are all one piece, there's no joint to grout and keep intact.

A much better low-maintenance countertop material than plastic laminate is Corian (E. I. Dupont de Nemours Company, Corian Building Products, Wilmington, DE 19898), which looks like marble and ranks right up there with it in price. Corian has advantages over laminate in that it is a much more permanent installation. Its cultured marble appearance runs completely through the thickness and so wear doesn't show. Nor does it need to be glued to a plywood or other substrate like laminate does. You can sand away scratches and blemishes like cigarette burns, and the repair is not noticeable. Stains are easier to clean up on Corian than on most marbles, and it can be cut and worked like hardwood (using special blades), so you can custom-fit it to any situation. One of Corian's biggest sellers is its one-piece counter/sink combination. It's great for low maintenance on wet bars, tabletops, desktops, island tops, telephone counters, and windowsills. In bathrooms, it gives the look of cultured marble to one-piece vanity tops and tubs and matching shower walls, windowsills, and baseboards.

Ceilings

Structurally, ceilings face a problem not shared by the rest of the house. Unlike a wall or floor, most of the ceiling's weight has no underpinning but *hangs* from the joists overhead on the relatively frail strength of nails, screws, or adhesives. To make matters worse, style dictates heavy plaster ceilings, or heavier drywall panels overlaid with textured plaster. It is no wonder that the first sign of aging in a house is usually cracked or sagging ceilings. Plaster is the lesser of two evils in this case because it is not as heavy as drywall. Because of its weight, drywall *must* be installed with screws, not nails.

Textured plaster ceilings are relatively cheap. In a room where dirt is not a particular problem, they are fairly easy to maintain if the rock or metal lath is solidly fastened to the joists and if the joists are dry and solidly braced before installation. The key to any kind of plastering is a very well-built house frame that keeps expansion and contraction to a minimum. Finely textured plaster is okay, but heavily textured plaster should be avoided; it is difficult to paint and impossible to clean.

In a kitchen or bathroom, a smooth plaster ceiling has the advantage of not having any grooves or indentations to make cleaning more difficult. But greasy kitchen stains can rarely be scrubbed *completely* from the ceiling; streaks remain. Here is where paint is wonderful (in my opinion the *only* place paint is wonderful). Once reasonably clean, the smooth plaster ceiling can be painted to like-new condition. And repainted as necessary. In the long run, this is easier maintenance than trying to clean unremovable ceiling tile.

Lightweight wood panels or planks would make very good low-maintenance sense for ceilings, but only recently have they been merchandised, and homeowners appear hesitant to use them this way, not just because of cost. A tongue-and-groove "siding" could make a very practical ceiling nailed directly to the joists, but few like the idea of wood grain over their heads, especially the darker shades of wood. Ceilings must be light-colored, and the fact that wood can be blonded or painted white never seems to occur to many people.

Ceiling Tiles

Instead of wood panels or planks, ceilings are now very often wood fiber, mineral fiber, plastics, and fiberglass, shaped into tiles usually a foot square, but sometimes 2 feet square. When these tiles are factory finished for easy cleaning, they are the best low-cost solution for low maintenance. The acoustical kinds absorb noise very well. But the biggest advantage of these tiles is that if the ceiling is damaged by roof leaks or anything else, you can remove individual tiles rather than having to do over a whole ceiling. The choices in tile design are many, both in the new look of real wood panels and the old traditional look of embossed paper or fancy plaster.

The suspended ceiling tiles that rest in metal or vinyl frames (and that now can be purchased in colors that match or complement the tiles) are particularly nice for cleaning. You merely lift them out of their frames and wash them at the sink instead of having to break your back, neck, and arms reaching above your head to scrub them.

Suspended ceiling tiles are, of course, only practical if you have enough headroom. Suspended ceilings came into vogue to lower high Victorian ceilings so that the rooms wouldn't be so expensive to heat. They have proven so handy for hiding plumbing and light-fixture wires that buildings, especially office buildings, are built with enough headroom to allow for them. However, today you can use suspended ceilings in almost any standard height room—if you don't plan to invite many 7-foot 10-inch basketball players in for a party.

As I said a bit earlier, these tiles are designed to hang in metal or vinyl frames, but they can alternatively be nailed directly to furring strips that are nailed to the overhead joists. Installation information is easily available when and where you buy the tiles. It pays to use quality wood for furring strips—straight, clear kiln-dried pine or fir in 1-by-3-inch or 1-by-4-inch dimensions. This is no place for knotty, warped boards.

Ceiling Moldings

If you are doing over an old Victorian house authentically, you may be staring up at some once-beautiful plaster molding that is cracked or chipped. Small cracks can be filled with plaster of Paris or Spackle, and chips can be built up with new plaster. You can even replace whole sections of damaged molding with new by making a new mold from the existing molding—many books and magazines show you how. But it is all high maintenance. I think it's much better to replace it, when possible, with new lightweight polyurethane moldings that look exactly like old plaster, or, in other forms, like fancy wood molding. That advice is probably anathema to authentic restorers, but at least if you desire fancy molding in a new room or an old one not previously so ornate, these synthetic cornice moldings, chandelier bases, etc., etc., look as good as plaster and can be cut, sawed, sanded, and painted. Vinyl moldings that look like wood are good for low maintenance, too, if you can be satisfied not using real wood. I can't. Though in this case wood may mean slightly more maintenance because it may chip or scratch more easily, but you can repair gouges, scratches, and chips in it better than in vinyl.

Metal Ceiling Panels

Some 60 years ago, metal ceiling panels were very popular, and you can still find them by the thousands in shops and businesses along the Midwest's Main Streets. Today, stamped metal ceiling panels usually re-

Individual metal panels have been pieced together here to re-create a lovely old patterned ceiling.

ferred to as tin ceilings are enjoying a minor comeback, even in residences. They can be used as they are finished from the factory, usually in some metallic luster, or they can be painted. Be sure to wash the panels with paint thinner to remove the protective coat of oil before painting. Prime with an oil-base metal primer and topcoat with alkyd (enamel) paint unless manufacturer's directions advise otherwise. Stamped metal for ceilings or walls is available from W. F. Norman Corporation (P.O. Box 323, Nevada, MO 64772); and from A. A. Abbingdon Affiliates (2149 Utica Avenue, Brooklyn, NY 11234).

Exciting new metal panels for ceilings and/or walls are available in brass and aluminum. Contact especially Wilsonart (Ralph Wilson Plastics Company, 600 General Bruce Drive, Temple, TX 76501). And they come in a variety of colors—polished black aluminum, polished brass aluminum, polished gold aluminum, polished smoke aluminum, solid-polished brass, stain-brushed bronze aluminum, and others. Although their use in residences has been limited so far, they make extremely stunning ceilings.

The polished or brushed surfaces will scratch or mar rather easily, which makes the panels better for ceilings than walls. The panels come from the factory with a protective film to prevent scuffing and this film should not be removed until the panels are safely installed. (They are bonded to ceiling or walls with prescribed adhesives.) Care must be taken not to bend them too much or the panels might crease. Clean with warm water and mild soap; abrasive cleaners could scratch the decorative sheen of the metal.

CHAPTER 13

FURNITURE AND CABINETS

From the standpoint of low maintenance, we should gauge furniture value first of all by its construction; how long it will last without breaking or falling apart. Then we should determine how long various treatments will preserve the wood from decay due to moisture or insects. Thirdly, we need to look at what finishes will preserve the desired color or patina of the wood the longest, and which of these means less work in keeping the furniture clean and presentable. Unfortunately, these practical considerations are often superceded by fad and fashion before which there is no defense. I can tout the advantages of one furniture style over another, or one finish over another until I'm blue in the face, and if fashion or fad dictates something else, something else it will be, except for those sensible enough who don't mind taking the road less traveled.

Determining Furniture Construction

For example, some Chippendale chairs of great value have backs that are too fragile to even score a C for low maintenance. George Grotz, in his *The Furniture Doctor* (Doubleday, 1983), goes so far as to say that "Chippendale chairs are fragile pieces that you either have to keep in glass cases or continually repair." The reason he says that, not altogether tongue-in-cheek, is that Mr. Chippendale liked to dress up his furniture with all kinds of fancies popular at the time—ornate carvings, or in the case of some of his chair backs, with intricate cutouts in the back rails. Structurally, these ornate holes in the wood did nothing but weaken it, especially when a really stout lord of the manor leaned back while sitting in one.

Length of the Grain

An even worse design flaw in my opinion is the Hepplewhite shield-back chair. Especially in less expensive imitations of the originals, these chair backs are glued together from several short curved pieces of wood and will not hold up to heavy use. In fact, whenever you see any wood furniture design that incorporates round or excessively curved lines, be-ware. Most curved crest rails on chairs, particularly the round balloon-back Victorian chairs, are structural disasters. As Desmond Gaston says in his *Care and Repair of Furniture* (Doubleday, 1978), such chairs should never be lifted with only one hand at the middle of the crest rail, but with two hands, one on each back upright. Better still: Avoid furniture with structural pieces of wood in round or smartly curved forms, *unless the wood is bent to form the curve,* as in a good Windsor chair.

The reason is that wood's structural strength derives from what car-penters refer to as "long grain" wood. If you cut a board lengthwise with the grain—the only way you can cut a long board—it has strength. Try cutting a thin strip of wood off a wide board cross-grained, and you will find the subsequent stick or strip very weak—you can snap it in two over your knee. "Short grain" has no tensile strength.

Keeping that in mind, take a look at the grain in any board. It usually runs fairly straight down the length of the board. If you cut a curved or rounded piece out of that board, as for a crest rail or whatever, you have a comparatively weak piece with lots of short grain. Any sharply rounded piece cut from a board will be extremely weak. Therefore to maintain long-grain strength in a curved form, you either have to bend the wood or tenon two, three, or more slightly curved pieces of wood together, each piece maintaining as much long grain as possible. Strength in the latter case depends on how well the glue and tenon joints hold up over the years, and the usual answer is, not so well in a chair back.

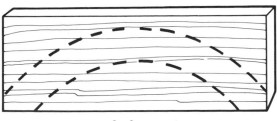

A weak wood curve.

**a weak short grain;
will break easily**

Three stronger wood curves.

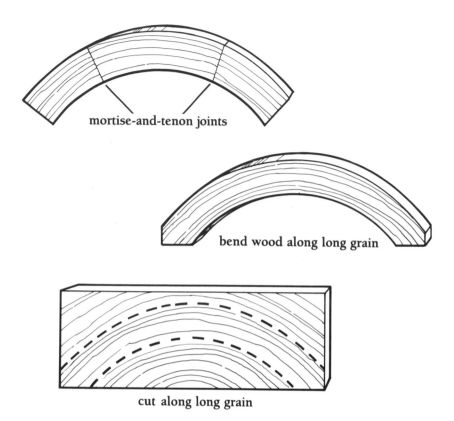

mortise-and-tenon joints

bend wood along long grain

cut along long grain

There is a third and best way to get a curve and that is to use only naturally curved-grain wood for curved shapes. Thus in James Krenov's masterful pieces of cabinetry, invariably curved pieces are made of curved grain. You can see the grain flow with the curve. Handcrafters in wood always keep their eyes open for such boards in lumberyards or limbs or tree trunks in the woods. For example, the best old farm wagon sled runners are cut from ash trunks that grow out in a short curve at the base of the tree. Rockers on rocking chairs should come from curved-grain boards or from curved branches thick enough to cut into rocker boards. If a rocker is cut out of a straight-grained board, it is bound to be weaker.

Joinery

A second characteristic of wood that affects structural soundness is its tendency to swell and shrink with changing humidity. Therefore, how pieces of wood are joined in furniture is of crucial importance. If there is no allowance for wood movement, the joints will shrink and loosen or swell and break. Chair rungs and back spindles are the worst sinners in this regard. If you simply drill a hole in wood and glue a rung or spindle in it, in time it will loosen and pull out and/or break off. On good furniture, extra measures are taken to lock the joint. To use Thomas Moser's current furniture as but one example, rungs and spindles go all the way through the chair seat or back rail, then they are spread at the socket with a wooden wedge—the same technique that's used to keep a hammer handle in its head.

At the very least, rungs and spindles should be heat-dried down to 8 percent moisture or lower (which is lower than the prevailing humidity in a house) and then seated tightly in their holes. The spindle or rung then swells a bit in ordinary room humidity, locking it almost irrevocably. Even if room humidity in winter gets down to where the wood shrinks a bit, it will not shrink enough to break the glue joint. When heat-dried rungs or spindles are used with green seat or leg wood, as in good handmade Appalachian ladderback chairs (such as you can find for sale in Berea, Kentucky, where Berea College has long been supportive of traditional crafts), the joints are the strongest possible: the green wood shrinks and the heat dried spindles or rungs swell a little. No glue is used at all. This

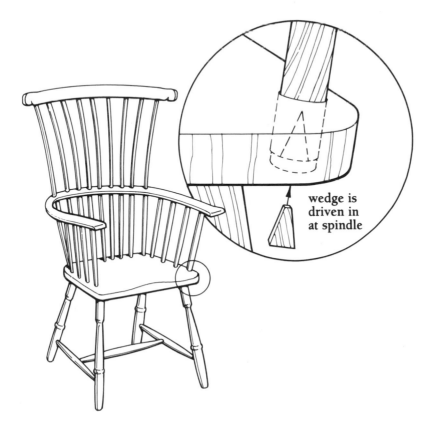

Locking a furniture joint.

wedge is
driven in
at spindle

was (and with the Amish still is) the way mortised-and-tenoned barn beams were joined so permanently together in traditional barns. After 200 years, sometimes the only way to take such a joint apart is to cut it apart with a chain saw.

You can't tell by looking at a chair if the rungs and spindles have been joined this way. Price may be an indication—a Moser chair, so made, will cost around $500 and after you have fussed with cheap chairs half a lifetime, you know the price is worth it. You can, however, check for through-wedges. Cabinetmakers who use them let them show proudly where they come through the seat or leg or back rail, handsomely sanded down, the wedge a dark line across the face of the spindle. Usually this is a sign of good furniture. But the ultimate Cadillac, or maybe I should say Rolls-Royce of a chair rung joint is a *hidden* through-wedge. Instead of boring a hole completely through a chair leg, which of course weakens the leg a bit more than a hole only partially through, the hole is bored about halfway, wider at the rear than at the opening. Then a slot is made in the rung, the wedge started in the slot, then the rung inserted, wedge first, into the hole. As the rung is driven home, the wedge spreads the rung end to fit the hole and lock it in place. It takes great skill to do this right, because once the rung is driven in, you're going to have a hard time pulling it out again if the fit is not right.

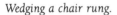

Wedging a chair rung.

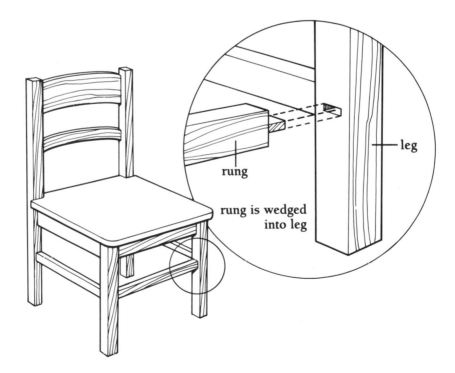

rung

leg

rung is wedged
into leg

Another never-failing joint for spindles is seen today only on some good handmade furniture, though it was often used on Windsor chairs a century ago. The back rail on a good Windsor is all one piece, bent to the proper curve and the ends through-wedged into the seat. The intervening vertical spindles were through-wedged at the top. But where these spindles join to the seat, instead of through-wedging, old-time cabinetmakers cut slots in the back of the seat board and left a knob on the end of the spindles. The spindles were then inserted into the slots and the slots closed by one of a number of ways. It was then impossible for the spindles to pull out because the knobs on each spindle end were larger than the slot. Such spindles last for generations without glue. They may get loose, but they can't come out.

In carcase construction (any furniture in box form like cabinets and chests), there are many ways to join the corners, from simple gluing to intricate dovetailing. Simple gluing of a butt end of a board to the side edge of the one perpendicular to it, without any kind of joinery notching the boards into each other, is the least durable. Miracle glues we may have, but they won't keep wood from swelling and shrinking. At least dowels (pegs) ought to accompany gluing, if not grooves that allow horizontal boards to fit into vertical ones in some way that spreads the stress of the joint to the wood as well as the glue. Countersunk metal screws are never as strong as dowels but will hold wood together fairly well in cheaper furniture. The problem with screws as with wonder glues is that the temptation in using them is to avoid good joinery methods instead of using them in combination with such methods. And if good joinery methods are used, there is no need for screws or wonder glues. Incidentally, in repairing furniture, using nails and screws hardly ever gives long-lasting results. Wood and glue alone will make a stronger and more durable repair every time. Nails will only cause problems for your furniture repair shop when you finally take the piece there for proper fixing.

With plywood and veneer, you might get away with cheaper joinery methods, maybe even glue alone, because these products do not move—swell and shrink—as much as solid wood. We tend to look down on good veneered furniture as inferior to solid wood, which it is in strength and repairability. But laminated wood does not warp like solid wood can. And you can cut more gracious curves in laminated wood without worrying about short grain.

Most furniture-makers would agree that the best carcase joint of all is the dovetail. Trapezoidal-shaped notches are cut into one edge of a board and matching notches are made in the edge of the board that it is joined to at right angles. The two slip together so that you see a row of little dovetails on one side and, if you go around the corner of the joint, so to speak, you'll see a row of little rectangles. Sometimes, depending on fashion, the dovetails are hidden, but today they speak so much for quality that furniture-makers display them grandly, often using contrasting woods to make them

Dovetails at drawer corners.

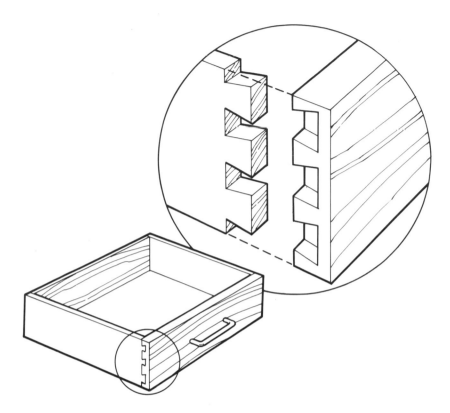

show up better. Dovetail joints can be machine made, and almost all better furniture will have at least the side joints of drawers dovetailed. Hidden, machine-made dovetails (cut with a power router) are weaker than hand-made ones because the router groove cuts away about a third of the dovetail's thickness.

In good frame-and-panel construction, as in a door or paneled cabinet, the frame boards are mortised and tenoned into each other at the corners, and a groove is cut all along the inside of the frame. The panel fits into these grooves and is not glued. Rather, the panel "floats" in the grooves, having enough room so the wood can swell and shrink without splitting the wood. This is especially necessary on an exterior door exposed to the weather.

Mortise-and-tenon joints are also used to join braces to legs, chair back splats to uprights, like the "ladders" in a ladderback chair, and table aprons to table legs. This kind of joint provides a much greater area for gluing than the usual round hole of a rung or spindle and so is much stronger. Sometimes in handcrafted furniture, the artisan will put a wood pin or two through the mortise-and-tenon joint, which locks it even more permanently.

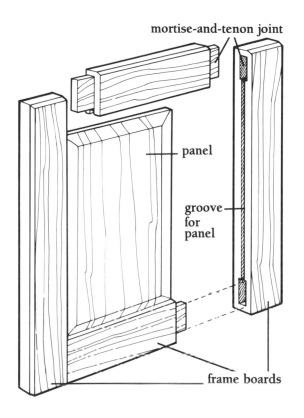

mortise-and-tenon joint

panel

groove for panel

frame boards

"Floating" frame-and-panel construction.

On really good furniture, the cabinetmaker will almost always use a clear finish so that the pins, the mortise-and-tenon joint itself, and any other kind of fancy joinery will show clearly. Beware of furniture that is stained so dark and heavy that you can't see grain or joinery details. Before I knew better, I bought a set of spindleback chairs that loosened in three years. The uprights on the back were indeed through-wedged to the seat, but the wedges had not been properly driven in, nor did the uprights reach completely through the seat. Close inspection showed that the ill-made joints were hidden under a varnish-stain glop. I should have been suspicious anyway, because the chair legs were reinforced under the seat with little metal braces. In quality chairs, these braces are entirely unnecessary.

The best furniture in terms of structural strength is what is called knockdown furniture, most often exemplified by the trestle table. Knockdown furniture, as the name indicates, comes apart easily and is favored by people who know they are going to change residences often. Because it is not glued or screwed together, knockdown furniture must depend on structurally sound and skillful joinery, keyed together with wedges. If you try to wiggle a knockdown trestle table and it doesn't wiggle, you know you are in the presence of first-rate cabinetry. The piece is made to swell

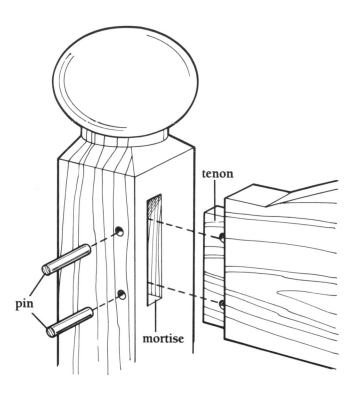

Mortise-and-tenon joint with wood pins.

and shrink in season with no worries about breaking glue joints. I have a little spice cabinet that remains fairly tight though it has no glue in it and comes completely apart. The mortising, dovetailing, and pegging necessary in such knockdown furniture, however, takes so much handwork that it is rarely done commercially even in small handcraft shops.

Another detail to look for in furniture design is the triangle. Oddly, except for a few mavericks, furniture incorporating triangles has not been

Arms Add Strength to Chairs

Chairs made for use around the table do not usually have arms. And such chairs must rely almost solely on the joints between the back and the seat for strength. Since the weight of the person leaning against the chair back is more toward the top of the back, the leverage engendered puts great stress on the joints at the seat. And this is the main reason so many chair backs come loose. This problem is greatly alleviated if the chair has arms because the arms act as an extra brace higher up on the chair back, greatly relieving the stress at the seat joints. The moral of the story? For greater durability, buy chairs with arms even if they don't fit under the table. The armrests add considerable comfort to sitting, too.

Can Leaning Back on a Chair Weaken It?

It is not altogether correct to say that a chair can be ruined by leaning back in it on the back two legs. With cheap furniture it certainly is true, and more might be ruined than just the chair. But a well-made chair should hold you safely on two legs as easily as four, as Appalachian makers of good ladderbacks love to demonstrate. One maker has even developed a trick of hopping around on *one* leg of his chairs just to show how strong they are.

---

popular for several centuries, the rectangle being the approved geometric unit. But try this experiment sometime: Nail four boards together in a rectangle, with one nail at each corner. You can easily move it into any parallelogram shape you desire. Now nail three boards into a triangle with one nail at each corner. It won't budge. Using triangles, you can build stout furniture even with relatively flimsy components. The moral: If you see chairs, tables and sofas with triangular bracing, you know they have inherent strength.

Other Signs of Quality Furniture

• Is the chair seat flat or is it carved out to take the shape of the buttocks? The flatter the cheaper, the more deeply sculptured, the higher the quality.

• Are carvings or inlay work well done or sloppy? Such decoration in itself neither adds to nor detracts from the durability of the piece, but it does indicate care and skill in the cabinetmaker.

• Are the inside and underside corners of cabinets, chests, etc., reinforced with glue blocks? They should be.

• Open the drawers of bureaus and look inside. Are there dust panels between drawers? If so, this is almost always a sign of quality furniture.

• Lay the extension leaves of a table you want to buy on top of the table. Do they match the tabletop precisely? On good furniture they will. On poor furniture, they might not. Also, both the top and bottom of table leaves should be finished exactly the same way. If not, the side with less finish will pick up moisture or dry out at a different rate than the other side, causing warping.

• Look through the butt edge of a board on your piece. The more vertical the grain that runs through the thickness of a board, the more stable it will be. The more curved or horizontal the grain through the thickness, the more it will be inclined to warp. The former is called quartersawn, the latter flat-sawn. Quartersawing wood wastes some of the log and is not commonly done anymore, but it is superior structurally.

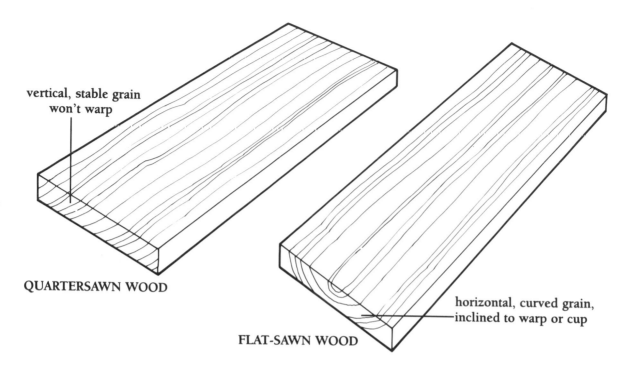

vertical, stable grain
won't warp

QUARTERSAWN WOOD

horizontal, curved grain,
inclined to warp or cup

FLAT-SAWN WOOD

*Edge grains in wood
boards.*

Upholstered Furniture

In upholstered furniture, the best seats have coiled springs tied together with lots of fabric webbing. But such springs demand a heavy framework to hold them from breaking loose after a few years, especially when Uncle Filbert breaks his diet and drops 245 pounds of flesh into them. You might be better served with light furniture, and the cheaper flat intertwining S springs. They are not as comfortable and hopefully not as inviting to Uncle Filbert, and so less likely to need costly repair work. Rubber and other light, springy kinds of webbing to support seats alone are not practical no matter how cheap. They soon sag out of shape. Better to have a solid wood seat with foam rubber cushions.

Vinyl coverings for upholstery are the easiest to clean and maintain. Whether you want to cover richly upholstered furniture to keep it clean is a matter of opinion, I suppose. What is the use of having grand furniture if it is never seen except when you throw a party (which is just when it needs a covering the most)? It reminds me of people who buy expensive cars with a beautiful front grille and then cover the grille with an ugly bug screen. But a good compromise in furniture is to cover chair and sofa arms with little pads of an attractive, matching pattern. The arms are what get dirty quickest and where the most wear takes place. And armrest coverings can be easily washed.

Feel through the upholstery on a chair or sofa you want to buy. Is the wood ample at the bottom rail of the frame? It should measure at least 2 by 2 inches. Grab the top of one back upright in one hand and the front of the arm diagonally opposite to it in the other hand. Pull toward each other. Then pull the two arms toward each other from the front. In both cases if there is a lot of give, the joints are no doubt bad. Keep this little technique in mind when buying used pieces. If there is much give in a new piece, then it is really bad stuff.

On used furniture, look for worm holes. By the kind of mysterious obstinancy human beings are regularly capable of, a dent or gouge in furniture may be unforgiveable, but worm holes give added value. But if the worm holes are active, there's nothing attractive about them. Look for frass (fine sawdust) under a piece of furniture—it indicates active worm holes. Spraying a few times in the holes with an insecticide usually gets rid of the borers, but if they have been in the wood a long time, they may have weakened it badly. Furniture that sits near fireplaces is often the first to be infested with borers. The reason is most logical. The borers come in with the firewood brought in to burn. The best remedy is to bring in wood only as needed for the fire. Borers will chew in most woods but seem to favor beech, birch, and elm. And there's a kind that loves to eat wicker furniture.

Which Woods Make the Best Furniture?

Generally speaking, hardwoods make more durable furniture than softwoods. Hardwoods, again generally speaking, come from broad-leaved trees and softwoods come from coniferous trees. Oak, cherry, walnut, and mahogany are prime hardwoods for furniture but many others are used including beech, elm, birch, ash, gum, hickory, pecan, plus many exotics such as teak and ebony. In fact, there are very few hardwoods (including all the fruitwoods) that are not used for furniture. In the softwoods, white pine is the principal furniture wood used in this country, although others might well be substituted. Good white pine furniture might last as long as good walnut furniture, and some from colonial times is certainly as valuable today as some finer furniture of that age. So softwoods are not necessarily inferior.

Generalities are hard to make where wood is involved. One must first specify how or where each type of wood is used in furniture. In colonial times, for example, no respectable country carpenter would use pine in the chair rungs or anywhere else strength was important. Pine chairs had pine seats. Legs might be oak, rungs almost always ash or hickory. A cupboard on the other hand, being largely made of wide flat boards, might be all pine and plenty strong enough for the purpose. But because it was soft and easy to work it was rarely used for tabletops, which took much abuse. Pine has no distinctive grain, but the colonials invariably painted their furniture and did not give a hoot about grain anyway. Wood grain was one of the most common sights in their world so it had little standing decoratively.

One finds beech, birch, and gum often used in cheap furniture, but this is not a slur on the strength or durability of the wood itself. These are common woods and so cheaper woods, but they can make good furniture from the low-maintenance point of view. Because beech, birch, and especially gum have little in the way of showy grain, they can be stained to resemble more expensive woods. Thus they get the reputation of being cheap imitations of good furniture. That being the case, their presence in a piece of furniture *may* indicate less quality—not because of the wood's inherent characteristics, but because the furniture-maker was not intent on making quality furniture when he used them. If he intended to take the time to make a good chest of drawers, he'd use cherry or walnut. Thus today, a factory-made chest of white ash stained to look like walnut or cherry, or passed off as white oak, could be very moderate in price and cheap in construction—and therefore rank far down the list of low-maintenance furniture. The same ash, cut and assembled by an accomplished cabinetmaker like James Krenov, could rank at the top of the list—and be very, very valuable to boot.

Look, for example, at upholstered furniture from the first part of the twentieth century, if not earlier. If the back legs are beech or birch instead of mahogany, oak, or walnut like the wood that shows in front, the piece is invariably of lower quality. The wood doesn't make it lower quality, but only indicates that less time was taken in quality construction, and that quite possibly, cheaper springs were used.

In other words, except for specific structural demands, like the supple tensile strength of hickory and ash for spindles, rungs, and bentwood, the kind of wood used depends in large part upon whatever fashion dictates as desirable at the moment. Thus white oak goes in and out of fashion—it was all the rage at the turn of the century and is so again today. As a woodworker I dislike it because it is open pored and requires more work to get a smooth, glasslike finish. And because it is so hard. Planer blades dull twice as fast on white oak as on black walnut. But white oak (unlike red oak) is very strong and even where (as in table legs) you must mortise holes that are quite large and reduce the actual thickness of the leg by half, oak will stand up to it where walnut might not. Incidentally, in such a case a couple of dowels that require only two small holes might make a better joint for low maintenance than a large mortise-and-tenon joint, even though it is now fashionable to think of doweling as cheap factory joinery and mortise and tenon as quality handcrafted work.

Cherry is a fairly hard wood too, but excellent for carving, which is one reason why so often antique carved furniture in Chippendale or whatever is cherry. Although many carvers prefer softer woods, like basswood, cherry (as is true of many fruitwoods) can be carved with good crisp detail and does not split out in carving into the grain. Cherry, of course, is also considered extremely beautiful in color if not in grain.

Black walnut and Honduran or African mahogany are not as hard as cherry or maple but have both the color and grain the human eye has always found irresistible. Their presence in furniture almost always denotes high quality.

Many exotic woods are used by handcrafters in furniture-making and their use denotes quality furniture, whether or not the wood itself is all that great. For instance, American woodworkers have a current penchant for brash sassafras. But some exotic woods, like teak, have inherent high quality. Teak is extremely hard and oily and will decay hardly at all, even if left out in the weather.

Maple can be both a common furniture wood and exotic (such as curly maple or bird's-eye maple). The appearance of these maple grains in furniture indicates high quality, since no woodworker would commit such valuable wood to cheap work. Bird's-eye maple is almost always found on old furniture as veneer. Veneer can be high maintenance since a dent or gouge might go all the way through it. Also glues, especially before about 1950, were not what they are now, and older veneers may delaminate due to glue failure. But, as mentioned earlier, veneered furniture does not tend to warp as solid woods do and so should not be sneered at.

Plain hard maple is an excellent furniture wood and takes a superior finish. Being lighter in color than cherry or walnut, it can be stained to almost any color desired.

How to Tell Woods Apart

You can't by eye. Black walnut has a dark brown to purple natural color, unlike any other American wood. If you see it unfinished, you can tell it rather easily. Raw cherry wood has an orangeish-pinkish tint to it that is also fairly easy to identify. Beyond that, however, only practice and experience can tell, and then even experts are often fooled unless or until the wood is examined microscopically.

Clever wood finishers can make cheap woods look very much like expensive ones. Also the way the log is sawed—flat-sawn or quarter-sawn—can make the same wood look quite different in grain. As with jewelry, you must usually rely on the honesty of the furniture-maker or dealer. And hope they know what they are talking about. You can make walnut and mahogany look like each other, gum look like cherry, even maple look like cherry. The point is, if the piece is well made, does it matter if it is really walnut or really mahogany? If you pay cherry prices for gum you have of course been cheated, but all else being equal, one table will probably last as long as the other.

Finishes for Wood Furniture

Because my son makes new furniture professionally and sometimes repairs old furniture, I get a lot of phone calls meant for him inquiring about better ways to finish furniture. Since I consider myself a little knowledgeable on the subject, I used to make the mistake of trying to answer the questions myself. Before long I realized most callers were not really interested in what I had to say but were only looking for an excuse to trumpet their own favorite concoctions. It appears that anyone who has ever lifted a paintbrush is an expert on wood finishes, just as anyone who has ever lifted a pencil is sure he can write a book if only he had the time. So when I'm asked about varnish, shellac, lacquer, oil, and how to solve the state of the economy, I have a stock answer. I pause a moment or two, which I hope denotes to the caller that I'm mulling over the case he or she has presented. Then I say: "I can think of several possibilities and I bet you can, too." Then they tell me just what possibilities they can think of, and I learn more than they do. Summing up: There's an almost unlimited number of ways to finish wood and any of them are fine if the result is what you want. For instance, sheep dip makes a nice finish if you are striving for a grain color of deep cobalt blue. Honest.

Even the experts delight in disagreeing with each other. Consider tung oil, for example. To listen to certain ads on television or to certain woodworkers, tung oil comes directly from the hand of God for our everlasting happiness, by way of Homer Formby's refinishing secrets (Formby's being a quality brand name in tung oil).

But Marc A. Williams, senior furniture conservator at the Smithsonian Institute indignantly challenges some of Formby's notions in the June 1986 issue of *Rodale's New Shelter* magazine in a letter to the editor: "It is totally inappropriate to 'feed' wood with oil products," he writes. "Linseed oil and tung oil are absorbed into a surface and react with oxygen in the air to polymerize and harden. With time they become difficult to remove, can darken almost to black, and attract dust and dirt." He further states that Formby's refinishing secrets are based on age old "myths."

Then George Grotz comes along (my favorite expert, cited earlier) in his book *The Furniture Doctor* and disagrees with both. He doesn't think oils' darkening wood is such a problem, but on the other hand, he is positively disrespectful to the worshipers of tung oil, calling it nothing but floor sealer at a higher price. In some instances that might be right, but one must be careful dealing with experts. Grotz goes on to describe tung oil as being made by "squeezing the juice out of resinous pine trees in Louisiana." As probably thousands of his readers have told him by now, he appears to be inadvertently confusing turpentine with tung oil, which comes from the seed of the tung tree. Almost all finishers (even Grotz) agree that tung oil is a good finishing product, but Tage Frid, another expert, says it darkens wood much less than linseed oil does in his book *Tage Frid Teaches Woodworking* (The Taunton Press, 1981).

Who's right? They all are in one way or another. We are dealing with art as much as science. The idea is to keep everyone slightly confused, and when all else fails in that goal, the experts start talking about some esoteric formula, perhaps from sixteenth-century China, that uses seedlac varnish scraped off banyan trees that is diluted with urine from a Tibetan llama. Of course, it reaches its potential only if you put on 32 coats and rub it between coats with rice chaff moistened in castor oil. And of course again, seedlac varnish is available only from two hermits who live in the forests of northern California.

This whole business of furniture finishing is a game humans love to play. How many times have I seen a homeowner look over a newly delivered piece of furniture from the store and nearly have an apoplectic fit upon finding a scratch so small and out of the way he almost needs a magnifying glass to find it. He then pounces upon the hapless delivery-man, demanding his money back or another piece of furniture. This very same homeowner, on another occasion, shows me a newly purchased piece of "antique country" that appears to have been dragged out of a barn. He proudly points out the cracks, gouges, peeling paint, and mouse gnawings that make the piece "authentic." The truth is we finish furniture (or refrain from finishing it) mostly for reasons of fashion and in the long run little of the art and science involved has anything to do with maintenance, although we determinedly pretend otherwise.

In discussing low maintenance and furniture care, we must first admit that plain old bare wood, rough sawn or sanded, will last forever within the shelter of a house, as long as the atmosphere is reasonably dry and bugs or animals don't eat it. All that wood finishes can do is make the furniture easier to keep clean and perhaps preserve a certain desired color of the wood. If the truth be told, preserving the wood itself is more in the capabilities of environmental control than in finishes. Finishes can do very little about moisture because they do not penetrate far enough to have much effect. If you really want to control swelling and shrinking in wood, use humidifiers and dehumidifiers, as any museum curator will tell you.

With that caveat, I will proceed through the various clear finishes with an eye to maintenance, not beauty or fashion. We think of these finishes—shellac, lacquer, oil, varnish, and polyurethane—as separate and distinct substances, but as a matter of chemical fact, they overlap. Specific finishes may contain both oil and varnish or shellac and lacquers. The lac in shellac and lacquer originally stood for the same thing—a bug, or the excretions of this parasitic insect. Today, commercial lacquer is something quite different from that old Chinese lacquer. The first "varnishes" came about when shellac was boiled with linseed oil. Polyurethane is really a varnish that may contain cottonseed oil rather than linseed oil to which tough plastic formulations have been added. The main purpose of all these materials is to enhance the beauty of the wood in some way. But some are better than others in terms of maintenance, as I hope to make clear here.

Shellac

This is one of the easiest finishes to apply. It dries fairly fast, is very clear, and takes polish very well. French polishing is usually done on shellac. Liquid shellac does not store well, and it is better to buy the dry flakes and mix or "cut" your own as needed with denatured alcohol according to directions. Shellac readily dissolves in alcohol and so is easy to remove if you want to apply another finish. By the same token, it is not a good *top*coat for furniture, especially tabletops, because alcohol will dissolve it. Water is also a bane of shellac—a wet glass makes white rings on it. And if shellac is applied in an excessively humid atmosphere, it may develop a whitish blush. Better to use shellac for low maintenance as an undercoat, as a sealer between a stain and a varnish, or as a sealer for varnish alone. Unless labels say otherwise, you should not varnish directly on stain. Some people mistakenly think it is wrong to varnish over shellac; most professionals do it because shellac can be rubbed smoother than a first thin sealer coat of varnish and is cleaner than sanding sealers.

Lacquer

Lacquer today is almost always nitrate cellulose and acetone in varying formulations. It is much tougher than shellac and dries very fast. In fact, it was developed to answer the need of assembly line factory furniture that required a very quick-drying finish. Some of these lacquers dry almost instantaneously upon hitting the wood or other surface you're covering, so you have to spray them on if you don't want to leave brush marks. Brushable lacquers are available if spraying is not your strong point, but even with these, quick drying can make brush marks a problem. Most store-bought, mass-produced furniture is finished with this lacquer. Though it is more durable than shellac as a topcoat, it suffers from some of the same drawbacks: water causes white stains, and waxing the lacquered surface only delays the appearance of the white stains a little longer. Such stains, like white rings from wet glasses, are, however, rather easy to remove by smearing a little mayonnaise on them, waiting a few minutes, and then wiping off.

Factory-applied lacquer also won't hold up well to frequent contact with human skin. Where arms or hands rub a lot on tabletops, chair arms or back rails, the lacquer finish will soften, get muddy, and then dry rough and ugly. Then you have to remove the mess with lacquer thinner and apply a good polyurethane varnish or a hard carnauba wax.

Since there are so many variations in formulas and in woods themselves, not to mention people's attitudes, I'm aware that nearly anything I say can prompt an exception, but there's one hard-and-fast rule about lacquer that's agreed upon by all: Do not apply it over an oil or varnish finish. It won't dry. Since so-called sanding sealers have become popular to use to seal wood before other finishes are applied, they are often used under lacquer. I suppose it's a matter of taste, but this somewhat dulls the high-gloss effect we use lacquer for, and some finishers have observed that under such a finish, wood pores may turn whitish after a few years. Skip the sealer and apply three to four coats of lacquer instead for better effect. Practice makes perfect, and the high gloss achieved is much easier than French polishing on shellac.

Chinese lacquers and seedlac varnish lacquers that come from the lacquer or varnish tree are more like shellac than commercial lacquer. Furniture finished with them is beautiful, but they must be painstakingly applied in several thin coats. Unless you are going to make a serious hobby out of wood finishing, such finishes are beyond practical interest and beyond the scope of this book.

Oil

Oils are the easiest materials for a good practical furniture finish in my opinion. You can more or less smear them on any old which way and then wipe them off. How long you should wait before wiping them off is a matter of opinion, even in this simple operation. This, of course, means you have plenty of leeway and not to worry. Oils were one of the earliest finishes, and linseed oil, from the seed of flax, continues to be one of the most-used ingredients, not just used alone as a finishing for wood, but in combination with varnishes and paints as well. Many materials that go by fancy names like "antique finisher" or "aging polisher" are little more than linseed oil and petroleum distillates with perhaps some drying resins or other driers to speed up drying time. Oils dry slowly, especially linseed oil, which in fact never dries completely in pure form. Tung oil, its leading competitor for Favorite Oil of the Century, dries faster but is still slow. Other admixtures of oils and resins, called generically "Danish oil," dry better to a harder, more durable finish than pure linseed oil. Pure oils, because they dry slowly, do catch dust, which can be rubbed in with subsequent applications. Over the centuries this may or may not lead to a significant darkening of the wood, which may be desirable.

Most finishers, except those like the Smithsonian curator I quoted earlier, believe that oil finishes improve with age. The ones who idolize linseed oil claim, after an ancient adage, that a linseed-oil finish needs to be renewed periodically for years, perhaps forever, each thin coat deepening the luster and beauty of the finish. This is a matter of taste, not maintenance. But an oil finish is much easier to repair than a lacquer one, all finishers agree. And that is what mainly concerns us here.

Don't use oils in drawers or bookcases. On hot days, oiled wood may bleed a little and clothes or paper might get stained. Also, to some noses, oil in an enclosed drawer or cabinet gives off a kind of rancid odor.

Varnish

Varnishes contain oil, usually linseed oil, with resins and other substances added to make tougher, stable, more durable finishes than shellac or lacquer. For tabletops especially, varnish ought to be the preferred finish for low maintenance. Because of the oils in them, varnishes dry rather slowly compared to shellac and lacquer. This is good from the standpoint of avoiding brush marks, but bad from the standpoint of attracting dust and lint on the wet surface. But drying times get shorter and shorter with new formulations coming on the market. Whatever varnish you choose (or any other finish for that matter) always apply it in a room temperature of 70° to 80°F for best results. Varnishes give a slightly yellow cast to the wood (or stain) but it is a toss-up whether this is an advantage or disadvantage. Again it is a matter of taste. Varnishes are more resistant to heat, water, and alcohol than other finishes.

POLYURETHANE

Polyurethane varnishes need a category separate unto themselves. They are varnishes, but the ingredients and formulations are more complex and the refining process more sophisticated, resulting in products that wear well, resist scratches, and are almost impervious to household chemicals, detergents, alcohol, boiling hot water, and vegetable stains. They apply easily with urethane foam applicators (no brush marks) and dry fast and so, for all these reasons, are of particular interest for low maintenance. (One drawback of polyurethane is the shiny, sort of plastic gloss that results. And another is that such a tough finish is harder to repair if it does get scratched deeply.)

There are so many urethane and polyurethane formulations on the market that even the experts give up and say that for the average layperson the best advice is to stick to good brand names and avoid cheaper products. Basically, the main ingredient in the oil-base kinds (which is what you should use for furniture) is good old linseed oil, although it might also be soybean, safflower, or cottonseed oil. When the word alkyd is added to the description of oil-base polyurethanes, *and this is true in paints and enamels as well as clear finishes,* it means they contain a synthetic polymer binder derived from linseed or other vegetable oils. The difference is slight. Alkyds improve adhesion and reduce cost. The different blends and formulations between oils and alkyds are legion. Don't worry about it too much. But, especially for exterior furniture, linseed oil–base alkyd polyurethanes are generally considered more durable than soybean or safflower oils. The latter, especially safflower oil, are less darkening, however.

There are both gloss- and satin-finish polyurethanes. The former contain silicates to gloss up the finish a bit. These silicates give the glossier varnish a harder finish, making it more durable and preferable for outside use over the satin. Satin finishes hide imperfections in the finish, glossy polyurethanes make them more visible. Polyurethane varnishes do not take the kind of rubbing I describe below. Buffing alone, however, will increase luster, even without wax—another low-maintenance plus. As with any finish, several thin coats are better than two thicker ones. And as with regular varnish, if you use polyurethane as a first coat sealer under a second coat of polyurethane, thin the first coat with mineral spirits for better penetration. Label directions should specify details.

Stay with One Brand

A smart rule to follow, whatever kind of finish you decide to use, is to stick with the same brand name when applying two or more different materials. If, for example, you decide to go the complete route of starting with bare wood and applying a filler, then a stain, then a sealer, and finally

---

No Finish at All

Wood furniture in some cases, especially where blemishing stains are not likely, does not have to be finished at all. My son has a little bedside stand he made, and its bare wood has displayed its beauty now for several years, none the worse off for no finish at all, and to his eye, more beautiful without any. As the famous cabinetmaker James Krenov says: "Left natural, elm and ash are beautiful; they look fine hand-planed, or planed and then sanded very lightly so as to give a misty effect. *Any* finish put on such wood will detract from, rather than add to it

. . . .For whatever reasons—smell, color, feel—wood as it is after being worked with skill is for me a matter of pride, almost a boast. Many of the pieces I make are intentionally of wood that need not be sanded—or even finished at all." (From *The Fine Art of Cabinetmaking*, by James Krenov, Van Nostrand Reinhold Company, 1977.)

As much as I agree with Krenov (and my son), a good lacquer or varnish finish will help keep warping at a minimum and enhance the beauty of most furniture woods.

---

topcoats—or any combination thereof—it's best to stay with the same brand name because of possible slight variations in formulas between different manufacturers. Behlen is one of many good companies, and I mention it only because its many products are available conveniently by mail, through the Garrett Wade catalog of woodworking tools and supplies (161 Avenue of the Americas, New York, NY 10013). Minwax products (Minwax Company, Inc., P.O. Box 99, Flora, IL 62839) and Deft products (Deft, Inc., P.O. Box 2476, Alliance, OH 44601) I have found to be very good, and Watco finishing oil (Watco Corporation, Santa Monica, CA 90406) a nice substitute for pure linseed or tung oil. And as I said at the beginning of this section, I'm sure you know of some even better. All three of them are readily available in most hardware stores.

When the Finish Is Not Quite up to Your Expectations

Theoretically, whether you use shellac, lacquer, or varnish for a finish, if you do things right, the finish should be the finish. Unfortunately, this is usually not the case, and for a real professional look, you need to finish these finishes by rubbing. Most of us will leave brush marks in shellacs and lacquers and specks in varnish. (Always finish furniture in as dust-free an environment as possible.) The specks may be dust or sawdust particles or tiny bits of resin that gather in varnish sometimes, especially after the container has been opened a while. Or the finish might turn out too shiny to suit you, rather than possessing that deep glowing luster you fancy. Sometimes you can *lightly* sand out surface roughness, brush marks, or runs; then wipe with a lint-free rag and apply one more topcoat. But the proper way is to do a professional rubbing job, which is not difficult, and which, in addition to smoothing and cleaning the surface, also removes undesired shininess.

Get some 3M brand abrasive paper from your hardware store or auto-supply store, in 400-, 500-, and 600-grade grit. Fold a small section of the paper around a rubber block. Dip it into a tray of mineral spirits and gently rub with the grain in as long a stroke as possible. You have to be careful not to sand through the finish, which is easy to do at the edges. Keep the surface wet with mineral oil while rubbing and wipe away glop that gathers on the surface with a paper towel and clean mineral spirits. Start with the 400 grit and repeat with the 500 and 600, always very gently. Try to avoid overlapping as much as possible and look at the surface against the light to see any skips. When all surface imperfections have been removed, wipe clean and let dry completely. You can leave the surface as is, if you like a matte finish or buff it for a deeper luster. If you want more glow, use wax.

There are other ways to polish furniture, but they are all harder than this method. And since traditionally they are done with shellac, they are not particularly low maintenance.

Wax or Oil?

Once you have furniture finished to your liking, you'll want to keep it that way, and this is where the biggest argument ensues among experts and nonexperts. Should you wax or should you oil? The answer is: it depends. It depends who you ask. If you opt for wax, it should be a hard wax—with a goodly proportion of carnauba in it. A good waxing twice a year is sufficient. With furniture polishes (mostly linseed oil with lemon scent), you go over the furniture every week or so, but it is far easier than waxing. Waxes build up; furniture polishes darken. A good wax on lacquer will inhibit blushing and water spots somewhat; furniture polish won't. The best choice in my opinion is Renaissance Wax. It cleans and protects (even against alcohol) and does not obscure the beauty of the wood. It's what most museums use to maintain their priceless treasures, and that's good enough for me.

Repair Sticks

Scratches in varnish and oil can often be rubbed out. Crinkles, cracks, and crazes in old shellac or lacquer can be obliterated by dissolving these finishes—alcohol for shellac and acetone or lacquer thinner for lacquer—and allowing them to flow together and harden again, but this is very tricky business. (Low-maintenance buffs should stick with oil or varnish.) Deeper scratches can sometimes be obscured with furniture retouching crayons, which are about the same things the kids use for coloring books but come in colors more likely to match wood tones.

But for filling and hiding dents, gouges, and deep scratches, the best option is what are called "lacquer sticks." They are the consistency of crayons, too, but are actually shellac with drying and solidifying resins added, of about candy bar shape and size. They come in most wood colors used in furniture. You melt a little of the lacquer stick onto a hot knife (300°F is perfect) and let the liquified shellac then flow into the hole or gouge. About any knife will do; you can even buy electric ones just for this job. When the filler solidifies again, you can sand it smooth and cover with any topcoat. If sanding is too risky on furniture already finished, there are other products to smooth the surface without harming the surrounding area, like Abrisol and Burn-In-Balm from Behlen. All the products mentioned in this paragraph are available from the Garrett Wade catalog (see Appendix B).

Painted Wood Furniture

Though the prevailing mood is for clear finishes that show the natural beauty of the wood, there has always been a modest interest in painted furniture. In terms of low maintenance, paint on furniture has the same advantages and disadvantages as paint on walls. Chips, gouges, and mars will show more visibly on painted furniture than on clear-finished furniture, and that is just about the whole maintenance story.

In most cases, whatever is used (even enamel paint unless label directions specify otherwise), whether it needs an undercoat or not, or whether the wood ought to have a filler applied before paint is applied to smooth and close the pores (read label directions to find out), the paint ought to be covered with a clear finish. Lacquer is sometimes used for an extremely high-gloss finish on paint. Better for low maintenance is to seal the paint with shellac and then top-coat with a satin varnish. The shellac sealer is important, even on tough, hard enamel, because otherwise the varnish can lift some of the paint color and give the finish a dirty cast; the varnish "pulls off the paint" as a finisher would say.

Oil-base enamels seem to be the preferred (though by no means only) paints used on furniture. A favorite is Waterlox (Waterlox Chemical and Coating Corporation, 9808 Meech Avenue, Cleveland, OH 44105). Some painters will mix a tung oil additive or something similar to make the enamel flow better and dry quicker. You can also mix Waterlox and similar products alone with dry pigments to get any color you desire. But this subject opens up a vast range of information that has little relevance to maintenance, pro or con.

Metal and Plastic Furniture

Chrome dinette sets are very much out of style right now. They are, or were anyway, fairly low maintenance. The biggest problem: tears in the plastic seat and back covers. The only handy way to mend a tear was with tape—ugly to say the least. But the chrome frames of the chairs and the plastic-topped chrome tables will last a long time without half the upkeep of wood.

Metal furniture moves in and out of fashion as continuously as the rising and falling of hemlines. Brass beds can be very big one year and ho-hum the next. I think this inconstancy is connected more with age than with era. At some point in our lives (not always the same point with everyone), brass beds make the heart throb and two years later make the mouth yawn. The same with iron beds.

Brass and copper can be lacquered to prevent tarnishing. Brass beds and other brass furniture are usually factory finished this way. If or when lacquer begins to peel from the metal it can be removed quite easily with denatured alcohol and the surface then relacquered. Use a transparent metal lacquer. Do not use a metal polish or cleaner on a lacquered surface. To clean, simply dust or wipe with a damp sponge.

Stainless steel would make heavy and costly furniture, but think how beautiful this burnished surface would be. Usually where ordinary steel is used in furniture, as in the office or on the patio, it is painted, and the paint wears and chips with use in a manner we would not tolerate in the living room. But if steel were treated like good wood, burnished and finished with clear oils and polishes and gone over regularly with polish to prevent rust and renew the shine, how beautiful it would be, and with far less maintenance than wood. Metals have grain, too, and laminated metals, as for example Damascus steel, have very beautiful grain indeed. But such furniture awaits a new twist in postmodern styles.

The plastic lucite furniture of the '50s was wonderfully indestructible stuff. Because plastic can be molded to any shape or curve, it is much more amenable to the human body than wood, and many times more stable. But modern man associates (often justifiably) plastic furniture with mass-produced junk and continues to hunger after wood. Somehow, low maintenance to the contrary, I'm glad.

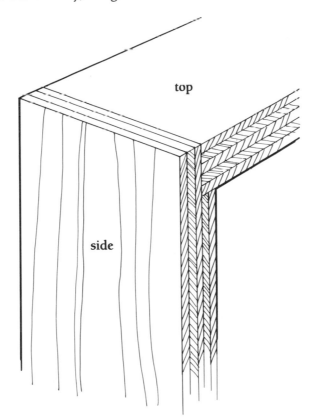

Rabbeted and glued corner joint.

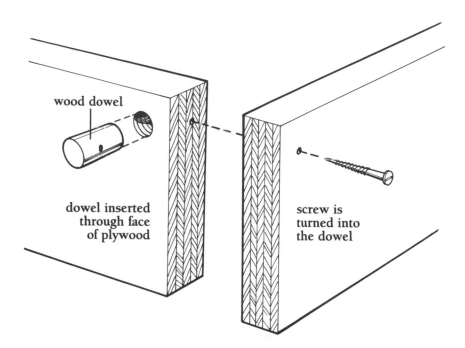

wood dowel

dowel inserted
through face
of plywood

screw is
turned into
the dowel

*Doweled and screwed
corner joint.*

Cabinets and Shelves

What has been said about wood furniture applies to wood cabinets as well, with one exception. Cabinetry often calls for rather large expanses of flat wood, as in doors, tops, or sides. In solid wood, large flat expanses are hard to keep from warping and so in this case, low maintenance applauds the use of plywood with birch or other hardwood facing. Plywood makes very strong boxwood construction since it cannot rack, and only in joining corners is there a problem. A screw, nail, or even dowel will hold well in the *face* of plywood (driven through its thickness). But when you try to insert any of these into the *edge* of the plywood (directly into the layers of laminated wood), they will not hold well at all. Thus, corners should be rabbeted and glued—the rabbeting makes more corner area to glue.

Carpenters have a little trick to make the screws hold in the laminated edge of the plywood. They ascertain where the screw will go into the edge, then they insert a dowel through the face of that edge so that the dowel will intersect the screw going at right angles into the laminations. The screw then screws into the dowel, not just into the laminated edge, and holds solidly.

Where plywood less than ¾ inch thick is being used, cabinet corners should all be backed on the inside with glue blocks to hold the corners solid.

In choosing kitchen cabinets for durability, clear-finished wood still gets the nod from me over anything painted because paint will show blemishes quicker than clear-finished wood. Cabinets covered with plastic laminates are easier to clean than wood, although a smooth factory finish on good hardwood cleans nearly as easily. (If water drops turn white on the finish, you don't want the cabinet.)

A feature to look for in kitchen cabinets is a door pull backed by a metal or other long-wearing plate of some kind. Ours are of antique brass (you don't have to be forever shining them) and they keep fingers and rings from blemishing the wood when you open a door or drawer.

The best low-maintenance cabinet door latch is a magnetized hinge, with no latch at all. When these first came out, the little magnets in the hinges, which not only keep the doors closed but pull them closed if they are left ajar, would pop out after about seven years. Improvements generally have solved this problem.

In checking kitchen cabinets, another good indication of durability is the way drawers are made. On the best ones, the fronts are dovetailed to the sides to endure generations of pulling. The bottoms of the drawers are held in grooves (dadoes) in the bottoms of the front and side—not glued—and the backs sit on top of the bottoms to which they are only lightly tacked. All this leaves the drawer bottom free to "float" in its grooves. It can contract and expand with changing humidity without pushing the drawer sides out so that they stick.

Bookshelves

Bookshelves are rather straightforward cabinets. Shelf boards really ought to be dadoed into the side boards, not just butted up and nailed or

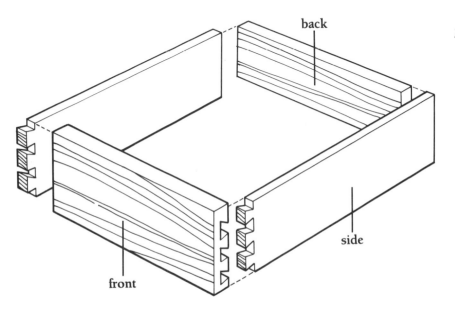

Drawer construction.

back

side

front

screwed. At any rate, remember that books are heavy, and shelving using 1-inch boards (which are really ¾ inch) should have a support at least every 2½ feet. Any less support than that and the shelf can sag under a full load of books. Incidentally, book collectors say that glass-enclosed bookcases are *not* better for books. They may keep dust from accumulating, but in open shelves there is more air circulation to ward off mildew-related problems, which is a bigger problem for books than dust.

CHAPTER 14

APPLIANCES

If furniture reveals some amusing contradictions about human nature, appliances would speak entire volumes on the subject if they could talk. For the most part, behaviorists have not studied this fertile field for signs of our communal sanity or insanity, but when they do, we shall all be greatly entertained, noting how the human spirit can rise and fall from the sublime to the ridiculous. Behold, for example, modern man, who insists on all the laborsaving devices he can't afford, and then, lacking for something to do with his softening body, he buys yet one more "appliance"— an exercycle—and works and sweats over it harder than grandmother did doing the wash.

Refrigerators and Freezers

No appliance illustrates both the sublime and the ridiculous in human nature like the refrigerator. On the more or less sublime level, refrigeration has certainly meant progress in healthfulness and in preventing food from going to waste, not to mention convenience. And though refrigerators use more energy than any other home appliance except water heaters and furnaces, they are for the most part marvelously maintenance-free over a lifetime of 20 years. The one my family recently replaced worked 21 years for us. It cost about $250 new and perhaps another $100 in service bills over that period of time. We received $90 on a trade-in (after the dealer had knocked $100 off the list price of the new one). I figure it cost us about $15 a year plus electricity to run, certainly a great value in today's world.

Unfortunately, over that same period of time, energy use in refrigeration rose to a ridiculous level, mostly due to fashion, style, and taste. For example, there are many refrigerators still running today that are 40 years old or more, but not in people's houses. They have been relegated to garages or vacation cabins because they are "ugly." The motor and compressor are mounted on top of the units in plain sight rather than being hidden integrally into the innards like modern refrigerators. Heat from these top-mounted compressors dissipates away into the air rather than seeping up through the unit, which is one reason they last so long. Amory Lovins, the environmentalist who has become the energy conscience of our society, says that in many if not most refrigerators made between about 1950 and 1980, nearly half the cooling energy was and is spent in getting rid of the heat of the motor.

In addition to having the compressor in the wrong place, the design of the modern upright refrigerator and upright freezer is all wrong. When you open the door, the cold air tumbles out. Chest freezers avoid this problem and should be the first freezer choice for low maintenance. Unfortunately, it's somewhat unhandy to find what you want in a chest freezer. Because you open a refrigerator much more often than a freezer, lost cold air is much more of a problem with refrigerators. Some statistical gadfly has calculated that about 75 percent of the cold air is lost when the door is opened wide, and that in a typical household, the door is opened maybe 50 times a day. At that rate, there's a waste of 2,000 Btu per day on a 16-cubic-foot unit. That's about $20 of electricity a year, depending on your rate per year. While that won't break anyone, it is only one of the costs you have to pay if you linger in front of an open refrigerator deciding what you want to eat or drink several times a day. And opening the door increases frost buildup within, requiring more frequent defrosting, which eats into the Btu in a most voracious manner. The electrical cost of operating the watt-guzzling refrigerators of the early '70s (when flagrant energy consumption was at its peak) was well over $100 a year. Contrast that with the experimental refrigerator Lovins uses, a $1,900 Sun Frost (Box DD, Arcata, CA 95521), which is said to use only 5 to 8 percent of the electricity conventional refrigerators use. One of its many cost-saving features is its ability to utilize cold outside air in winter, rather than the warmer indoor air. If all Americans had low-energy refrigerators like this one, says Lovins, the savings would eliminate the need for 20 large power plants. Equally efficient freezers could eliminate another 15.

Of course, not everyone can afford or would choose to spend $1,900 on a refrigerator, but the good news is that the refrigeration industry is improving efficiency in its standard refrigerators for little or no extra cost to you. Energy consumption of a typical refrigerator today is about half of what it was in 1975. The latest step in energy conservation is the electronic defrost control system. Instead of a defrost cycle every 12 or 24 hours whether needed or not, this electronic control system initiates a defrost cycle only when necessary—as seldom as every 60 hours. Whirlpool appears to be leading the way with its Systems Sentinel II; it's already available on some Whirlpool and Kenmore models. But by the time you read this, more refrigerators will no doubt come equipped with similar devices.

Other manufacturers are currently using a less expensive way to cut down the defrost cycle time with more sensitive thermostatic controls that switch on the defrost cycle for the minimum length of time necessary to get rid of the frost. Older refrigerators without such sensitive controls have warm-up periods unnecessarily long that warm up the refrigerator unnecessarily high. On our ever-faithful 21-year-old Frigidaire, a thermometer laid on the freezer shelf could register as high as 50°F during defrosting.

I hesitate to mention any specific features and the brand name appliance on which they can be found, good or bad, because it suggests that some brands are better than others. In refrigerators, that makes no more sense than saying Chevys are better than Fords, unless you just want to start an argument. First of all, different brand names in refrigerators do not necessarily signify different companies. GE owns Hotpoint—our Hotpoint dealer says few people know that and he has customers who swear by Hotpoints but say they'd never have a GE in the house. White owns Westinghouse and Gibson and may own more (or less) by the time you read this. Whirlpool makes Kenmores for Sears. This is especially noteworthy for those of us in the habit of thinking that Sears and other mail-order companies deal only in midpriced to cheaper appliances. Whirlpool makes excellent refrigerators by any standard, and so Kenmores don't have to take a back seat to anyone. (The addresses of all these appliance companies can be found in Appendix A.)

It is also ridiculous to assert one brand is better than another today because the parts in various makes can come from the same independent manufacturers. The real guts of a refrigerator are its motor, compressor, capacitor, and freon-filled coils, and these parts can very well be the same in two different brands. When the capacitor needed replacing on our Frigidaire refrigerator, the repairman used one from a washing machine of a different make! Tecumseh makes compressor motors for many refrigerator manufacturers. At least one company, Franklin, makes whole refrigerators for the brand-name companies to put their names on. Franklin made a model for Hotpoint for three years because Franklin could manufacture it cheaper than Hotpoint could. Our Hotpoint dealer told me that both Hotpoint and GE used exactly the same compressor one year. The compressor worked fine for Hotpoint but caused problems for GE—a mystery that engineers solved only when they realized the Hotpoint factory was sealing in a different oil than GE. The latter's type of oil wasn't compatible with the compressor.

If all refrigerators today are more alike than different, why do people occasionally have trouble and others don't? If you listen to complaints, you notice soon enough that no one brand gets singled out more than others. An independent repairman who works on all brands told me what I've concluded to be the judgment closest to the truth. "Actually," he says, "It's a matter of luck. Every so often, a lemon is going to come off the assembly line, I don't care whose brand it is." Most often problems with lemons can be fixed during the warranty period, but sometimes the difficulties don't show up until about the tenth year when the refrigerator should be only at midlife. Then its owner will forever swear at the brand name. If he had gotten the very next refrigerator off the assembly line, he might have forever sworn by the brand name. This is of course true of almost all mass-produced items and a fact of life in modern times.

You never hear a refrigerator company brag about its compressor, which is what it should do if it wants to attract intelligent buyers. A refrigerator will last with minor service repairs until its compressor goes out. That's a $200 to $300 replacement job, and so most people trade in refrigerators at that point. Nor do manufacturers talk about how well their units resist freon leakage. In most refrigerators, you'll have to have the serviceman add a little freon to your unit some time after it is ten years old.

Instead, the manufacturers advertise the frills they put on their units, for in truth that's what many American consumers care most about. Thus we now see a profusion of electronic readout panels that are mostly ridiculous. The only good thing I can say about them is that the microchips that power them use virtually no energy, so the gadget-lovers who want to waste their money this way can do so without wasting energy. I suppose it is nice (and a way to impress poorer friends) to touch a panel and learn that the inside refrigerator temperature is 37°F, but a cheap thermometer placed on a shelf is easy to read when you open the door to take out some food. I suppose it is nice when a red light flashes or an obnoxious beep erupts if the inside temperature rises to 40°F, indicating something is wrong. And what does your fancy electronic diagnostic digital readout tell you IF something is wrong? It will flash a Code B or E or whatever, and when you look that up in your operation manual, it turns out to mean that you should call your serviceman!

Interestingly, none of these ultrafrill models are on display in my hometown. Dealers say they can't sell them, so they don't stock them. "In the '70s, you could sell the more expensive accessories but not today," one dealer said. "Money's tighter now and people will pay only for honest value around here."

Ice makers are very handy frills, but their value is debatable from a low-maintenance point of view. In their favor, they add surprisingly little to your energy bill. How long will they last? No one knows. The cost for a modest one is about $120, including the job of tapping into your water line. The manuals that come with refrigerators equipped with automatic ice makers say that it should be shut off along with the water supply to it when you go on vacation, which suggests possible problems could occur. One of the things that factored into our decision not to invest $120 was that only on rare occasions do we need a lot of ice cubes, and we can freeze them up and store them in the freezer ahead of time using the traditional trays. The clincher was a recollection of a family we know with four thirsty youngsters who complained that their ice maker could not keep up with demand. We observed that the children would cram a glass with ice cubes so that it held very little liquid. After a brief sipping, the cubes got dumped into the sink. In a short time, the kids were thirsty again since they had drunk very little the first time. Then the process was repeated.

Today a simple ice maker is almost passé. The big deal now is to be able to get ice cubes through an outlet without opening the door. Then there's automatic crushed ice. And ice-cold water through a door dispenser. These are expensive gadgets, begging for maintenance problems. But fun if you have the money. (We know a young couple who are way ahead in this game. In their house stands an older refrigerator with a spigot in its side. Give it a twist and out pours beer. Inside the fridge there is a cold keg with a pipeline to the spigot. Great for parties and cheaper beer than the bottled kind in the long run. Maybe.)

But even more and better frills are being developed. Admiral already has models that will ejaculate 12 pounds of ice cubes a day, which ought to cover the needs of the most profligate family. Units with quicker and colder deep freeze compartments are great for automatic ice cream makers—you pour ingredients into a canister and a special stirrer blends them while they freeze. Projections call for automatic cream whippers and mousse jellers eventually. Eventually? At the rate things are going and as long as the flush money holds out, we may get miniature soda fountains self-contained in our refrigerators. You can already buy an ice cream maker from Sears (Kenmore label but made by Osrow Products) that plays "Happy Days Are Here Again" when a batch is ready to eat. That costs $80. One that won't sing anything costs $50. See what I mean? A fool and his money are soon parted.

New refrigerators (as well as some other major appliances) now by law must bear the black and yellow tags indicating their energy costs per year. These figures are about as valuable as the Environmental Protection Agency (EPA) miles-per-gallon rating on cars. They give you a basis for comparison, maybe, and that's about all. Opponents of the energy tags say the government testing specifications are too arbitrary and lead to more confusion than clarity. Not to mention that it costs lots of taxpayers' money for the program. The Department of Energy (DOE) dictates the testing procedure but the actual tests are carried out by independent labs *or by the manufacturers' own facilities*. The DOE is supposed to keep testing under careful surveillance and there are various checks and balances, supposedly, to discourage a proliferation of little white lies. But the history of this kind of governmental regulation over the past 20 years leaves little room for credibility.

Textured surfaces obscure fingerprints, thus reducing daily maintenance. But the doors still get dirty whether you can see the fingerprints or not, and doors need to be wiped off regularly, so the advantage is not much.

On many models you can get designer door panels and trim to jazz up the external appearance or match it with your decor. Black glass is all the rage now, followed closely by custom-made wood panels. Designer panels are practical in that they take into account the quicksilver nature of fad and fashion. You can keep in the mainstream, or just ahead of it, by changing doors instead of whole refrigerators. My theory is that even if a refrigerator came encased in solid gold etched with the most artistic skill since Ghiberti did the church doors of San Giovanni, people would tire of it in ten years and replace it over with something else. Probably avocado, which by then would be fashionable again.

Tempered glass shelves cost a little more than the standard wire shelves (about $40 more) but are an aid to cleaning maintenance. If something drips, it doesn't drip on down through the entire refrigerator and can be more easily cleaned off the shelf.

For Maintenance Sake

You have only one important chore to do regularly: Clean the condenser coils. They are located underneath the refrigerator, usually reached by lifting or removing a panel at the bottom front. Some have coils in back, in which case you have to pull the unit out from the wall to clean them. Obviously units with the coils underneath are handier so long as you can reach them from the front of the refrigerator. You must vacuum dust that gathers in these coils at least once a year (twice or thrice is better), or as your operating manual calls for. This little chore will add years to the unit's life and subtract dollars from your energy bill.

The operating manual should tell you other practices that save you money, too:

- For one thing, plastic parts in most refrigerators should not be washed in automatic dishwashers. The heat of the water might soften and warp them a bit out of shape.
- Don't stuff the refrigerator too full. Overloaded fridges have a much harder time keeping everything cool enough.
- Don't put things in the refrigerator that don't need cooling. This rule seems obvious but it's often violated.
- Be sure doors align well with the body of the refrigerator when it is closed. Overloading deep door shelves may cause the door to cant a bit so the seals don't fit flush. (Actually, this is most likely to be a problem with upright freezers, not with refrigerators.)
- Develop the habit of checking the refrigerator door to make sure it is closed. Children are inclined to leave it ajar and turn the fridge into a rather expensive room air conditioner. Here's where some of that gadgety electronic monitoring can be useful; it issues a warning sound if the door is ajar. But then every time you opened it, you'd be beeped to death.
- Wipe off moisture on bottles and other containers before putting them back in the refrigerator.

• When you turn controls to the coldest positions for quick chilling, don't forget to turn them back later.

• Locate the unit as far from the stove or heat vents as you conveniently can. It's not good to place the refrigerator where the sun through a window will shine on it steadily, either.

• Finally, a caution that may not have much to do with maintenance: If you decide to trash an old refrigerator, remove the door first. Every year, still, kids die in old or abandoned refrigerators. If you are going to store the unit rather than get rid of it, keep all the shelves in place to discourage a child from crawling inside. Then render the door inoperable in some way. You can do this by gluing wood blocks to the inside top of the door so the door can't close. A better way is to wrap several rounds of that untearable tape from the hardware store around the whole refrigerator. If the door handles connect with the door at both ends, you can run a chain through the handles and around the body, top and bottom, and then padlock the chain. Magnetic doors alleviate the problem since they can be kicked open from inside. But why not be certain; take the door off or chain it closed.

Ranges, Cooktops, Microwaves

For purposes of low maintenance, much of what I've said about refrigerators applies to other major appliances too, especially cooking appliances. Like refrigerators, a range can last a long time—one lady in our town still uses one made in the '40s and says she wouldn't part with it for all the electronic gadgetry in today's kitchen. Burners burn out on ranges but are simple and fairly inexpensive to replace. (Have you noticed that as burners get easier to replace, they tend to burn out quicker, too? Is that progress?) On gas ranges, there are no burners to go kaput as such. Once in a blue moon the gas ports might get plugged but a poke or two with a length of wire can solve that. There are really ancient ones with original equipment still alive and well. My sister has one in her garage modified for LP gas, which she uses for electric blackout emergencies and for boiling off maple sap.

The only other major range problem that can develop is linked to the self-cleaning oven. Early and/or cheap models sometimes do not have enough insulation in them, and the oven walls crack during self-cleaning. But such bad luck with today's models would be a rarity. Self-cleaning ovens are a great way to lower maintenance. The increase in energy usage is at least partially balanced by a decrease in energy in normal baking because the added insulation keeps more heat in the oven. Statisticians say it costs 39 cents to run a self-cleaning oven at average electric rates.

The other maintenance bugaboo with cooking ranges is wiping up around the burners and cleaning the drips and spills that fall through them. Designers have made it relatively easy to lift the burners out or up and clean the porcelain pans underneath. Now you can get solid "black burners." They're caulked around the edges so that there's no space for anything to drip through. Some new ranges sport a one-piece "upswept" burner that has no cracks to trap dirt around the edges. In effect, the rim of the burner and the cooktop are one piece. Some burners allow you to adjust the size of the heated area to the size of the pot or pan you are heating. This saves energy. If you don't have this feature, you should try to use the burner that more closely fits the utensil you are cooking in, as I guess everyone who has taken a course in home economics knows. To put a small pan on a large burner is wasteful.

One more design feature I have found in some new ranges that makes cleanup easier is an oven vent duct that is not directly at the lowest center part of the catch pan. This prevents large spillovers from going into the oven.

If you are thinking of buying a new cooking appliance and haven't been keeping up with new developments, you will be in for a surprise when you go to your favorite appliance store. First of all, the word "range" is heard less and less, in favor of the word "cooktop." A cooktop essentially is a range top installed someplace other than on a range and it has no oven under it. (If it has an oven under it, it is generally called a "drop-in.") A cooktop may be installed in almost any countertop or kitchen island. Cooktops can be equipped with several different choices of burners— changeable plug-in modules (to use the latest language) that can function as a grill, griddle, or even a rotisserie. Whether the griddle burner is really any improvement over the old iron fry pan is arguable. And whether a grill burner on the cooktop is any real advance over grilling in your conventional oven is also debatable. But the new cooktops do offer greater freedom in designing a kitchen. Fashion rules and practicality follow, stumbling, after it.

Inductive Heat Cooktops

But the big advance in cooktops is in the incorporation of a really new kind of burner that uses inductive heat, not the usual conductive kind. When the word "cooktop" is used now, and especially by the time you read this, it refers almost always to inductive burners. An induction cooktop has its heating coil embedded in a ceramic plate. What you see as the "burner" is the ceramic plate upon which you set your pot or whatever. But that ceramic plate does not get hot. Instead, when you switch on the burner, the heating coil inside sets up a magnetic field. An iron pot, a porcelainized iron pot, or a magnetized stainless steel pot set on the burner attracts the heat magnetically through the ceramic plate. The pot heats up, not the burner. (In the old conductive way, the heat had to first spread through the burner, then flow by conduction into the utensil on it.) Great claims of efficiency are being made for induction burners—up to 60 percent more efficient than conductive electric burners and up to 15 percent more efficient than gas burners. In addition, these burners have a safety advantage over the old ones; you are not likely to get burned if you accidentally touch them. Induction burners appear at this time to be very much the wave of the future despite their higher cost right now.

Convection Ovens

Another relatively new development is the convection oven. Standard ovens are heated by simple radiant heat coming from the heating elements. Convection ovens add a fan to circulate that heat more uniformly. The advantage is faster, more even cooking than standard ovens. Many cooks like convection cooking for lots of uses but prefer radiant heat for food that burns easily, or where a slower roasting can mean greater flavor. You can buy new ovens that come equipped with both and enjoy the best of both types of cooking. You convert from radiation to convective heat at the flick of a switch.

Microwave Ovens

Microwave ovens have become the most popular new ovens of all— "microwaving" is our newest verb. Because they heat and cook so fast, they are beloved by busy families. In a way, microwaves and the fast lane people deserve each other. Microwaves are great for heating up food that otherwise is ready to eat, like TV dinners, and for lightly cooking vegetables. But every person I meet who enjoys good food says that microwaving will never take the place of slower range cooking. Meat and pastries just don't taste as good out of the microwave. And a frozen casserole will take as long to thaw and cook in a microwave as in an ordinary oven. Improvements may negate my statements, but as of now, these drawbacks are significant for anyone with even a touch of gourmet in their souls.

In their favor, microwaves use far less electricity than ordinary ranges. But since most homes will continue to have both standard and microwave ovens, this advantage might be less than the energy watchers calculate—if you count in the energy of manufacturing and distributing all those microwaves in addition to all those conventional ranges.

The electronic monitoring gadgetry on cooking appliances, especially microwaves, is literally fantastic. It reminds me of Christmas decorations, and some of the gadgetry is not much more useful than that, either. Whereas previously you turned knobs to activate and deactivate a stove, now you touch panels. Lots of the digital readouts give you information you don't need to know or maybe don't want to know, like the date, which has nothing to do with cooking anyway. It's the language of touch paneling that deludes you. "Electronic programming" sounds like a big deal, but more often than not it enables you to do with your stove exactly what you have always been able to do, minus the pretty lights. For example, here is a description of one of the features you get on a microwave, as I quote verbatim from the catalog of a leading manufacturer: "Temp Cook/Hold cycle that cooks food by temperature and maintains selected temperature until Clear/Off is touched." Wow. You do that on an old range by twisting a few knobs.

But I don't want to make too much fun of electronic gadgetry because some of it is real progress. And with microwaves, ultrahandy touch panels that monitor everything except whether you have let the dog out yet are really almost necessary. Why? Because the microwave works so fast it would be folly to leave the cooking time up to human manual control. The food would more often be annihilated than cooked. I'm sure by now everyone has heard the story of the misguided soul who put his poodle, fresh from a bath, in the microwave to dry off and then the phone rang . . .

How long will a microwave last without major repairs or replacement? There's not much about them that can go wrong, really. But they haven't been around long enough yet for us to find out.

Washers and Dryers

Washers and dryers probably shouldn't be expected to last as long as refrigerators and cookstoves because they have more hardworking movable parts. At any rate, the modern versions don't last as long without major repair. Maytag's older wringer-washers lasted 20 years, easily, with good care. Maytag's reputation for durability was made with that machine, not their modern automatic appliances. I don't mean that their automatic washers and dryers aren't considered among the best, but in maintenance terms they can't hold an agitator to the old wringer type. Alas and alack, Maytag no longer even makes a wringer-washer. No one wants to take the time to feed clothes through a wringer except the Amish who are trying to find a way to manufacture washers like the old Maytags themselves now that they can't buy them anymore.

It is not Maytag's fault their new models, or anyone else's, last only 10 years or so on the average. It's the nature of the beast. New washers are asked to do more, faster and better, than the wringers. Some repair workers suggest that the reason Maytag's washers may last longer even now is because of an ingenious use of belts that break before anything major wears out when a moving part is jammed or overloaded. At any rate, surveys reported in *The Durability Factor,* edited by Roger Yepsen (Rodale

Press, 1982) indicate that while Maytag's washers and dryers head the list for durability, their lead is very slight over Whirlpool, Gibson, Westinghouse's front-loading models, and GE. Maytag ranks first in least number of service calls by only .1 percent over GE products, and Maytag *dryers* required more service calls than GE, Whirlpool, or Frigidaire. (However, I must mention that while Frigidaire has overall poor showings in the surveys mentioned, at home our Frigidaires have performed very well. Our washer worked faithfully for 15 years until it needed to have its water pump repaired, and our Frigidaire dryer has run for 17 years without any repairs. Both appliances have far exceeded the survey average.)

Careful Use Means Low Maintenance

What experience teaches, if repairmen don't, is that low maintenance on washers and dryers is much more a matter of how the appliance is used, not what brand name is on it. Compact washers and dryers do not last as long as full-sized because people overload them more frequently. The single most devastating practice with washers is overloading. Some people just can't discipline themselves not to do it. They want to get the washing finished too fast. If the tub's load limit is 18 pounds and they have 28 pounds more to go, they shove it all in. Careful owners whose machines last far longer than the average do just the opposite. They will back off and put in two small 14-pound loads, adjusting the water level indicator to low or small. Following this procedure can save you the cost of at least two washers in your lifetime, so long as you follow a few other easy rules.

For example, don't use more soap than specifications call for. The same person who overloads wants to oversoap, too. The soap bubbles into places it isn't supposed to go, carrying scum with it to gum up timer switches, etc.

Rust is another major destroyer of washing machines. If the washer sits in a wet basement, the bottom and/or back will rust so badly that the repairman can't remove it except with cusswords and a hacksaw. Scratches on the sides or nicks in the porcelain top will give rust a place to get started. Wiping the washer off with a dry rag after each use helps immensely. A dry laundry room floor helps more. (Keeping the door of the washer open so that any water inside evaporates instead of sitting there inviting rust, will help, too.) Look for warranties, like Maytag has, of five years against rust on the zinc-coated steel sides and porcelain tops. Porcelain on both inner and outer tubs is so far superior to plastic as to be well worth the cost.

Choose a washer that allows you to select whatever water temperature best suits the fabric being washed. Cold water washes and rinses are often practical and cut down on energy costs. Many people I know rarely use hot water at all anymore—just warm and cold.

If you throw a couple of sneakers alone in the tub, expect one to jam the agitator eventually. Happens all the time. (Washing a sneaker along with a few towels or other clothes is much better.)

Dryers should last longer than washers (which is one reason you might not want to buy one of those over-under combination washer-dryers). There are minor breakdowns—a thermostat goes out, a drive belt breaks. But if you burn out a motor in less than 12 years it is probably your own fault. As with washers, overloading shortens the life of dryers.

New dryers allow you to select more precisely the drying temperature you desire, another possible cost-cutting feature. Some models have automatic sensors that monitor dryer temperature continuously and shut off the heater when it is not needed, another good energy saver. Lint traps on dryers need regular cleaning, and so models with traps that are handy to remove and clean out are an advantage.

The best dryer for low maintenance is of course the clothesline. Our dryer has lasted so long because we dry outside at least half the year. The smell that sun and wind give to sheets and clothes is a greater reward than the money saved or time "lost." If you want to make hanging wash out faster and more convenient, rig up a clothesline on pulleys—one pulley on your deck or porch, the other high on the side of a nearby building or tree. You may not have a proper tree or other elevation handy, but if you do and you don't take advantage of it, you're missing out on an easy clothesline. (More details on this in my book *Gene Logsdon's Practical Skills* [Rodale Press, 1985].)

Dishwashers

The number of home appliances seems never-ending, and people who are low-maintenance minded forever try to draw a line of defense: I will buy this one, but then no more. But Christmastime leadeth us into temptation, so we buy one more. Everyone else has one, and friends are beginning to give you that queer look reserved for hermits and lepers. At least that's what has happened to us because we don't have a dishwasher. I am branded as being unkind to my wife, although I wash dishes, too. I have little regard anymore for the harried mother who rolls doleful eyes at me and moans that there is nothing for her children to do around the house to teach them the discipline of work. At the same time, she would sooner part with her husband than her dishwasher.

Most people are going to have a dishwasher, come what may, and there is little use discussing the possibilities for family life and even congenial party conversation when everyone pitches in and does the dishes by hand. It's just one of those hateful jobs no one will do if he (especially he) can get out of it. Even though you must still scrape the dishes and rinse them, which is half of the hand-washing job, people still insist on the dishwasher to do the other half.

Dishwasher Do's and Don'ts

One plus is that dishwashers don't waste as much as they used to. And if you *will* rinse the dishes before putting them into the washer, the machine will last longer. There's a little timid disposal in the newer washers that feature a "prerinse cycle" but to depend on it to take the place of manually scraping and rinsing the dishes is to invite breakdowns due to plugging up the water outlet. There are two materials you should be especially wary of. Unpopped popcorn kernels go right through the grinder and plug the outlet. So will twist-ties, which can inadvertently get into the dishwasher because of careless scraping and rinsing. Little bits of bone can also plug the outlet.

Various types of food residue also work their way into the holes in the inner door where wiring, etc., come through. The residue is then exceedingly hard if not impossible to clean away. The best you can do is to keep the buildup at a minimum by rinsing dishes manually before putting them in the washer.

To save money and possibly repairs, don't use the supplemental heat elements to dry dishes. Most times, you aren't going to need the dishes until the next meal, and they can dry slowly with ordinary room air. Just open up the washer door, roll out the racks, and let the dishes dry by themselves.

Dishwashers that heat their own water usually save money since it is cheaper to have properly heated water just for the dishes than to keep all your water that hot. Most dishwasher detergents call for water at about 120° to 140°F.

If you run out of regular dishwasher soap, DO NOT use a laundry detergent. Don't even try to use "just a little bit." In the dishwasher, Tide will turn into a real tide of suds, and you'll have to rinse the dishes by hand to get it all off.

Where well water is used, even though softened, it may still contain minerals that play havoc with the plastic-covered wire baskets in your dishwasher. Some water deteriorates baskets more than others, like the water in our neighborhood. Our neighbors just have to replace baskets periodically—and that's $60 a crack. This is another reason wise country dwellers should have cisterns, though few do. Rainwater saves plumbing, saves softening costs, saves soap, washes hair, skin, and dishes better, saves appliances, and saves dishwasher racks.

Electronic timers on dishwashers allow you to save money in a way that few thought of before the rise in electric rate prices: They allow you to program the wash cycle in the middle of the night. Good idea. Utility companies have to gear up to serve customers at their highest electric usage—the peak hours, which are usually about 5:00 P.M. until 9:00 P.M. Demand for electricity is much lower from about 1:00 A.M. to 5:00 A.M., and in some states utility companies charge much less for it during these times to encourage use in off-peak hours.

Some manufacturers are making it easier for homeowners to do their own minor repairs on washers, dryers, and kitchen appliances. GE has a "Quick-Fix System" of easy-to-follow repair manuals and color-coded parts. Toll-free hotlines can also bring needed advice (see the box "Appliance 800 Numbers"). These are steps in the right direction. There's no reason a society that can journey to the moon can't make an appliance with easy-to-replace parts. It costs $20 to $30 just to get a repairman to step into your house.

Appliance "800" Numbers

Several manufacturers provide toll-free numbers for locating parts and service for their products. In addition to service help, some hotlines also handle consumer inquiries about the company's products, plus general questions on appliance selection, use, and care.

Admiral Home Appliances
(800) 447–8371
(800) 322–6302 in Illinois

Carrier Corporation
(800) 227–7437

Emerson Quiet Kool Corporation
(800) 447–4700
(800) 322–4400 in Illinois

Fedders USA
(800) 621–5199
(800) 972–5855 in Illinois

General Electric Company
(800) 626–2000

Hamilton Beach Division/
Scovill, Inc.
(800) 334–2785
(800) 672–5872 in North Carolina

Kelvinator Appliance Company
(800) 245–0600
(800) 242–0580 in Pennsylvania

Patton Electric Company
(800) 348–1930

Roper Corporation
(800) 447–6737
(800) 323–7778 in Illinois

Tappan Company
(800) 447–2882
(800) 322–4400 in Illinois

Whirlpool Corporation
(800) 253–1301
(800) 632–2243 in Michigan
(800) 253–1121 in Alaska and Hawaii

White-Westinghouse Appliance Company
(800) 245–0600
(800) 245–0580 in Pennsylvania

Water Heaters

Next to your furnace, the water heater is the biggest energy user in the house. Therefore, any way you can devise to use less hot water or preheat it some cheap way, the more money you can save. Some systems have a water holding tank where water rises to room temperature before it is heated. A supplementary solar system that would preheat water to 70° or 80°F may be more practical than one built to heat water to 120°F for direct use. Such systems add their own upkeep to maintenance, however, and for the low-maintenance buff, this must be weighed shrewdly against the cost of conventional water heating. Those using conventional electric water heaters might find such solar systems well worth the management time they require, while those with gas or oil heaters or improved-efficiency electric ones would probably not.

I have to use "howevers" and "probabilities" because the price of fuels ranges widely from coast to coast, and oil prices are so volatile. Electricity in New York City costs seven times what it costs in Seattle. Natural gas is very cheap in Alaska, very expensive in Hawaii, and twice as expensive in New England as in the Plains states. And many of us don't have natural gas lines to tap into anyway.

Electric water heaters cost twice as much to operate as do gas heaters, using average fuel prices. But the good news is that new electric heaters are getting more efficient. If you are shopping, be content with nothing less than one with an "Energy Factor" of 95 or better. Such a heater coupled with new water-saving shower heads and other economical uses of hot water can cut the cost of electricity considerably. Other economical uses? Limit showers to 5 minutes, bathtub levels to 5 inches. Wash clothes only when they are dirty, rather than when just wrinkled, and ditch the hot tub and the dishwasher. The maintenance work you would save with such unpopular measures is amazing. And I'm not just talking about the extra wear and tear on all the appliances involved; you will also not have to repair the shower and bathroom wall nearly so soon—or maybe never. Oh, yes, to learn simplicity and from that true happiness! As an unknown poet wrote in 1775: "Lost is our old simplicity of times, / The world abounds with laws—and teems with crimes."

An even more complicated and less-efficient way to save money on heating water electrically is with the new electric heat pump water heaters. They use only half the energy of conventional electric heaters, but cost three times as much initially. Also, the heat pump process works efficiently only where winters are not so severe (see "Heat Pumps," below). Moreover, to heat the water, they have to pull heat out of the house, meaning your furnace has to work that much harder. To my way of thinking, you're robbing Peter to pay Paul.

Natural gas water heaters (and oil as long as the price stays down) are much cheaper to operate than electric ones. But conventional gas heaters are not nearly as efficient as they should be, either—much energy is lost just keeping unused hot water hot. One solution to this problem is the combination furnace/water heater such as the Polaris (Mor-Flo Industries, 18450 South Miles Road, Cleveland, OH 44128), which heats water for the heating system and water for other uses as a sort of by-product. Of course, during the nonheating season, these appliances still need hot water, and whether the Polaris system will be any cheaper than the conventional way is doubtful.

A Little Maintenance for Longer Life

In locales that have hard water, lime scale or other minerals build up inside the tank walls and on the heating elements, even if the water is softened. This scale needs to be cleaned off about every five years or sooner. You can do it yourself, but most maintenance manuals advise calling in a serviceman; so do I. If your heater is hissing internally (rather than from a relief valve), it is probably due to scale building up. The noise does not necessarily signify a problem, but indicates a cleanup job might be in order. Periodically (twice a year or as your manual suggests), you should open the drain valve at the bottom of the tank and let water run out until it is clear. This can slow scale and sediment buildup on the elements and especially on the bottom of the tank.

Most water heaters are set at 150°F at the factory, or at least they used to be. If you want to save money with a lower setting, adjust the thermostats. Normally there are two, one at the top of the tank and one at the bottom.

Excess water pressure causes undue strain on your plumbing system. Pressure of about 55 pounds per inch is ample. Have a plumber check yours sometime when he's there on a call. Sometimes excessive water pressure builds up just in the heater tank when the hot water expands. This can cause the relief valve to leak. There are several solutions, but all require a serviceman.

In conventional water heaters there's a magnesium rod extending down the middle of the tank that corrodes quicker than the tank—the theory is that it draws corrosive elements in the water to it rather than the tank and puts a rust-inhibiting coating on the tank wall so the tank or at least the heating element resists rusting longer. This rod is called in some maintenance manuals the "sacrificial anode," which sounds to me like something out of Dante's *Inferno*. Anyway, if you are confronted with some unexplicable water odor not controlled by softening, remove the sacrificial anode and throw it into the Inferno or wherever. That's what a plumber did for us when we had a water odor problem, and it worked. Otherwise, you are supposed to replace the sacrificial anode (I love repeating that name for some odd reason) whenever it corrodes down to about the diameter of an ordinary wire. Since our heater tank seems alive and well after 13 years without one altogether, I have to wonder if the whole idea was not dreamed up by some frustrated poet in the plumbing business.

Water Softeners

Water softeners are high-maintenance appliances, not because they break down but because you have to keep feeding salt into them. The only way I know to avoid this kind of maintenance is to live where "city water," as we call it, is available. Indeed, city living indirectly avoids several maintenance problems. If you look into my typical country basement, you find four, yes four, tanks standing mutely in the corner waiting for me to turn my back so they can malfunction. There's a pressure tank (the submersible pump is outside in the well), the water softener, the tank for the salt flush, and the water heater. The city dweller needs only the water heater. (Of course the chlorine in his water may be slowly killing off the urban society, but that is another matter not to concern us here.)

Timers on softeners often malfunction, and there are some little rubber and plastic seals in the mechanism that control the flow of water in and out that need to be replaced every eight years or more. You'll know when it's replacement time because the soft water won't be soft anymore. The repairman showed me exactly how to replace those seals, but I always forget such things (on purpose, I think) and will have to call him back next time. Bye, bye another 20 bucks.

Space Heating Systems

As you'll quickly see, my preference in heating systems is electric radiant ceiling heat. If you're planning to build a new house, you should consider it seriously. But if a new house or a major renovation is not in your future, then read on; there are other good choices for upgrading or replacing your present system.

Electric Radiant Ceiling Heat

The most maintenance-free house heating system is electric radiant heat cables embedded in the ceiling plaster. That statement will no doubt start an argument anywhere, but *all things considered,* it's hard to disagree with. There's no furnace whatsoever to maintain, no ducts to find a place for, no chimney or flue to clean, no baseboard radiators to get in the way of furniture or to look ugly, no gas leaks to worry about, no blower noise, no oil truck to wait frantically for, no wood to chop and carry or ashes to take out. Radiant ceiling cables also produce the cleanest heat. Time spent dusting and repainting ceilings is halved.

So what are the drawbacks? Once in awhile you have to replace a thermostat. On very rare occasions, a break develops in the network of cable that needs to be repaired. Electricians familiar with ceiling cable systems have ways to pinpoint such gaps exactly and repair them by removing only a very small amount of plaster. But in this regard, you run into the main drawback. Not many electricians want to mess with the intricate web of cable in a ceiling. Installing it requires an attention to detail that is almost craftsmanlike. We are fortunate to have an electrician who is in my opinion a genius. He can fix gaps in ceiling cable, but as he likes to point out, almost all the repairs he makes are in ceilings someone else installed. Lesson 1: If you can't find electricians enthusiastic about radiant heat ceiling cables, better choose some other system.

As is the case so often, the best low-maintenance systems are among the costlier ones. Installing ceiling cables costs as much or more as a gas or oil furnace, and it requires a plaster ceiling or plaster on drywall. The cost, however, is not so great when you compare it to the ductwork required for hot air furnaces or baseboard radiators or water-heating systems. But since electricity is not a very efficient way to heat, so common wisdom says, you pay more for it than for oil or gas. Even in this respect, radiant ceiling heat is not as expensive as an electric resistance furnace, and there's a good argument, all things considered, that its expense is reasonable.

It amazes me when experts say that gas and oil are more energy-saving than electricity for heating a house when they don't count the enormous amount of energy used to manufacture and distribute gas and oil furnaces, ducting, fuel tanks, etc. Nor do they count the enormous amount of energy spent in carting oil around in trucks and boats and pipelines. They talk about how efficient the new gas furnaces are, which is true, but some of that efficiency is gained by using electric ignition rather than pilot lights, and in the new condensing furnaces (see "Gas and Oil Furnaces," below), there is an electric inductor motor and perhaps other electric accessories that help circulate air and combustion gases to attain that efficiency. And remember, blowers on gas and oil furnaces are run by electricity. All things considered, I have a hunch radiant heating cables might be much closer to gas and oil in total energy use than we are led to believe.

Radiant ceiling heat is weird stuff. It doesn't really heat the air the way a warm air furnace does, but rather heats objects in the air. Thus, if you have your feet under the table they may feel a bit chilly (one of the minor drawbacks of this kind of heating) while your head is comfortably warm. By not heating or moving the air radiant heat saves energy. And you feel warmer than when a hot air furnace or heat pump circulates warm air around the room. Moreover, radiant heat is a very even heat since it is the same all over the room—no cold corners that a furnace must work twice as hard to warm before the thermostat turns it off. And best of all, you can adjust the heat in every room as needed or turn it off completely in rooms not occupied. Carefully used (and of course that is the key to everything), this kind of heat in our experience is not so terribly expensive in spring and fall, when temperatures are between 30° and 60°F, *if* the house is very well insulated, as it must be for electric heat. In really cold weather, the meter can spin merrily away, but how much this really costs in comparison to gas or oil heat in really cold weather I can't say from experience because we heat with wood in December, January, and February.

But a friend here in cold northern Ohio heats entirely with radiant electric ceiling heat and he swears by it. His electric rate is 6.2¢ per kilowatt-hour, and last year he paid out $672 for electric heat for a house of 2,700 square feet. Considering the convenience and the lack of any maintenance, can you beat that? One reason (I think) for his economy is that the house is a split-level, like ours, and the bottom floor nestles into a hill on three sides. Ground temperatures of about 55°F keep that level from ever getting real cold, and so it is easier to keep warm. My friend discounts this because his house, at least on the top level, is not very well insulated, he says, since it was built before the energy crisis. He believes this type of heat is just not that wasteful of energy, and that electric heat gets its bad name from electric resistant furnaces and baseboard heaters. "And a lot of people tend to throw their heating bill into one lump with their air-conditioning bill. We don't have air-conditioning," he says.

Heat Pumps

Nevertheless, electric radiant ceiling heat is not a popular choice. Where people want electric heat, they are choosing the heat pump more and more, because it cuts electric usage to nearly half of electric resistance heaters or ceiling cable. Also heat pumps are air conditioners, too, and save the price of buying a separate unit for that. Indeed, heat pumps are better air coolers than they are space heaters. Improvements may alter the following advice, but as of now, air-source heat pumps are really economical only where winters are mild. When the temperature drops below about 15°F they kick into a conventional electric resistant mode of heating and that will kick up your utility bill real fast.

Some new units, called dual-fuel heat pumps, are made to work in tandem with another fuel, so that in cold weather the heat pump turns off and a gas or oil heater comes on instead of using an electric resistance heater. Their purchase is questionable because if you have to have a gas or oil heater anyway, the heat pump can be justified only as an air conditioner.

Our electrician believes the all-around "best" heating system, as a compromise between low maintenance and cost, is a *water-source* heat pump. Instead of drawing heat out of cold winter air, it draws it out of groundwater, which maintains a temperature of about 50° to 55°F. The most economical water-source heat pump can be enjoyed only by those who have a well. Systems that circulate water and antifreeze through pipes buried in the ground are more costly to install.

Electric Thermo-Storage

The very latest experiment in energy-saving electric heat is called electric thermo-storage, and my electrical genius acquaintance has installed a few such systems. The savings come from the discount you can get from many utility companies by using the bulk of your electric energy during off-peak periods. Some electric utilities are encouraging electric thermo-storage for this reason; if they can keep electric usage down during peak periods, it means lots of money saved overall. Ohio Power right now offers an off-peak rate of only 3 cents per kilowatt-hour to encourage developments like electric thermo-storage. (In our area, water heaters have a control on them that the utility company can turn on or off at central headquarters. If peak load starts going too high, they shut off our water heaters and turn them back on in the wee hours of the morning when not much electricity is being used. So far we have never lacked hot water, nor have I heard anyone else complain, while the utility company has been able to save enormous amounts of money, which hopefully they are passing on.)

In electric thermo-storage, a massive heat storage sink is built in the ground under the house. The material might be stone, brick, or another storage mass—experimenting is still underway. This mass is heated with off-peak electricity, enough to keep the house warm until the next off-peak period. Homeowners claim an 80 percent decrease in heating costs over conventional electric heat. This is something to ask about, especially if you are building new, although the system can be integrated into an existing house. However, where winters are cold you'll need a supplementary source of heat: electric thermo-storage will raise the temperature on cold days only to the mid-60s at best.

Such a system is obviously low maintenance—mostly electronic monitors and fans for air circulation. With a heat pump there is considerably more to maintain. Generally there's a unit installed in your house and another outside. The compressor and one heat exchange coil are outside, and a blower and another heat exchange coil are inside. Freon refrigerant moves the heat back and forth between outdoors and indoors, in one direction in summer and another in winter by means of a clever reversing valve.

Gas and Oil Furnaces

The cheapest way to heat if you have to buy fuel, is with gas—or oil when it is as inexpensive as it is right now in late 1986. Improvements, especially the new condensing furnaces as they are called, in both gas and oil heaters have increased their efficiency remarkably. Condensing furnaces have *two* heat exchangers in them capable of wringing almost all the heat out of escaping combustion gases. Gas condensing furnaces have efficiency ratings of 90 to 95 percent, while those fueled by oil have ratings of 85 to 90 percent, which justifies their higher price over conventional furnaces (they sell for about $2,000). Another great advantage is that gases are cooled so low that a real chimney is not needed. Oil needs a galvanized pipe; gas only a plastic one. But in shopping, pay particular attention to how the condensation is handled. By the time circulating air scrubs the last heat from combustion gases, they have cooled to where condensation occurs. This condensate can cause corrosion on the heat exchanger. Check to see how the warranty covers that.

There are many good condensing furnaces on the market and by the time you read this every dealer should have one to sell. If not, Amana, Whirlpool, and Lennox (see Appendix A for addresses) are good brands with which to start your investigation. Lennox is also a front-runner in the much ballyhooed pulse combustion furnaces. These are even more expensive (around $3,000) but use gas so conservatively by employing intermittent combustion rather than a steady flow of gas that payback may well justify the price. But pulse combustion requires more intricate electrical devices, and as my electrician says: "They are wonderful as long as everything is working, but there's a lot that can go wrong."

FURNACE MAINTENANCE

Maintenance on gas and oil furnaces is about the same: clean the blower at least once a year, clean or replace the filter, clean the flue, and make sure the fuel nozzles aren't partially plugged. On water-heating systems, you also need to bleed air out of the radiators about once a year. Oil furnaces get dirtier quicker than gas ones and are more complicated to service. Many fuel companies or furnace dealers have a regular service program well worth the cost. But if you want to do the work yourself, it's much easier to watch carefully and ask lots of questions as a serviceman does the work than try to understand printed language about heat exchangers, electrodes, transformers, cartridge gaskets, etc.

A good indication that your oil furnace needs cleaning is lots of soot in the flue inside the damper on the flue. You can check easily by lifting the damper door and peeking inside. A gremlin often overlooked is a plugged filter in the supply pipe from the oil tank to the furnace. The filter is sort of a little cup in the line, usually right outside the tank.

Other overlooked potential troublemakers are the pump and blower motors. The motors on older furnaces need a few drops of oil twice a year or more in their little oil cups with the snap-down lids. If you ignore that detail long enough, the motor will freeze up.

The main filter above the blower is easy enough to replace or wash if it is the washable kind. The fans on the blower itself need cleaning less often, but if you shirk this job, you will pay for it in higher fuel bills and shorter motor life. Since the blower is a beast to get to in most oil furnaces, I think the annual servicing by a professional is well worth the cost.

Gas furnaces are somewhat easier to clean, but the whole job is one I think you should watch a serviceman do at least once. In order to get to the blower fins the blower usually needs to be removed from the furnace. Although that is not particularly complicated and well within the capability of anyone mechanically inclined, I still suggest getting a briefing from your serviceman and/or studying closely the maintenance manual that comes with your particular furnace.

A usual maintenance repair job on gas furnaces is replacing the thermocouple device that automatically turns off the gas if the pilot light goes out. Of course, with the newer electronic controls, pilot lights are obsolete and so are thermocouples.

If the blower is belt-driven, replace the belt when it begins to fray or show serious wear. Or at least have a new belt ready. Otherwise, the old belt will break on a Saturday night when the temperature is below zero and your serviceman is out of town.

Adjusting air ports on the burners is simple if you know what you are doing, but again, I suggest having your furnace dealer or serviceman do it. Money spent for real technical expertise is seldom wasted. At any rate, if you do decide to do it yourself, be sure to heed your manual and turn off all necessary switches and valves beforehand.

Combination furnaces—usually wood or coal combined with gas or oil—increase your security, and, if you have your own wood, may decrease your fuel bill. But there's no maintenance advantage—in fact, more things can go wrong on a combination furnace than on a regular one.

Wood Stoves and Fireplaces

Heating with wood is high maintenance no matter how you split it. Wood stoves themselves are premium examples of low-maintenance technology, since if made properly they should last nearly forever without repair work. But of course handling the wood and the ashes is very high maintenance, not to mention regular cleaning of the flue and chimney. If you have your own wood or can get some free for the cutting and you consider the work enjoyable exercise, then wood heat pays enough to justify itself, despite high maintenance. Otherwise, it can be justified only as a backup heating system during winter power failures. In this case, you would be foolish to buy a stove that depends on electric fans to circulate the heat unless the stove will also function without fans.

The wood stove business has slumped sharply with the fall of oil prices—at least, that is the reason given. I fail to see the connection since only 12 percent of American homes are heated with oil (compared to 11 percent for wood) anyway. Gas prices certainly haven't slumped, and electric rates continue to climb. I think rather that the wood stove business has declined because the faddists who run after every trend dropped out of the wood heating mania as soon as they realized the amount of work involved. This is unfortunate, perhaps, because most of the "bad" stoves have been purged from the market and the ones remaining are mostly "good" ones with much improved efficiencies.

I put quotes around "bad" and "good" when talking about wood stoves because there is much hype and hoke connected with marketing them. I still don't think the general wood-burning public, or prospective wood-burning customer especially, understands the proper connection between efficiency and airtight stoves. Nothing would burn in an airtight stove. People have problems with "airtight" stoves because they won't open them up enough so the wood can burn hot and clean. So we invent the catalytic burner that burns smoke, more or less, and so increases the efficiency of the stove (at considerable increase in cost and regular replacement of the catalytic burner). This is better than polluting the air with unburned combustion gases, but it is not the best solution. In fact, some stove manufacturers are redesigning their stoves with more sophisticated internal heat exchangers (somewhat along the same lines as the new heat exchangers in oil and gas furnaces) and can get just as much efficiency and lack of pollutants as the catalytic burners. In fact, *most* of the first nine stoves to pass the stringent tests of the Oregon Department of Environmental Quality did *not* have catalytic burners. Lopi Energy Systems (10850 117th Place NE, Kirkland, WA 98033) is an example.

I almost hate to mention wood stoves by brand and do so only as information to start you on your own market research, not as an endorsement. *The Woodheat/Woodstove Directory* (Street Enterprises, Box 255, Menomonee Falls, WI 53051) is a good source of further brand-name information. There are too many variables in the art and science of burning wood correctly, and the brand name is the least significant of all.

The Oregon Certification test has about as much real significance as government gas mileage tests, but the Environmental Protection Agency (EPA) is lumbering toward some kind of standard testing in an effort to cut down on air pollution. Air pollution from wood stoves is a problem only in some relatively small areas, but as usual we are all going to be made to suffer impractical regulations. Operator skill makes a stove burn cleanly, not EPA regulations. And strangely enough, with operator skill, an inexpensive "leaky" stove will burn cleaner than a more expensive "good" one, simply because it is not "airtight." (And those powders you can buy to sprinkle on your fire to clean out the creosote in your flue won't help much if you're not using your stove properly. Interestingly, such cleaners come with instructions on how to burn a more efficient, cleaner fire in your stove or fireplace. Following those directions will be much more effective than using any commercial creosote cleaner.)

I know a couple who heat primarily with an ancient box stove they paid $35 for. It is so far from airtight that you could stick a knife blade through the cracks between various seam lines. It has air vent controls below the door and a damper up in the flue in the old-fashioned way so that you can control draft very accurately, but you can't shut it down so that the flue only smolders. The firebox is very small (the experts now say that this is a requirement to get very hot, clean-burning fires). Also, the chunks of wood these people fuel with are very small—no more than 3 inches thick and about 8 inches long, which is also a way to get a good hot fire, so long as there is plenty of air getting to it. They rarely put more than two or three pieces of wood in the stove at once (admittedly high maintenance) extracting from it a nice hot fire. I will bet that they get more heat per pound of wood than the best Oregon-certified, catalytic equipped dual heat-exchanging Fisher Tech IV on the market.

Be that as it may, modern wood stoves are so attractive they will fit any decor. Tile stoves, now becoming popular, hold and radiate heat well, are not burning hot to the touch, and are easy to clean off. Whether they are worth the extra cost over steel or cast-iron stoves is mostly a matter of taste, although steel and cast iron do need more surface polishing and cleaning than tile or soapstone. Ashpans make taking out ashes a little easier (not much). A wood bin beside the stove confines dirt and bark on the wood to a single place, but you still have to sweep up around the stove quite often. One of those hand-held little vacuum cleaners powered with rechargeable batteries is very handy for this purpose. We keep ours by the wood box.

The good news in catalytic burners is that the new ones are guaranteed for five years, rather than needing replacement every other year as was generally the case with the first ones that came on the market a few years ago. Don't expect miracles from them (even with catalytic burners, you should not let your stove smolder with a cold, smoky fire), but they will cut down considerably on creosote buildup in a poorly operated stove. Supposedly a catalytic burner will enable your stove to use wood more efficiently so that you will ultimately burn less wood—some say a third less wood—for the same amount of heat generated, but as I say, that depends on who is operating the stove.

Fireplace inserts today are really stoves made to fit into fireplace openings. Such inserts will make simple fireplaces more efficient, but no matter what the dealer tells you, they will not deliver heat out into the house the way a freestanding cast-iron stove of similar size will. The Mark IV Fisher (Cesco Industries, Inc., P.O. Box 7817, Roanoke, VA 24019) has an efficiency rating of 79 percent, excellent for an insert and very good for a stove. But a stove entombed in a fireplace still loses radiant heat that, in my opinion, it never makes up in the convective heat it is designed to produce.

The ultimate in wood-burning low maintenance is the huge masonry fireplace, used for centuries in many parts of Europe and referred to sometimes as a Russian fireplace. It is in essence a very large fireplace, which is an integral part of the house. Its mass makes it a good heat storage sink. In the large fire chamber, a very hot (and traditionally large) fire is burned, heating the whole masonry storage sink as the hot smoke finds its way through a labyrinth to the chimney. The warmed masonry then slowly and steadily heats the house until another big intense firing is necessary. Little or no creosote forms with the hot fire, nor is a large amount of wood used because the fire burns perhaps only 2 hours for every 10 or so hours of heating it supplies via the warmed masonry. Thus the fireplace becomes in reality a central heating furnace. The drawback is the cost of construction and the lack of know-how in this country to build them. (Alex Wade, in his book *A Design and Construction Handbook for Energy-Saving Houses* [Rodale Press, 1980], describes Russian fireplaces much better than I do here; he also provides sources for more information about them.)

If you are interested in an open fireplace with much more efficiency than a normal fireplace, there is an American version of the masonry fireplace on the market called the Tess 148 (Thermal Energy Storage Systems, Inc., P.O. Box M, Mine Road, Kenvil, NJ 07847). As with all open fireplaces, there is no appreciable buildup of creosote, and in addition, its Rumsford design and heat storage capability mean you get a lot more heat; your fireplace becomes something more than just an expensive luxury.

Small Appliances

In a way, small appliances are very low maintenance because when one of them breaks, which is often and soon, we simply throw it away and buy a new one. Thus we pass on maintenance to public officials who must figure out what to do with the junk we so wantonly toss away in the garbage. I have an acquaintance who loves to fix things, and he says just about every appliance is fixable if you can get the new part from the manufacturer. This takes time. Manufacturers would much rather you lose patience and buy a new one.

To avoid fixing, I am tempted to say never buy an appliance priced at $19.95, or for that matter $29.95. But that would not be totally true, and besides we will have these appliances whether we want them or not for the same reason men have closets full of ties. Small, cheap appliances make such nice Christmas gifts. But given a choice, it is always better to pay a little more rather than a little less.

Better than that, whenever possible, investigate *manually* operated appliances. Our manually operated ice cream maker is *much* more satisfactory in our estimation than the electric one we used to use. A hand-cranked pasta maker we bought last year suits us much better than an electric one. Our hand-operated Victoria Strainer (from Vitantonio Manufacturing Company, 34355 Vokes Drive, Eastlake, OH 44094) is perfect for preparing apples for sauce, tomatoes for juice and catsup, baby foods, etc. Our hand-cranked flour mill and hand-cranked meat grinder are perfect for a normal kitchen's needs. These tools don't suddenly quit working and are usually easy enough to fix if something does break.

Vacuum Cleaners

Vacuum cleaners can be high maintenance if you try to run them when the bag is full of dirt, or mercy, without the screen that keeps dirt from being sucked into the motor. A high-priced Electrolux will generally be a better buy than a cheap _____ (fill in the manufacturer of your choice). But for real low maintenance, a central cleaning system is best. The suction motor is much more powerful, the lightweight hose and attachments easier to handle, and cleaning becomes a very quiet job for once. I thought surely the pipes carrying away the dirt would get plugged, but after observing central cleaning in a friend's house for a good many years, this evidently doesn't happen. Another advantage is that a central cleaning system does not exhaust air right back into the room like a conventional vacuum does, blowing nearly as much dust into the air as it sucks up.

Irons

The ports in steam irons get plugged in time, more so if you are using well water, even if it's softened. It will pay anyone to catch a little rainwater or save the water from a dehumidifier to use in steam irons to lengthen the time before the ports become plugged. A wire will unplug the holes somewhat. A solution of half vinegar and half water allowed to steam away is supposed to clean out mineral buildup, but doesn't always work. Buildup on the bottom of the iron, from spray-on starches, for instance, can be removed by rubbing gently with a nonabrasive cleanser like Bon Ami. Do not use regular scouring powder; it will scratch the bottom.

Toasters

Don't forget to pull the crumb pan out of your toaster once in a blue moon and dump it. And remember Logsdon's Law of Small Appliance

Repair: When it doesn't work, check the electric plug and cord first. Invariably appliances that you plug in and out frequently develop loose connections or breaks in the wire.

Air Conditioners

It is interesting to try to imagine urban development without the air conditioner. The proliferation of high-rise apartments and tall office buildings would never have happened, especially in the South. Most likely factories, stores, and offices would have expanded underground. Or squatted in low profiles in woodland. There would be a premium on tree shade and cities would look more like forested suburbs. Sounds like a pretty good idea to me.

At any rate, air conditioners are now considered an absolute necessity by most people even in the North, which is a pity. There is so much energy waste with them. I have worked in air-conditioned offices and ridden in air-conditioned cars, and visited air-conditioned homes where I had to wear a sweater to stay warm. I have seen air conditioners in the North roaring away when opening a window would have brought in a cool breeze far more pleasant than conditioned air. In the North, there are about 20 days a year when air-conditioning really helps, not enough to justify an efficient central air-conditioning system.

The cheapest and most maintenance-free air-conditioning is a house built at least partially into the ground. The lower level of our house stays naturally comfortable all summer—but some of that economy is lost because in-ground rooms invariably need a dehumidifier. The cost of a small dehumidifier is, however, much less than air-conditioning.

An attic fan and/or window fans provide cheap and effective air-conditioning when the weather is only mildly hot. In well-insulated houses that become uncomfortably hot only in the late afternoon, you can turn on such fans to pull in evening and night air to cool a house down as effectively for sleeping as any air conditioner.

To cool one or two rooms, a room air conditioner may be more economical, even though these kinds are less efficient and involve more maintenance than a central system. (For a more or less complete listing of efficiency ratings of various brands of air conditioners, you can send for *The Most Energy-Efficient Appliances,* from the American Council for an Energy-Efficient Economy [Suite 525, 1001 Connecticut Avenue NW, Washington, DC 20036].) The central air Carrier Premium IV (Carrier Corporation, Carrier Parkway, P.O. Box 4808, Syracuse, NY 13221) and the Lennox Power Saver (see Appendix A for address) head the list with ratings around 15. Friedrich (Friedrich Air Conditioning & Refrigeration

Company, P.O. Box 1540, San Antonio, TX 78295) and Carrier room air conditioners head the list in room air conditioners with ratings of about 11. These ratings are not any more significant in themselves than other energy ratings given in this book but serve as a sort of comparison. And since efficiency and running time are related, the more efficient, the less the maintenance, generally speaking.

The Japanese have developed a central air-conditioning system different from those in the United States. As in regular American central systems, the compressor sits outside. The difference is that there is an evaporator in each room; tubing carries refrigerant to each evaporator. The advantage of this design is that there is no ductwork, so installation is easier than regular central air. The evaporators are positioned high on the walls for better air circulation and are out of furniture's way. By the time you read this, American manufacturers should be offering these "split" systems. They are worth looking into.

Maintenance Tips

A few timely maintenance tips will add years of good performance to your unit:

- If you can position your outside condenser in the shade, so much the better. Make sure the air intake is not blocked by bushes or debris.
- Clean or replace the filter(s) regularly.
- Clean the coils in the condenser.
- Put a few drops of oil in those little cups at each end of the motors. Oiling too much is as bad as oiling not enough because the excess attracts dirt into the motor. Once a year is usually enough, twice if you are really energetic.
- Don't set the thermostat lower than the temperature you desire, thinking that it will cool down quicker that way. It will just run longer and so the sooner maintenance problems will develop.
- You should consult with an experienced cooling contractor for recommendations on the proper size air conditioner for your needs. No use paying for more than you need, and anyway, an air conditioner with more capacity than you need will cool too quickly for you to get the full dehumidifying action from it. A unit too small will use more electricity trying to cool a space larger than it can handle. It will do a poor job no matter how hard it tries, and the extra strain will cause it to wear out too soon.

Details on how to do these service jobs are in the service manual you purchased with your machine or are available from your dealer.

Toilet Fixtures

The float that controls the water intake in the toilet tank sometimes gets stuck or may (very rarely) get a hole in it and not float. In either case, water runs continuously through the tank rather than filling. Normally, the float rises with the water level until it closes off the incoming water. You can lessen the amount of water you use for every flush by bending the float rod so it closes the valve sooner.

There are water-saving toilets you should know about. Although these toilets will not result in direct household maintenance savings, they will save us larger-scale maintenance costs because in the long run they cut down our use of an important natural resource—clean water. We waste water terribly, and from scientists comes the sad word that water will be (not may be) our next big crisis. Among the new water-saving toilets, Rodale's Product Testing Group found in tests that those listed below used the least amount of water while still doing a satisfactory job of flushing. (Using less water per flush doesn't help if you have to flush twice.)

- The Ultra One G (Eljer Plumbingware, Three Gateway Center, Pittsburgh, PA 15222)
- The Superrinse (Thetford Corporation, P.O. Box 1285, Ann Arbor, MI 48106)
- The Cashsaver MX (as in missile?) (Water Control International, 2820 West Maple Road, Suite 224, Troy, MI 48084)

There is a maintenance problem with all toilet bowls that I daresay has never been discussed in print, because of its somewhat delicate nature. (Where are you, Ann Landers, now that I need you?) The toilet bowl is not a men's urinal, yet thoughtless men try to pretend it is. To put it more frankly, a stream of liquid descending from a height into a toilet bowl *splashes* when it hits the water. The splashing has surprising distance to it. Splatterings hit the walls on either side of the bowl. In other words, men, *sit down*. Sitting does no harm to your masculine ego. I discussed this little maintenance detail with my wife and several sisters, all of whom said housewives would bless me for bringing this nefarious practice out of the (water) closet. If splattering the walls does not make you macho types flinch, be aware that it is also splattering your pants legs.

Wastewater Systems

Away go troubles down the drain—hopefully, but unfortunately, not always. Prevention is again the solution.

Drains

Hair is the main culprit in bathtub drains, but modern tubs handle the problem easily, with a screen in the drain. To get it out for cleaning, you may be able to twist the drain plug, lift it out, and clean off the screen at the bottom of it. But today, usually, you have to remove the little lever above the faucet that turns on the shower. You then can lift out a longish rod with a coil spring and a screen on the end of it that catches the hairs. This should be done once or twice a year at least.

Children are the leading cause of toilet plug-ups. They are fascinated by the way things disappear down the bowl and are liable to try to get rid of everything from dirty pants to the family cat in this convenient manner. Plumbers looking for more work love such children, but nothing can tempt a parent more toward child abuse.

Garbage Disposals

At the kitchen sink, the garbage disposal is both bane and boon to plumbing maintenance. By grinding table scraps into a paste that water can carry away through the plumbing, disposals save many a clogged drain of yesteryear. However, as is so true of most modern technology, in solving one problem, they create others. Because it seems no longer necessary to be careful how much plate scrapings, etc., go down the drain, all sorts of things go down, including silverware and scouring pads, which plug or break the disposal. Plugging, say users and plumbers both, is most often caused by not using enough water to flush away the ground-up garbage. "On ours you have to have the faucet on full force when the disposal is running," one homeowner told me. This, of course, is wasteful. Most disposals also require a larger than standard drainpipe—at least a 2-inch size rather than a 1½ inch. Putting in the larger is definitely a wise way toward lower maintenance.

"A disposal seems fairly low cost, but by the time you make all the necessary plumbing and installation changes, I'm not so sure," says another householder. Banana skins, citrus rinds, onion skins, unpopped popcorn kernels, and bones are materials you are advised not to try to put through disposals. This fact greatly negates the claims for convenience that disposals enjoy; if you have to dispose of these things some other way, why not all the table scraps?

At least homeowners with land, a garden, chickens, etc., are better served composting or feeding or at least burying table scraps rather than putting up with the expense and high maintenance of garbage disposals. There is tremendous waste involved. If someday we can recycle sewage sludge back to the land handily, dumping garbage into the sewer system might make sense, but homeowners will pay dearly for the convenience, sooner or later.

Septic Systems

Flushing ground-up garbage into septic systems is another way to overload them before their time. Bacteria will digest garbage, however, as well as it will digest excrement, but as the list of rules that came with our septic system says: "Do not discharge excess grease or fatty materials into the system . . . use garbage disposals sparingly."

Other no-no's listed are:

- backwash water from water softeners
- cigarette stubs
- cloth
- colored toilet paper; use only *white* toilet paper
- disposable diapers
- large amounts of acids or caustics like lye, cleaning materials that have a high or low pH factor; use low-suds detergents
- petroleum-base materials like motor oils, grease, kerosene, gasoline, paint thinner, etc.
  - paper towels
  - plastic materials
  - rubber products
  - sanitary napkins and tampons
  - sump pump discharges
  - tissues

When you add to the inevitable violations of these rules the typical family's extravagant use of water, it is no wonder that so many septic systems ooze to lawn surfaces, especially in subdivisions where soil percolation just barely meets minimum standards to begin with. Then, of course, the septic tanks, which in these conditions are no more than cesspools, have to be pumped out every other year or sooner.

New septic systems that can be used where leach beds are impractical will produce an effluent, if the above rules are followed, suitable for discharge in accordance with Environmental Protection Agency (EPA) regulations. These require an outlet for the effluent, of course, and so are applicable only in country areas. They are expensive (ours cost about $2,000 ten years ago) and are relatively high maintenance, since there is an agitator motor and an aerator motor and two timers that wear out over a period of five to ten years. Waste from the house is agitated regularly in the first chamber and the effluent aerated and filtered in the second chamber before it is released.

These units are serviced regularly by a company in that business, and you pay for the service, which is better than trying to do the repairs yourself. The pollution problems with these units are that if they malfunction, they can continue to discharge effluent, albeit not properly treated effluent, and there are homeowners who are careless enough to let such a condition continue as long as possible. Hence the twice yearly check by a service company. But homeowners should call the service company immediately upon a malfunction—it will save them money in the long run. We have had one of these units for 12 years now and by following the rules as much as we can, we have never had to clean out the tank, and never should have to, since theoretically, a biologically healthy septic tank will work forever.

One of the main problems with septic tanks is that they get overloaded—especially in crowded suburbs. Homeowners are then forced to plunk down a good amout of money for hooking up to a sewer, thereby pushing the problem onto city officials, who have to deal with all that wastewater. Another big problem with septic tanks is that many old ones in more rural areas are not working, or work only as cesspools, and the polluted effluent flows off in tile lines into streams and rivers. This is illegal, but the EPA can't afford the monumental task of enforcing the rules. Eventually these cesspools have to be replaced, and then the EPA requires a proper system. It will take awhile, but eventually country streams should be reasonably clean again, at least of sewage.

The Automatic House Ha Ha

The computerization of the world is well underway and will bring great blessings, the salespeople tell us, to civilization. An end to war? Well no. An end to totalitarian government? Well, no. An end to the ecological destruction of the universe? Well, no. As a matter of fact, computerization is a great aid to war, totalitarian governments, and ecological destruction. But, anyway, electronics promises good things, too, like enabling people to walk who otherwise would remain crippled for life.

For our purposes here, computerization is not only a way to ease household maintenance but to save energy, a few examples of which we have already seen. Often the only energy saved is energy used merely because we don't have the discipline to use it carefully and efficiently in the first place.

Now, looking for more worlds to conquer, the computer business wants to turn the whole house into what it calls the "automatic house." The new electronic thermostats already discussed are part of that automation, controlling heat output economically so you (hopefully) don't have to worry about at what temperature you left the thermostat. New on the market are electronic digital scales that weigh small amounts of food handily and accurately. Even newer is a faucet that automatically releases a flow of water whenever an object interrupts an infrared beam from an electronic photocell in the nozzle. One such faucet is available from Sloan

Value Company (10500 Seymour Avenue, Franklin Park, IL 60131). There are also dozens of timers that can be programmed to start or stop everything except the lawn mower. And that might be next.

Is this all practical? How often anyway do you really need an automatic stream of water? Your two-year-old will find it great sport, that's for sure. And let us contemplate more deeply the computer salesperson's dreams of combining all these electronic marvels into the "total electronic house control." By that they mean a software program you put into your personal computer that controls lights, appliances, security systems, and almost any kind of gadget you desire, turning your house on and off "on a schedule tailored to your requirements." (I'm quoting from one of those glib and naive, rosy-future articles that magazines love to publish so people run out and buy their advertisers' products.)

The reason this won't work is that human beings have very little notion about what their requirements are going to be in the near or distant future. They can be relied on in only one respect: they will change their minds. Accordingly, it may be impossible to program a weekly or even daily schedule to regulate lights and appliances. Human nature would soon rebel as it already is rebelling to those sickening electronic voices that tell you your car lights are still on.

Here is a quote from an article describing "Jonathan," a sort of computer robot built into the "Tomorrowhouse" complete electronic programmable system (Compu Home Systems International Ltd., 1660 South Albion, Suite 806, Denver, CO 80222). "Each morning, Jonathan's voice synthesizer awakens you by announcing 'Good morning, Master.'" (Already I am running the other way as fast as I can.) "Then Jonathan reports the time, the outdoor temperature, and your appointments for the day." So now the work office has insinuated itself even into the sanctuary of the bedroom. The last thing I want to hear when I wake up is a list of the appointments I'm supposed to keep that day.

If a security sensor is triggered, Jonathan turns on all the lights and dials the police with a distress call. Great, but I bet the police don't think so. Think of the false alarms this is bound to lead to. But anyway, you can silence Jonathan with a quick command, thank God.

Seriously though, just how regimented and automatic do we want to live at home? How many people really want to schedule their daily activities, or their house's functions as much as nine weeks ahead? If the ultimate is to live in a house where everything is accomplished automatically, what will we *do?* Watch yet more TV? Play yet more games? Perhaps it will become possible to transmit *The Decline and Fall of the Roman Empire* into our brain without reading it—while simultaneously watching one program on TV and three more on VCRs from last week.

I would end this book with a plea for the ultimate maintenance feature every home should possess: *Sanity.* Home should be a retreat from a "real" world that runs on the cowlike logic of the computer and a disregard for every value except profitability. This has driven Americans to embrace in their leisure time sports and crafts that use their bodies, their hands, their wits, and physical skills, which automation has so thoughtlessly tried to rob us of. Let us be terribly careful how much of all the automatic world we bring home with us. It is expensive. It means more maintenance, one way or another. And much of it is insane. Even Timothy Orr Knight, editor of *Personal Robotics* writes ("Will You Own a Robot," in *New Shelter,* Nov./Dec. 1984): "Indeed like the personal computer of a few years ago, the personal robot seems to be an answer in search of a question." Enough said.

APPENDIX A: PRODUCTS

Here is a list of the brand-name products and/or suppliers that I mention in the text of this book. Certainly I cannot say that these are the only good products of their kind available. They are, rather, the products that I am most familiar with, and I like what I know about them. You may very well know other brands that are equally good.

Appliances

appliance manufacturers

Admiral Home Appliances
1701 East Woodfield Road
Schaumburg, IL 60196

Amana Refrigeration, Inc.
Amana, IA 52204

Frigidaire Company
973 East Congress Park Drive
Centerville, OH 45459

General Electric Company
9500 Williamsburg Plaza
Louisville, KY 40222

Gibson Appliance Company
635 West Charles Street
Greenville, MI 48838

Hotpoint
General Electric Company
9500 Williamsburg Plaza
Louisville, KY 40222

Kelvinator Appliance
  Company
White Consolidated
  Industries
300 Phillipi Road
Columbus, OH 43218

Kenmore
Sears Roebuck & Company
Sears Tower
Chicago, IL 60684

Lennox Industries
P.O. Box 809000
Dallas, TX 75380-9000

Magic Chef, Inc.
740 King Edward Avenue
Cleveland, TN 37311

Panasonic
Matsushita Appliance
  Company
Electric Corporation
  of America
One Panasonic Way
Secaucus, NJ 07094

Sun Frost
Box DD
Arcata, CA 95521
(superefficient refrigerator)

Tappan
White Consolidated
  Industries
300 Phillipi Road
Columbus, OH 43218

Whirlpool Corporation
Appliance Information
  Service
2000 M-63 North
Benton Harbor, MI 49022

White-Westinghouse
  Appliance Company
White Consolidated
  Industries
300 Phillipi Road
Columbus, OH 43218

central air-conditioners

Carrier Premium IV
Carrier Corporation
Carrier Parkway
P.O. Box 4808
Syracuse, NY 13221

Friedrich Air Conditioning &
  Refrigeration Company
P.O. Box 1540
San Antonio, TX 78295

Lennox Power Saver
Lennox Industries
P.O. Box 809000
Dallas, TX 75380

**combination furnace/
water heater**

Polaris
Mor-Flo Industries
18450 South Miles Road
Cleveland, OH 44128

computerized house system

Tomorrowhouse
Compu Home Systems
  International Ltd.
1660 South Albion
Suite 806
Denver, CO 80222

efficient, clean wood stoves

Lopi Energy Systems
10850 117th Place NE
Kirkland, WA 98033

fireplace inserts

Mark IV Fisher
Cesco Industries, Inc.
P.O. Box 7817
Roanoke, VA 24019

hand-operated food mills

Victoria Strainer
Vitantonio Manufacturing
  Company
34355 Vokes Drive
Eastlake, OH 44094

Rumsford fireplaces

Tess 148
Thermal Energy Storage
  Systems, Inc.
P.O. Box M
Mine Road
Kenvil, NJ 07847

Ceilings

**stamped metal for ceilings
or walls**

A. A. Abbingdon Affiliates
2149 Utica Avenue
Brooklyn, NY 11234

W. F. Norman Corporation
P.O. Box 323
Nevada, MO 64772

Wilsonart
Ralph Wilson
  Plastics Company
600 General Bruce Drive
Temple, TX 76501

Doors and Windows

**exterior rolling
window shutters**

Perfecta
American Reflexa
31843 West 8 Mile Road
Livonia, MI 48152

Security Shutters
Security Shutter Corporation
109 James Street
Venice, FL 33595

fiberglass insulated doors

Therma-Tru Corporation
P.O. Box 7404
Toledo, OH 43615

multiglazed skylights

Velux
Velux-America, Inc.
P.O. Box 3208
Greenwood, SC 29648

patio doors with footbolt

Bilt Best Windows
175 10th Street
Sainte Genevieve, MO 63670

solid wood doors sold by mail

Kirby Mill Works
Box 898
Ignacio, CO 81137

Exteriors and Framing

**facsimile stones fashioned
from concrete**

L. B. Stone Company
Box 276
Apple Creek, OH 44606

insulated concrete block

Insul Block Corporation
55 Circuit Avenue
West Springfield, MA 01089

**insulated exterior
brick paneling**

Pan-Brick
Pan-Brick, Inc.
3030 Saskatchewan Drive
Regina, SK S4T 6P1
Canada

Perma-Panel
U.S. Brick
Michigan Division
3820 Serr Road
Corunna, MI 48817

insulated stucco exteriors

Dryvit
Dryvit System, Inc.
P.O. Box 1014
One Energy Way
West Warwick, RI 02983

Penbar, Inc.
2808 North 2 Street
Minneapolis, MN 55411

steel house frames

Madray Building Systems
P.O. Box 712
Okechobee, FL 33473

Tri-Steel Structures, Inc.
1400 Cresent
Denton, TX 76201

strong concrete for stuccoing and patching exterior walls

Advocote
Coatings International
5123 Woodlane Circle
Tallahassee, FL 32303

Kan Kote
Kan Kote, Inc.
P.O. Box H
Parker, PA 16049

Rockite
Hartline Products
   Company, Inc.
2186 Noble Road
Cleveland, OH 44112

surface bond masonry

Surewall
W. R. Bonsal Company
P.O. Box 241148
Charlotte, NC 28224

timber framing

Riverbend Timber
   Framing, Inc.
9012 U.S. 223
Blissfield, MI 49228

Floors

brick veneer floorcovering

Pee Dee
Deiner Brick
P.O. Box 130
Park Avenue and
   Cuthbert Road
Collingswood, NJ 08108

ceramic tiles

American Olean
   Tile Company
1000 Cannon Avenue
P.O. Box 271
Lansdale, PA 19446-0271

Elon, Inc.
150 East 58th Street
New York, NY 10155
(especially imported tiles)

Olympia Floor and Wall Tile
1000 Lawrence Avenue
Toronto, ON M6B 4A8
Canada

concrete simulated brick, slate, or flagstone floors

Bowmanite Corporation
81 Encina Avenue
Palo Alto, CA 94301

Coronado Products, Inc.
1325 6th Avenue North
Nashville, TN 37208-0568

handmade rugs

The Barn
Box 25, Market Street
Lehman, PA 18627

Rastetter Woolen Mill
Star Route
Millersburg, OH 44654

hardwood flooring

Harris-Tarkett, Inc.
P.O. Box 300
Johnson City, TN 37605

linoleum

Krommenie Company
   (Holland)
L. D. Brinkman
   (West Coast distributors)
1251 South Rockefeller
   Avenue
Ontario, CA 91745

Oriental rugs

Charles W. Jacobsen, Inc.
401 South Salina Street
Syracuse, NY 13201

Kaoud Brothers Oriental Rugs
17 South Main Street
West Hartford, CT 06107

phenolic varnish for wood floors

Gymseal
The McCloskey Corporation
7600 State Road
Philadelphia, PA 19136

stamps for patterning concrete

Masonry Specialty Company
4430 Gibsonia Road
Gibsonia, PA 15044

synthetic rubber flooring
Noraplan Duo
Nora Flooring
4201 Wilson Avenue
Madison, IN 47250

vinyl floorcovering
Armstrong World Industries
150 North Queen Street
Lancaster, PA 17604

Foundations

*interior concrete block sealers
for basements*
Thoroseal
Thoro System Products
7800 Northwest 38th Street
Miami, FL 33166

Tuff-N-Dri
Owens Corning
    Fiberglass Corporation
Fiberglass Tower
Toledo, OH 43659

pressure treated wood
Osmose Sunwood
Osmose Wood
    Preserving, Inc.
980 Ellicott Street
Buffalo, NY 14209

Wolmanized Lumber
Koppers Company, Inc.
436 Seventh Avenue
Pittsburgh, PA 15219

*waterproofing panels
for foundation exterior*
American Wick
    Drain Corporation
301 Warehouse Drive
Matthews, NC 28105

Eljen Corporation
15 Westwood Road
Storrs, CT 06268

Geotech Systems Corporation
100 Powers Court
Sterling, VA 22170

JDR Enterprises
725 Branch Drive
Alpharetta, GA 30201

Mirafi Inc
P.O. Box 240967
Charlotte, NC 28224

Owens Corning
    Fiberglass Corporation
Fiberglass Tower
Toledo, OH 43659

Garden Equipment

small motorized tiller-weeders
Mantis
Mantis Manufacturing
    Company
1458 County Line Road
Huntingdon Valley, PA
    19006

Sunbird
Sunbird Products
R.D. #4
Box 462
Middlebury, VT 05753

walking tractors
Kinco
1669 Grand Avenue
Saint Paul, MN 55105

Paints and Other Finishing Products

paint removers
Restore-X
Restech Industries, Inc.
P.O. Box 2747
Eugene, OR 97402

paint sealers
Waterlox
Waterlox Chemical and
    Coating Corporation
9808 Meech Avenue
Cleveland, OH 44105

power paint rollers
Power-Flo Products
    Corporation
1661 94th Lane NE
Minneapolis, MN 55434

wood finishing products
Deft, Inc.
P.O. Box 2476
Alliance, OH 44601

Minwax Company, Inc.
P.O. Box 99
Flora, IL 62839

Watco Finishing Oil
Watco Corporation
Santa Monica, CA 90406

Plumbing

electronic faucets
Sloan Value Company
10500 Seymour Avenue
Franklin Park, IL 60131

low-water toilets
The Cashsaver MX
Water Control International
2820 West Maple Road
Suite 224
Troy, MI 48084

The Superrinse
Thetford Corporation
P.O. Box 1285
Ann Arbor, MI 48106

The Ultra One G
Eljer Plumbingware
Three Gateway Center
Pittsburgh, PA 15222

Roofing

aluminum- and zinc-plated steel roofing

Galvalume
Bethlehem Steel Corporation
Bethlehem, PA 18016-7699

ceramic roofing tiles

Ludowici-Celadon Company
4757 Tile Plant Road
New Lexington, OH 43764

Marley Roof Tiles
    Corporation
1990 East Riverview Drive
San Bernardino, CA 92408
or
1901 San Felipe Road
Hollister, CA 95023

coated stainless steel roofing

Terne
Follansbee Steel
P.O. Box 610
Follansbee, WV 26037

concrete asbestos roof shingles

Supradur Manufacturing
    Corporation
P.O. Box 908
Rye, NY 10580

gutters and downspouts

Raingo
7034 East Court Street
Davison, MI 48423

metal roofing that mimics clay tiles

Met-Tile
P.O. Box 4268
Ontario, CA 91761-4268

paints for metal roofing

Architectural Engineering
    Products
7455 Carroll Road
San Diego, CA 92121

Berridge Manufacturing
1720 Maury Street
Houston, TX 77026

Korad
Polymer Extruded
    Products, Inc.
297 Ferry Street
Newark, NJ 07105

Penwalt Corporation
Plastics Department
3 Parkway
Philadelphia, PA 19102

PPG Industries, Inc.
One PPG Place
Pittsburgh, PA 15272

pressure-treated cedar shakes

Koppers Company, Inc.
436 Seventh Avenue
Pittsburgh, PA 15219

protective finish for cedar shakes

Flood's Roof Grade
The Flood Company
P.O. Box 399
Hudson, OH 44236

roll waterproofing flashing

Ice and Water Shield
W. R. Grace & Company
62 Whittemore Avenue
Cambridge, MA 02140

rust-resistant steel roofing

Cor-Ten
USX Corporation
600 Grant Street
Pittsburgh, PA 15230

zinc alloy roofing

Microzinc
W. P. Hickman Company
P.O. Box 15005
Asheville, NC 28813

Walls

all-in-one molded PVC bath or shower and enclosure

Traco Bath Systems
Delta Faucet Company
55 East 111 Street
Indianapolis, IN 46280

anaglypta (textured wall covering)

Decor International
    Wallcovering, Inc.
37-39 Crescent Street
Long Island City, NY 11101

Rejuvenation Houseparts
901 North Skidmore
Portland, OR 94124

facsimile stones fashioned from concrete

Coronado Stone
Coronado Products, Inc.
1325 6th Avenue North
Nashville, TN 37208-0568

L. B. Stone Company
Box 276
Apple Creek, OH 44606

handcrafted tiles

The Moravian Pottery
and Tile Works
Swamp Road
Doylestown, PA 18901

Sax Tatterson
Box 15
Taos, NM 87571

The Tile Gallery
300 D Street SW
Washington, DC 20024

*interior wall panels
with brick facings*

Masonite Corporation
1 South Wacker Drive
Chicago, IL 60606

manufactured tiles

American Olean
Tile Company
1000 Cannon Avenue
P.O. Box 271
Lansdale, PA 19446-0271

marblelike materials

Corian
E. I. Dupont
de Nemours Company
Corian Building Products
Wilmington, DE 19898

*marble tiles
with adhesive backing*

Hearthstone Decorator Tiles
Hearthstone Way
Morrisville, VT 05661

*plastic laminates for walls
and countertops*

Formica Corporation
1501 Broadway
Room 1519
New York, NY 10036

Nevamar Corporation
8339 Telegraph Road
Odenton, MD 21113

Wilsonart
Ralph Wilson
Plastics Company
600 General Bruce Drive
Temple, TX 76501

*rock lath boards made
especially for ceramic tile*

Durock
USG Corporation
101 South Wacker Drive
Chicago, IL 60606

synthetic hardwood planking

Marlite
Masonite Corporation
1 South Wacker Drive
Chicago, IL 60607

APPENDIX B: CATALOGS, BOOKS, AND MAGAZINES

I refer to a number of publications in the text of the book that I found useful for information and ideas related to low maintenance. I include them here, well aware of the fact that there are many others that are also worth reading.

Catalogs of Tools and Supplies

Garrett Wade
161 Avenue of the Americas
New York, NY 10013
*(woodworking tools
and supplies)*

Goldblatt Tool Company
P.O. Box 2334
511 Osage Street
Kansas City, KS 66110
*(general tools, but especially
woodworking tools)*

Masonry Specialty Catalog
4430 Gibsonia Road
Gibsonia, PA 15044
(masonry supplies)

Smith & Hawken Ltd.
25 Corte Madera
Mill Valley, CA 94941
*(teak patio furniture
as well as fine tools)*

Speigel
1113 West 22 Street
Oak Brook, IL 60609
(household furnishings)

Thompson & Morgan, Inc.
P.O. Box 100
Farmingdale, NJ 07727
*(large variety of domestic and
imported flower and vegetable
seeds)*

Books and Pamphlets

American Council for an Energy-Efficient
Economy. *The Most Energy-Efficient Appliances.* Washington, D.C.

Ceramic Tile Institute. *The Ceramic Tile
Manual.* Los Angeles.

Dietz, Marjorie M., ed. *10,000 Garden Questions Answered by 20 Experts.* New York:
Doubleday, 1974.

Frid, Tage. *Tage Frid Teaches Woodworking.*
Newtown, Conn.: The Taunton Press, 1981.

Gaston, Desmond. *Care and Repair of Furniture.* New York: Doubleday, 1978.

Giles, Drs. Carl and Barbara. *Steel Homes.* Blue
Ridge Summit, Pa.: TAB Books, 1981.

Grotz, George. *The Furniture Doctor.* New
York: Doubleday, 1983.

Hoadley, R. Bruce. *Understanding Wood*. New-town, Conn.: The Taunton Press, 1980.

Hylton, William, ed. *Build It Better Yourself*. Emmaus, Pa.: Rodale Press, 1976.

Krenov James. *The Fine Art of Cabinetmaking*. New York: Van Nostrand Reinhold Company, 1977.

Logsdon, Gene. *Gene Logsdon's Practical Skills*. Emmaus, Pa.: Rodale Press, 1985.

Nearing, Helen and Scott. *Living the Good Life*. Harrisburg, Pa.: Stackpole Books, 1970.

Portland Cement Association. *The Concrete Approach to Energy Conservation*. Skokie, Ill.

Randall, Frank A., Jr., and Panarese, William C. *Concrete Masonry Handbook for Architects, Engineers, Builders*. Skokie, Ill.: Portland Cement Association.

Reader's Digest Association. *Back to Basics: How to Learn and Enjoy Traditional American Skills*. Pleasantville, N.Y., 1981.

Tile Council of America. *Handbook for Ceramic Tile Installation*. Princeton, N.J., 1977.

Wade, Alex. *A Design and Construction Handbook for Energy-Saving Houses*. Emmaus, Pa.: Rodale Press, 1980.

Wade, Alex, and Ewenstein, Neal. *30 Energy-Efficient Houses . . . You Can Build*. Emmaus, Pa.: Rodale Press, 1977.

Western Wood Products Association. *Our Real Wood Interiors Design Workbook*. Portland, Oreg., 1985.

Yepsen, Roger B., Jr., ed. *The Durability Factor*. Emmaus, Pa.: Rodale Press, 1982.

Magazines

Country Journal
2245 Kohn Road
Box 8200
Harrisburg, PA 17105

Fine Homebuilding
The Taunton Press
63 South Main Street
P.O. Box 355
Newtown, CT 06470

Fine Woodworking
The Taunton Press
63 South Main Street
P.O. Box 355
Newtown, CT 06470

New England Architect and Builder Illustrated
Norbrook Publishing Company
601 Washington Street
Norwood, MA 02062

Remodeling World
308 North Wold Road
Suite 203
Wheeling, IL 60090

Rodale's Practical Homeowner (formerly *Rodale's New Shelter*)
Rodale Press
33 East Minor Street
Emmaus, PA 18098

Victorian Homes
Renovator's Supply
Box 61
Renovator's Old Mill
Millers Falls, MA 01349

The Woodheat/Woodstove Directory
Street Enterprises
Box 255
Menomonee Falls, WI 53051

APPENDIX C:
TRADE ASSOCIATIONS

These groups were helpful to me in my research, and they can be helpful to you if you want good information about generic products.

Ceramic Tile Institute
700 North Virgil Avenue
Los Angeles, CA 90029

Marble Institute of America
33505 State Street
Farmington, MI 48024

National Concrete
   Masonry Association
2302 Horse Pen Road
Herndon, VA 22070

North American
   Fruit Explorers
Robert Kurle
10 South 055 Madison Street
Hinsdale, IL 60521

The Red Cedar Shingle and
Hand Split Shake Bureau
515 116th Avenue NE
Suite 275
Bellevue, WA 98004

Western Wood
   Products Association
522 Southwest 5th Avenue
Yeon Building
Portland, OR 97204

PHOTOGRAPHY CREDITS

Page 8: courtesy of Winter Panel Corporation; **Page 13**: Steve Solinsky; **Page 44**: courtesy of *Fine Homebuilding* magazine; **Page 45**: Richard Garrett; **Page 48**: Robert Perron; **Page 50**: Robert Reck; **Page 51**: Ezra Stoller © Esto; **Page 53 (both photographs)**: courtesy of *Metal Construction News*; **Page 60**: Dennis Barnes; **Page 74**: Rodale Press Photography Department; **Pages 76, 79**: Dennis Barnes; **Page 81**: courtesy of Monier-Raymond; **Page 93**: courtesy of Rolscreen Company/Pella; **Page 96**: courtesy of American Reflexa; **Pages 98, 110 (both photographs), 118, 119**: Rodale Press Photography Department; **Page 120**: Alison Miksch; **Pages 151, 152, 153, 155, 156, 157, 158 (both photographs), 160, 164**: Rodale Press Photography Department; **Page 172**: Dennis Barnes; **Page 178**: courtesy of Bowmanite Corporation; **Page 179**: courtesy of Coronado Products, Inc.; **Page 180**: Rodale Press Photography Department; **Page 199**: courtesy of Harris-Tarkett, Inc.; **Page 211**: courtesy of Decor International Wallcovering, Inc.; **Pages 215, 219**: Rodale Press Photography Department; **Page 221**: courtesy of Owens Corning Fiberglass Corporation; **Page 223**: courtesy of American Olean Tile Company; **Page 225**: courtesy of Coronado Products, Inc.; **Page 226**: Rodale Press Photography Department; **Page 227**: courtesy of Masonite Corporation; **Page 229**: courtesy of E. I. Dupont de Nemours Company; **Page 232**: courtesy of W. F. Norman Corporation.

INDEX